BG A. N. Farley
P.O. Box 2009
Pittsburgh, PA 15230

TWICE
the Citizen

A History of the United States Army Reserve, 1908–1983

RICHARD B. CROSSLAND
Lieutenant Colonel, USAR

JAMES T. CURRIE
Major, USAR

Office of the Chief, Army Reserve
Washington, DC
1984

Acknowledgments

The authors of this study owe debts of gratitude to numerous individuals who helped with what has been by history-writing standards a whirlwind project. Special support was offered from the beginning by Maj. Gen. William R. Berkman, Chief, Army Reserve, and after he joined OCAR, by Brig. Gen. Harry J. Mott, III, Deputy Chief, Army Reserve.

Our immediate supervisor, Lewis C. Brodsky, Director of Public Affairs, Office of the Chief, Army Reserve, has given the entire project his complete and whole-hearted support. We are grateful that amidst the more glamorous fanfare that accompanied the Seventy-fifth Anniversary celebrations for the USAR, he never lost sight of the usefulness and importance of the history project. We owe you a lot, Lew.

The people who helped us locate and collect materials for this study were many. Personnel in the Modern Military Branch of the National Archives were always helpful, particularly Will Mahoney. At the Army's Center of Military History, Hannah Zeidlik and Karl Cocke guided us to documents we might otherwise have missed, and Mr. Cocke and Col. Bettie Morden spent considerable time and effort reviewing the manuscript for us. Within the Army Library at the Pentagon, Patricia Tugwell was always ready to assist us in locating an obscure first name or resolving an inconsistency. Bill Hauser at the US Forest Service's Audio-Visual Archives furnished pictures of the CCC, while the Defense Audiovisual Agency Archives were a treasure trove of old photographs for the book.

Other individual historians who shared with us their knowledge and comments were the Chief of the Joint Chiefs of Staff Historical Office—Willard Webb—and some of his staff members, specifically Walter Poole, Helen Bailey, and Truman Strobridge. Capt. Leonid Kondratiuk, Historian for the National Guard Bureau, was critical, but perceptive in what he had to say. To all of you, we offer our heartfelt gratitude. We absolve you, however, from any remaining differences or errors of fact or interpretation, for we were sometimes too stubborn to take your well-thought suggestions, or our own research led us to different conclusions from yours.

To Lynda Poole, who alone bore the typing load for this project in addition to her many other duties, we give our thanks.

Finally, we want to recognize our families. The spouses of military personnel always put up with so much, and our wives—Maryanna Crossland and Janis Rabbitt Currie—have endured this project with the greatest of patience and understanding. We have enjoyed researching and writing this book, and we hope that it may prove useful and interesting to the reader.

RICHARD B. CROSSLAND
Lieutenant Colonel, USAR
United States Army Training
    and Doctrine Command
Fort Monroe, Va.

JAMES T. CURRIE
Major, USAR
Washington, DC

September 1983

Da Pam 140–14

Contents

Photographs follow Chapters Three, Five, and Eight

List of Tables

Acronyms and
Abbreviations

ACS	Assistant Chief of Staff (Army)
ADT	Active Duty for Training
AEF	American Expeditionary Force
AGF	Army Ground Forces
AGI	Annual General Inspection
AGR	Active Guard and Reserve
AIT	Advanced Individual Training
Amb	Ambulance
AMOPS	Army Mobilization and Operations Planning System
AMSA	Area Maintenance Support Activities
ARCOM	Army Commendation Medal; Army Reserve Command
ARMC	Army Readiness and Mobilization Command
ARNG	Army National Guard
ARR	Army Readiness Region
ART	Army Reserve Technician
ARTEP	Army Training and Evaluation Program
ATT	Army Training Test
AUS	Army of the United States
AW	Automatic Weapon
AWOL	Absent without leave
Bn	Battalion
Brig. Gen.	Brigadier General
BUT	Basic Unit Training
Capt.	Captain
CAR	Chief, Army Reserve
CASP	Civilian Acquired Skills Program
CCC	Civilian Conservation Corps
Cdr	Commander
CG	Commanding General

C&GSC	US Army Command and General Staff College
CMH	Center of Military History (Army)
CMTC	Citizens' Military Training Camps
CNGB	Chief, National Guard Bureau
Co.	Company
Col.	Colonel
COMUS MACV	Commander, United States Military Assistance Command, Vietnam
CONARC	US Army Continental Army Command
CONUSA	Continental United States Army
DA	Department of the Army
DAMPL	Department of the Army Master Priority List
DCSOPS	Deputy Chief of Staff for Operations
DCSPER	Deputy Chief of Staff for Personnel
Det	Detachment
DMZ	Demilitarized Zone
DoD	Department of Defense
DS	Direct Support
EO	Executive Order
Equip	Equipment
ERC	Enlisted Reserve Corps
ERRA	Executive for Reserve and R.O.T.C. Affairs
Evac	Evacuation
FDR	President Franklin D. Roosevelt
Fin	Finance
Fltg Cft	Floating Craft
FORSCOM	US Army Forces Command
FY	Fiscal Year
G–1	General Staff (Personnel)
G–2	General Staff (Intelligence)
G–3	General Staff (Plans and Operations)
GAO	General Accounting Office
Gen	General
GOCOM	General Officer Command
GPO	Government Printing Office
GS	General Support
	General Staff
HHC	Headquarters and Headquarters Company
Hosp	Hospital
HQ	Headquarters
H.R.	House of Representatives
IADT	Inactive Duty Training (drill)
IDT	Inactive Duty Training
IMA	Individual Mobilization Augmentee
Inf	Infantry
IRR	Individual Ready Reserve

JCS	Joint Chiefs of Staff
L&LD	Legislation and Liaison Division
Lt.	Lieutenant
Lt. Col.	Lieutenant Colonel
Lt. Gen.	Lieutenant General
M16	Standard Vietnam-era military rifle, caliber 5.56 mm
Maint	Maintenance
Maj.	Major
Maj. Gen.	Major General
MCAR	Military Construction, Army Reserve
M-Day	Mobilization Day
Med	Medical
MI	Military Intelligence
MOBDES	Mobilization Designee
MOBEX	Mobilization Exercise
MOBPERS	Mobilization Personnel Processing System
MOS	Military Occupation Specialty
Msg	Message
MSP	Mutual Support Program
MTCA	Military Training Camps Association
MUSARC	Major United States Army Reserve Command
NG	National Guard
OCAR	Office of the Chief, Army Reserve
OER	Officer Evaluation Report
OERRA	Office of the Executive for Reserve and R.O.T.C. Affairs
OMA	Operations and Maintenance, Army
OMAR	Operations and Maintenance, Army Reserve
OR	Organized Reserve [Corps]
ORC	Office of Reserve Components
	Officers' Reserve Corps
	Organized Reserve Corps
Ord	Ordnance
Ortho	Orthopedic
OSD	Office of the Secretary of Defense
Pers	Personnel
Petr	Petroleum
PIO	Public Information Officer
PL	Public Law
PMP	Protective Mobilization Plan
POL	Petroleum, Oil, and Lubricants
POM	Program Objective Memorandum
PX	Post Exchange
QM	Quartermaster
RA	Regular Army
RAR	Regular Army Reserve
RDF-A	Rapid Deployment Force—Army

RDJTF	Rapid Deployment Joint Task Force
REP-63	Reserve Enlistment Program—1963
RFA	Reserve Forces Act of 1955
RG	Readiness Group
	Record Group (National Archives)
ROA	Reserve Officers Association
ROAD	Reorganization Objective Army Division
ROPA	Reserve Officer Personnel Act of 1954
ROTC	Reserve Officers Training Corps
RPA	Reserve Personnel, Army
RRMRP	Ready Reserve Mobilization Reinforcement Pool
RROTC	Reserve and ROTC Affairs
RTU	Reinforcement Training Unit
RVN	Republic of [South] Vietnam
SARCA	Senior Army Reserve Commanders Association
Sec	Section
SGLI	Servicemen's Group Life Insurance
SP	Self-propelled
Spt	Support
SRF	Selected Reserve Force
SRIP	Selected Reserve Incentive Program
SSAA	Senior Staff Administrative Assistant
STRAF	Strategic Reserve Army Forces
Sup	Supply
Surg	Surgery, Surgical
Svc	Service
TAG	The Adjutant General, US Army
TAGO	The Adjutant General's Office
T/O	Table of Organization
TOA	Total Obligation Authority
TOE	Table of Organization and Equipment
Trans	Transportation
Trk	Truck
USAR	United States Army Reserve
USAREC	US Army Recruiting Command
VHA	Variable Housing Allowance
WAC	Women's Army Corps

Foreword

The United States Army Reserve (USAR) had its official birth on April 23, 1908, in an act "To Increase the Efficiency of the Medical Department of the United States Army." From this modest beginning and limited mission, the Army Reserve has grown into a force of almost a million men and women who are very much a part of today's Total Army. The roots of the Army Reserve go back much further than 1908, however, for the concept of the citizen-soldier was an old one even at the time of the American Revolution.

The idea of writing a history of the Army Reserve originated in November 1982 during the early stages of planning for the USAR's Seventy-fifth Anniversary celebration in 1983. It became evident to Major (now Lieutenant Colonel) Richard B. Crossland and to Lewis C. Brodsky, Director of Public Affairs for the Office of the Chief, Army Reserve, that there was no readily available source of historical data about the Army Reserve. There were bits and pieces of USAR history scattered about, and there were legends enough to fill a file cabinet, but there was no comprehensive, book-length history of the Army Reserve. Major Crossland was thereupon assigned the task of writing such a book. Given the time frame in mind for the project (less than one year), it was soon obvious that this was not a one-person job. Permission was therefore secured to bring in an Army Reserve officer on a special tour of six months or so to work on the book.

The Reserve Components Personnel and Administration Center in St. Louis was given the task of locating an individual to do the job, and the name of James T. Currie popped up. Major Currie was at that time (January 1983) serving in a civilian capacity as Historian for the United States Department of Education, and he accepted the assignment. Lieutenant Colonel Crossland and Major Currie co-authored this volume, which is the only existing history of the Army Reserve. The authors have of necessity worked rapidly, researching and writing a draft manuscript of 450 pages in less than 6 months. The authors realize that in any pioneering study there are almost certainly going to be errors, both of omission and of commission. They have attempted, however, to be as accurate as possible, and every statement of fact is based upon the most credible sources available. They have drawn conclusions from these facts where such seemed justified, but the conclusions are purely their own and do not necessarily reflect the views of the Chief, Army Reserve, the Department of the Army, or the Department of Defense.

The title of the book is taken from Winston Churchill's statement that "The Reservist is twice the citizen," a phrase that also figured in the Seventy-fifth Anniversary High School Essay Contest co-sponsored by the Army Reserve and the Reserve Officers Association. Indeed, since 1908, members of the Army Reserve have taken on responsibilities greater than those required of most citizens, for they have given of their weeknights and weekends and summertime leisure to learn and train and prepare for the day when their country might call upon them in time of war or national emergency. From 1908 until 1948, Army Reservists received no pay except for the time they were on active duty; the many hours devoted to inactive duty drills and training went unrewarded financially. Since 1948 Army Reservists have qualified for an increasing list of benefits, including limited post exchange and commissary privileges and, if they serve long enough and live long enough, for retirement pay. As the citizen-soldier concept has matured and become an integral part of the Army, the United States has gradually given tangible recognition to the value of the Army Reserve. This belated reward does not in any way, however, diminish the fact that the Army Reservist is indeed "twice the citizen."

Within this volume, LTC Crossland was responsible for Chapters I, II, VII, VIII, and X and Appendixes G and H. Major Currie prepared Chapters III, IV, V, VI, and IX and Appendixes A through F. The authors hope that publication of this book will stimulate a greater interest in the United States Army Reserve and that their study will serve as a reference work for persons whose position calls for them to understand the Army Reserve.

Readers who have corrections, suggestions, or additions are urged to send such to the following address:

Headquarters, Department of the Army
Office of the Chief, Army Reserve
Attn: DAAR-PA (History Project)
Washington, DC 20310

1

Before There Was An Army Reserve

The United States Army Reserve, the largest component of the Department of Defense with nearly one million men and women,[1] was officially created in 1908. However, the heritage of the volunteer or "citizen-soldier" goes back to colonial America and has its roots in the enrolled militia of Anglo-Saxon England.

The idea of supplementing Regular or full-time forces with Reserve or part-time forces is even older than the Middle Ages. The Roman Empire of the late fourth and early fifth centuries depended upon the *Comitatus,* a full-time, regular Army that was backed by the *limitanei* of part-time soldiers living on the land along the Empire's long frontiers and charged with defense in time of emergency.[2]

Likewise, the basic 13th century medieval military organization had the standing army of the king or overlord—a highly trained professional army equipped with the finest weapons available—backed by the enrolled militia or select fyrd.[3] While the King's full-time professionals were available for service anywhere, the enrolled militia was a

---

1. As of March 31, 1983, the Office of the Deputy Chief of Staff for Personnel in its DCSPER Report–46 listed the strength of the Army Reserve at 943,396 encompassing the Ready, Standby and Retired Reserves. On December 31, 1982, the active Army, the largest of America's active duty forces, stood at 778,577 men and women.

2. Louis A. Zurcher and Gwyn Harris-Jenkins, editors, *Supplementary Military Forces—Reserves, Militias, Auxiliaries,* (Beverly Hills, Calif.: Sage Publications, 1978), pp. 91–92.

3. Michael Powicke, *Military Obligation in Medieval England, A Study of Liberty & Duty,* (Oxford at the Clarendon Press, 1962), pp. 6–7.

minimally-trained and individually-equipped force of citizen-soldiers normally employed within a few miles of their homes. Except in times of emergency, they carried on their civilian pursuits as farmers, merchants and craftsmen.

Below the enrolled militia was its unenrolled counter-part, the great fyrd or *levees en masse*, which consisted of all reasonably healthy men. This large body of unorganized, un-disciplined and generally untrained men was the last-ditch force used to defend the homeland from invasion.[4]

Modified and formalized by the 1181 Assize of Arms, the Statute of Winchester of 1285 and the Instructions for General Muster of 1572, the fyrd became the militia of Elizabethan England. This militia tradition was among the English institutions carried to the American colonies in the early 17th century at a time when militias were falling into disuse in an age of professional armies.

However, in the words of historian Russell F. Weigley, "The American colonies in the seventeenth century were much too poor to permit a class of able-bodied men to de-vote themselves solely to war and preparation for war."[5] Manpower was scarce, and every colony except Quaker Penn-sylvania solved the problem of military protection by turn-ing to the traditional English practice of relying upon a militia.

Even though tradition and the law called upon every able-bodied man to provide his own weapon and be prepared for militia duty, few emergencies required the entire popula-tion to rally to arms. As early as 1643, the Massachusetts Bay Colony reorganized its militia by calling for 30 volun-teers from each company of the common militia to be ready for service upon 30-minutes notice. The remainder of the company, 65 to 200 men, was exempt from the militia call except under the most dire circumstances.

Other colonies adopted similar provisions, and more or less permanent formations of persons willing to volunteer for duty soon developed. This in effect created an elite, enrolled militia reminiscent of medieval England.

While this arrangement was more than adequate as long as a colonial community remained a frontier commu-nity, the prowess of the colonial community militia faded as

4. James B. Whisker, *The Citizen-Soldier and U. S. Military Policy,* (North River Press, 1979), pp. 4–5.
5. Russell F. Weigley, *History of the United States Army,* (New York: The Macmillan Company, 1967), pp. 3–4.

the frontier receded. By the time of the French and Indian War, Col. George Washington of the Virginia militia reported that the militia was no longer a match for the Indians.[6] This reality, and the inability of the colonies to muster sufficient forces against the French, led London to send regular British regiments to America.

Although accustomed to European warfare with its highly disciplined maneuvers and point-blank volleys of musketry on open, rolling plains, the British soldiers adapted to the wooded American environment. They did most of the fighting, won the war and set the standard of soldiering for the Americans. Washington was impressed, and his fondest hope was that his militia might pattern themselves after the British regulars.[7]

THE REVOLUTION

A decade later, Washington was fighting a revolution with troops that were essentially the same as his French and Indian War militia. Washington remembered well the weakness of his Virginia militia and urged the Congress to create a large, standing army that he could turn into a professional force. Indeed, Washington wrote that "no Militia will ever acquire the habits necessary to resist a regular force."[8]

Although Washington was able to build an effective force with which victory was ultimately achieved, he was consistently denied a standing army of the size he deemed necessary. Weigley suggests that the Congress was "acutely mindful that the Parliamentary Army of 17th Century England had turned upon its legislative creator and erected the military dictatorship of Oliver Cromwell."[9] On the other hand, it has generally been established that the Revolutionary leadership was by and large conservative and very much inclined to rely upon the traditional militia.

In addition, Revolutionary propagandists had emphasized that a large standing army was an example of tyranny and had used the presence of British regulars in the Colonies to whip up support for the Revolution. This very useful propaganda theme would have been undercut if the Revolu-

---

6. *Ibid.,* p. 11.
7. *Ibid.,* p. 28.
8. Robert K. Wright, Jr., Army Lineage Series, *The Continental Army,* (Washington: Center of Military History: 1983), p. 156.
9. Weigley, *History of the United States Army,* p. 30.

tionaries had established a large, permanent force of their own.[10]

Eighteenth century military practices also worked against establishing a large, full-time Army. In the 1700's, military campaigns began in the spring and lasted until winter brought a halt to operations. As a rule, the American Revolution followed this pattern, with the battles of Trenton and Quebec being December exceptions to the norm.[11]

It made little sense to the Continental Congress to maintain a large force over the winter with the need to pay, provision and generally care for soldiers who would not be needed until spring. It was far more economical, they thought, to disband most of the Army when the snow started to fall and to later call out the volunteers and militia after the spring planting was done.

Throughout the war, economic factors and the practical impossibility of raising a large, long-term army that Washington wanted caused him to rely upon the militia to build up his forces for major campaigns.[12]

The militia also made the Revolutionary Army ubiquitous. Any victory by the British was immediately diminished because a force of Minutemen seemed always to spring from the countryside and harrass the British columns and in general make life difficult for the British. This added an element of guerrilla warfare to the Revolution that would not have been possible if the Americans had relied totally upon a regular army to prosecute the war.

In *American Military History*, Robert W. Coakley makes the point that both the Continental Army and militia forces

---

10. Wright specifically makes this point, writing that "the rhetoric of protest against British policy had strongly denied the need for a large 'standing army' of regular soldiers in America on the grounds that the colonial militia forces, composed of virtuous citizens-soldiers, were perfectly adequate for local defense. The outbreak of hostilities in Massachusetts did not change this attitude. Lexington, Concord and Bunker Hill only seemed to confirm the validity of that assumption." See Wright *Continental Army*, p. 43. It should also be noted that "quartering of large bodies of armed troops among us" was one of Thomas Jefferson's themes as early as 1774, and this grievance is included in the 1776 Declaration of Independence.

11. Erna Risch, Special Studies Series, *Supplying Washington's Army*, (Washington: Center of Military History, 1981), p. 416.

12. Wright, *Continental Army*, p. 127. The consistent economic woes which plagued the Revolution are detailed in Risch's *Supplying Washington's Army*, particularly on pages 17 and 20. Today's situation where Reserve Components provide an economical means of rounding out regular forces in time of emergency is analogous to the manpower solutions achieved by the Continental Congress during the Revolution.

were necessary to win the Revolution. More importantly, in Coakley's words, "the Revolutionary experience provided ammunition for two diametrically opposed schools of thought on American military policy: one advocating a large Regular Army, the other reliance upon the militia as the bulwark of national defense."[13]

These two schools of thought remain in 1983, even though the issue of large regular forces versus heavy reliance upon reserve or militia forces was apparently resolved with the announcement of the Total Force policy in August 1970. This policy, which states that the Reserve Components would be the principal augmentation of active forces in emergency, has not been proven in wartime, and it is quite likely that the debate will continue after our next mobilization experience.[14]

THE PEACETIME ARMY

The question of the peacetime Army was one of the first issues addressed in 1783 prior to the Sept. 24 signing of the Treaty of Paris that formally ended the Revolution. The handicaps of short enlistments, over-reliance upon volunteers and militia and the lack of standardized training among the part-time forces were recognized by the Revolutionary leadership.[15] A Congressional committee was formed under Alexander Hamilton to study and recommend a military establishment. In the tradition of such committees, witnesses were heard and particular attention was paid to the views of Washington,[16] who recommended a small Regular Army and

---

13. Robert W. Coakley, "The Winning of Independence," in Maurice Matloff (Gen. Ed.), *American Military History* (Washington: Office of the Chief of Military History, United States Army, 1969), pp. 98–100. See also Wright, *Continental Army,* pp. 3–20.

14. The Total Force policy was not adopted without dissent. Military leaders, including Gen. William C. Westmoreland, thought that the Total Force decision placed too much reliance upon part-time Reserve Component soldiers. This issue is addressed in Chapter 10, and much of this book is devoted to the struggle to develop an effective Reserve Component policy to meet America's world-wide military responsibilities.

15. The lessons learned from the Revolution are summarized in Marvin A. Kreidberg and Merton G. Henry, *History of Military Mobilization in the United States Army, 1775–1945,* (Washington: Department of the Army, 1955), p. 22.

16. Morris J. McGregor, Jr., "The Formative Years, 1783–1812," in Matloff, *American Military History,* pp. 103–105.

a militia of all citizens 18 to 50, modeled after the Swiss militia.[17]

Washington's proposals, however, came to naught, as the Confederation was burdened with war debts and did not have the resources to enact his recommendations. The debate over the military question continued throughout the period of the Articles of Confederation, and the Constitution emerged in 1787 with two military clauses reflecting a compromise on the issues.

Specifically, Article I, Section 8 of the Constitution granted to Congress the power to raise and support armies, to provide for organizing, arming and disciplining the militia and to provide for calling forth the militia to "execute the laws of the union, suppress insurrections and repel invasions." Reserved to the states were the powers to appoint officers and train the militia.[18]

After establishing the Department of War and continuing the small Regular Army in 1789, Congress was faced in 1790 with a detailed proposal for regulating the militia. Drafted by Secretary of War Henry Knox, the plan featured the division of all able-bodied white male citizens, aged 18–60, into three classes:

Those 18–20 to be called the Advanced Corps and to be trained in state camps for thirty days per year and clothed and fed and armed by the United States at a cost of about $400,000 per year; those 21–45 to be called the Main Corps and to be mustered and trained for four days per year; those 40–60 to be called the Reserve Corps and to be mustered twice a year.[19]

A bill containing the main features of this plan was introduced, debated and tabled in 1790 and again in 1791. Finally, in 1792 a weaker bill passed calling for all able-bodied white male citizens, aged 18–45, to be enrolled in a general militia. This Militia Act of 1792 required each man to furnish his own musket, bayonet, belt, and cartridges. Thus, $400,000 was saved—a considerable amount in that day—and the tradition of underfunding Reserve Components began.

---

17. Russell F. Weigley, *Towards an American Army: Military Thought from Washington to Marshall.* (Westport, Conn.: Greenwood Press, 1962), pp. 10–12.

18. The literal interpretation of these provisions in 1912 by Attorney General George W. Wickersham was a strong argument for a federal reserve force.

19. William H. Riker, *Soldiers of the States,* (Washington: Public Affairs Press, 1957), p. 18.

The 1792 act became the permanent military policy of the United States at a time when European military leaders were turning to massed, conscript armies. While Napoleon was dominating Europe with his conscripts, grand tactics and superior logistics, the United States was rejecting conscripted service and relying upon a militia system obsolete by European standards for 200 years.[20]

THE WAR OF 1812

The American militia system was faced with its first foreign challenge in the War of 1812, and it was found wanting. When Congress voted for war with Great Britian on June 18, 1812, the Regular Army contained fewer than 7,000 men.[21] A call for the states to raise 100,000 men generally went unheeded, and the governors of Massachusetts, Connecticut and Rhode Island opposed the call completely, maintaining that it was unconstitutional and illegal.

During the war itself, militia under Maj. Gen. Henry Dearborn refused to invade Canada, a failure which was remembered a century later when arguments were presented for a federal reserve force.[22] Historically a home defense force, the militia's leaders claimed that the Constitution provided no clear authority for their use outside of the United States. The Madison administration, uncertain of its public support, balked at sending reluctant citizen-soldiers into Canada and skirted the issue.[23] In the future, calling the militia into United States service was handled by regarding militia companies as volunteers for federal duty, serving under the general authority of Congress to raise armies.

THE EXPANSIBLE ARMY

Following the War of 1812, Secretary of War John C. Calhoun produced a pivotal document in the history of American military thought when he prepared his Dec. 12, 1820, "Report on the Reduction of the Army." Building upon ear-

---

20. Weigley, *Towards an American Army,* pp. 20–24.
21. Kreidberg and Henry, *History of Military Mobilization,* p. 46.
22. Weigley, *History of the United States Army,* pp. 119–20.
23. In fairness to the militia and volunteer forces, McGregor states that the militia fared as well as the Regular Army in victory and defeat. While the refusal of New York and Vermont soldiers to enter Canada scuttled Dearborn's planned 1812 march on Montreal, militia forces served well in the defense of Baltimore and were the key to Jackson's success in the South. See McGregor, "Formative Years," pp. 129–47.

lier proposals, Calhoun emphasized the Regular Army and discounted the militia by calling for an expansible army as the basis for future mobilization. Calhoun wanted to form in peacetime all of the regiments which the Army would require in war. The companies were to be manned at approximately half strength and were to be expanded to full strength for war.[24]

Calhoun thought that the militia might be relied upon to garrison forts and act as skirmishers and raiders if supported by good artillery and some regular infantry; but he wrote, "To rely upon them beyond this, to suppose our militia capable of meeting in the open field the regular troops of Europe, would be to resist the most obvious truth, and the whole of our experience as a nation."[25]

A more obvious truth in Calhoun's time was that the militia had fallen into disrepair. The Militia Act of 1792 had contained no provision for federal enforcement of the militia system, but had relied upon the states to do the job. This did not always occur. In 1816, for example, Delaware abolished fines for men who did not attend "days of parade;" and by 1820, many other states had stopped enforcing annual muster laws. Liberal exemptions from service also abounded, until few states retained an effective militia system on the eve of the War with Mexico.[26]

MEXICO

According to Marvin A. Kreidberg and Merton G. Henry in their *History of Military Mobilization in the United States Army, 1775–1945,* the militia system had so deteriorated by 1846 that many states did not know how to mobilize the militia, and many did not even appoint officers. When President James K. Polk called for volunteers to fight in Mexico, the normal procedure was for governors to issue a proclamation directing militia officers to assemble their men. In cases where militia officers did not exist, county sheriffs called out the militia. Once assembled, the militiamen were asked to volunteer for federal service. Those who volunteered were enrolled into companies, battalions and regiments. In many cases, where the militia system still functioned, entire

24. This cadre concept dominated military thinking until 1912 when the "Report on the Organization of Land Forces of the United States," principally authored by John McAuley Palmer, called for a great army of citizen-soldiers organized into their own units.
25. Weigley, *Towards an American Army,* p. 31.
26. Riker, *Soldiers of the States,* p. 29.

units volunteered;[27] and units such as the First Mississippi Rifles under Col. Jefferson Davis served with distinction.[28]

By the time of the Civil War, the militia was still theoretically in existence, and the Militia Act of 1792 was still the law of the land. However, as a practical matter, the militia did not exist as an effective, well-equipped military force.

CIVIL WAR

Acting under the authority of the 1792 law, President Abraham Lincoln called 75,000 militiamen for three months service on April 15, 1861. When it came time to raise a more permanent army, however, Lincoln called for 42,000 volunteers. Congress subsequently seconded his call on July 22, 1861, by authorizing up to 500,000 volunteers for three years' duty.

As a practical matter during the Civil War, the Secretary of War assigned manpower quotas to states based upon their population, and the governors administered the volunteer system. The individual soldier was drawn from the ranks of volunteers; he was not being mobilized from a previously existing militia unit.[29]

Following the Civil War, the public attitude toward the militia was indifferent. Despite the pride exhibited by veterans' organizations such as the Grand Army of the Republic, this pride was not translated into functioning militia units. Citizen-soldiery, in the opinion of William H. Riker, was at its lowest ebb because the Regular Army was sufficient to control the Indians and because there was no threat of a foreign war.[30] The growing militancy of the labor movement in the 1870s, however, helped revive the state militia. There was a direct relationship between labor unrest[31] in a state and that state's appropriation for the militia which was now more commonly called the National Guard.[32]

---

27. Kreidberg and Henry, *History of Military Mobilization,* pp. 75–82.

28. Lida Mayo, "The Mexican War and After," in Matloff, *American Military History,* pp. 168–72.

29. Kreidberg and Henry, *History of Military Mobilization,* pp. 90–98. The National Guard has a different interpretation of this point, and Civil War unit histories give evidence to both points of view.

30. William H. Riker, *Soldiers of the States,* pp. 41–66.

31. *Ibid.*

32. National Guard Officials were quick to down play the strikebreaking role of the militia. The police function was de-emphasized by

WAR WITH SPAIN

By the time of the Spanish-American War in 1898, the regiments and companies of the National Guard were units of citizen-soldiers available for mobilization, but once again Guard units were not called directly into federal service. Instead, a Volunteer Army was formed. As in the past, the militia provided volunteers for the new army, and National Guard units were encouraged to volunteer en masse. In addition, the Secretary of War was authorized to form 16 special units recruited by the federal government from the nation at large. The 1st Regiment of United States Volunteer Cavalry, the "Rough Riders" of Lt. Col. Theodore Roosevelt, was one of these units.

Even though the National Guard provided most of the manpower for the 125,000-man Volunteer Army, the combat actions of the Spanish-American War were primarily a Regular Army affair. Except for the Rough Riders and two former militia regiments, the 17,000 troops of the Cuban Expeditionary Force were from the old Regular Army. And, when National Guard units performed well in the Philippines, they were characterized as volunteer units by the Army establishment.[33]

The reason for this characterization was that the officers of the Regular Army were in the late 1800's contemptuous of part-time soldiers, whom they considered to be incompetent in military matters. This attitude had been exhibited by many post-Civil War senior officers including Generals Ulysses S. Grant and William T. Sherman, and these attitudes were clearly expressed in Brevet Maj. Gen. Emory Upton's book, *The Military Policy of the United States*.[34]

EMORY UPTON

A West Point graduate who was only 26-years-old at the end of the Civil War, Upton was an innovative thinker who has influenced generations of professional soldiers. After the war he wrote a text on infantry tactics and was subsequently named Commandant of Cadets at West Point. While at West Point, Upton continued to write on tactics, and in

promoting the social aspects of the Guard and giving greater attention to military maneuvers.

33. Weigley, *Towards an American Army*, p. 168.

34. Emory Upton, *The Military Policy of the United States*, 4th Edition, (Washington: 1916).

1875 he was sent on a world tour as an official observer for the United States Army. Upon his return in 1876, Upton began writing *The Military Policy of the United States*. He had been impressed by the military achievements of Prussia with its general staff and mass army that was made possible by a federal system of reserve soldiers. To adapt the Prussian system to American military traditions, Upton proposed the maintenance of a Regular Army of not more than 25,000 men.

This army was to be made up of skeletonized battalions that could be expanded in wartime by a federal reserve which Upton called "National Volunteers."[35] Upton advocated leaving the militia to the states to execute the laws of the states and called "the employment of militia and undisciplined troops commanded by generals and officers utterly ignorant of military art" the first and greatest weakness in the American military system.[36]

Upton's disdain for the militia was not unique. Maj. Gen. John A. Logan in his *The Volunteer Soldier of America*, published in 1887, asserted that the West Point system crushed the aspirations of volunteers and that the majority of regular officers would do anything to prevent a volunteer officer from being successful.[37] It should also be pointed out that militia officers often showed great antipathy toward Regulars. It is in light of this animosity that the Army attempted reforms following the Spanish-American War.

Weigley states that the US Army was on the verge of seeking a federally-sponsored volunteer force under Regular Army control on the eve of the Spanish-American War and that following the war Secretary of War Elihu Root was strongly influenced by Upton's writings.[38] Vincent P. Jones seconds Weigley on the latter point, stating that Root took the lead in reorganizing the Army and reforming the National Guard.[39]

---

35. Stephen E. Ambrose, *Upton and the Army*, (Baton Rouge: LSU Press, 1964), pp. 54–135.

36. Upton, *Military Policy*, p. XIII.

37. "The Dangerous West Point Monopoly" by John A. Logan as republished from *The Volunteer Soldier in America* in Russell F. Weigley's *The American Military: Readings in the History of the Military in American Society* (Reading, Mass.: Addison-Wesley Publishing Company, 1969) p. 83.

38. Weigley, *History of the United States Army*, pp. 296, 320.

39. Vincent P. Jones, "Transition and Change, 1902–1917," in Matloff, *American Military History*, pp. 45–46, 52.

ELIHU ROOT'S PLAN

In his *Report of the Secretary of War* for 1899, Root stated that the regular establishment of the United States would never by itself be the whole machine with which wars would be fought. He further wrote that the Regular Army would form but a part of a great wartime body.[40] Root then proposed that a homogeneous body of regulars and volunteers "using the same arms, familiar with the same drill, answering to the same ideas of discipline, instilled with the same spirit, and capable of equal and even performance" be formed.[41]

By 1901 Root was calling for some means by which young men seeking volunteer commissions might spend their vacations in military study preparing them for commissions in the volunteer army. Root wrote that "it is particularly desirable that a large number of young men should be made competent to perform the duties of volunteer officers in the staff and supply departments. Without such a class at the outbreak of war, with a large volunteer force being called into being, there will always be confusion, waste, delay and suffering . . . ."[42] This creation of a source of volunteer officers was in addition to National Guard officers and was the germ of the idea later espoused by Maj. Gen. Leonard Wood and his allies in the Military Training Camps Association.[43]

In 1902 Root proposed the creation of two categories of Volunteer Reserve to augment the Regular Army and National Guard in wartime. Root's First Volunteer Reserve was to be such companies and regiments of the organized militia as had volunteered for unlimited service during war. The Second Volunteer Reserve was to be composed of men with prior National Guard, Regular Army or Volunteer Army training and would be led by officers whose fitness for commissions had previously been proven.

Root wanted to be able to expand the standing 60,000-man Army to a force of 250,000 well-trained men instantly upon declaration of war. Root asserted that the effectiveness

---

40. Elihu Root, *Report of the Secretary of War, 1899,* (Washington: War Department, 1899), pp. 45–46, 52.

41. *Ibid.,* p. 53.

42. *Report of the Secretary of War, 1901* (Washington: War Department, 1901), pp. 23–24.

43. The issue of commissioning volunteer officers in reserve is covered in Chapter 2, but credit can certainly be given to Root for recognizing the need to train volunteer officers in advance of hostilities.

of militia or volunteer units depended largely upon the aid which they received from the national government.[44]

As much as Root may have favored Upton's idea of a federally controlled and commanded Reserve,[45] he was a realist. The creation of a federal Reserve force conflicted with the fact that the National Guard already constituted a reserve of manpower, and, to a lesser degree, of equipment. As Weigley puts it, the National Guard "was a force in being, while any other kind of reserve was only hypothetical."[46]

Therefore, Root supported legislation in 1903 to fundamentally upgrade the National Guard while retaining its historical state militia functions. Working with Ohio Congressman Charles W. Dick, a National Guard major general, Root helped draft Public Law 57–33, commonly known as the Dick Act.[47]

THE DICK ACT

This legislation clarified the concept of a universal militia. The militia was divided into two groups. The first was the organized militia, known as the National Guard, which was defined as the regularly enlisted, organized and uniformed active militia of the several states and territories. The second

---

44. *Report of the Secretary of War, 1902* (Washington: War Department, 1902), pp. 34–38.

45. In *Upton and the Army,* Ambrose states that Root's reforms of the War Department contain most of Upton's specific proposals. It would appear that Root thought enough of Upton's work to take Upton's unpublished manuscript of *The Military Policy of the United States,* then in the possession of Sen. Henry duPont of Delaware, have it edited by two Army officers and finally published in 1904 under War Department sponsorship. It is clear that Root did read Upton's earlier book, *The Armies of Asia and Europe,* and that Root consistently wrote of the Volunteer Army—not the National Guard per se—as the ultimate Army of the United States. See Root's *Report of the Secretary of War* for the years 1899, 1900, 1901 and 1902. Also, see Ambrose, cited above, pages 151–57 for an assessment of the overall impact of Upton's ideas.

46. Weigley, *History of the United States Army,* p. 321.

47. In "Elihu Root and the National Guard," published in the Spring 1959 issue of *Military Affairs,* Elbridge Colby sets forth the thesis that Root preferred to create a federally-controlled, nationwide Volunteer Army as a Reserve along the European model but that he was compelled for political reasons to upgrade the National Guard as a partial solution to the need for a national reserve force. Colby also contends that Root was strongly influenced by Upton and that Root saw the National Guard as serving state functions and being useful nationally only as a training ground for the Volunteer Army.

group was the Reserve Militia, which consisted of all able-bodied male citizens 18 to 45. Resident aliens who had declared their intent to become citizens were included in the two militias. For the first time, the Dick Act provided that general military stores, as well as arms and equipment, were to be offered to militia units that drilled at least 24 times a year and maintained a summer encampment of not less than five days. The militia units were to be periodically inspected by Regular Army officers, and Regular officers were detailed to the militia. Additionally, National Guard officers were declared eligible to attend Regular Army schools, and Guardsmen were to receive full pay and allowances while on maneuvers with the Regular Army.[48]

In addition, the Dick Act reaffirmed the principles of federal funding, federal inspections, and federal standards for training upon which today's Reserve Components are built.[49] The Act was the first of a series of bills from the establishment of an enlisted Army Reserve in 1912 through the sweeping National Defense Act of 1916 and its 1920 amendments that laid the groundwork for the Army's contemporary Reserve Components.

Following the January 21, 1903, passage of the Dick Act, Root achieved another of his objectives when Congress created the General Staff Corps on February 14, 1903. With the new General Staff of 45 officers, the Army was able to formulate cohesive, continuing military policies for the first time and take those planning steps which are essential for a successful mobilization.[50]

Root's ideas for a reserve corps soon grew into concrete form with a 1908 act "to increase the efficiency of the Medical Department of the United States Army."[51] The new corps was believed necessary to overcome serious wartime shortages of physicians, which had been apparent during the Spanish-American War; and there was no thought at the time that the commissioning of a few hundred Reserve doctors would lead to a force that numbers more than 3,000 units plus an Individual Ready Reserve of almost 250,000. Root's General Staff creation was also important for the Army Reserve, for the General Staff provided a place where John McAuley Palmer could think and write and produce in

---

48. 32 Stat. 775.
49. *Ibid.*
50. Kreidberg and Henry, *History of Military Mobilization,* pp. 177–79.
51. 35 Stat. 66–69.

1912 a document entitled "The Organization of the Land Forces of the United States." This remarkable work had a considerable influence upon the establishment of a Federal reserve force prior to World War I. The impact of Elihu Root was indeed far-ranging.

2

The Early Years

Behind the regular army must always stand the great reserve army consisting of the able-bodied men of the nation, so trained as to be
promptly available for military service if needed, but following their normal occupations in time of peace.

MAJ. GEN. LEONARD WOOD, 1916[1]

THE MEDICAL RESERVE

The passage of Senate Bill 1424 on April 23, 1908, authorized the Army to secure a reserve corps of medical
officers who could be ordered to active duty by the Secretary
of War during time of emergency. These reserve doctors were
to be commissioned as first lieutenants and to rank below
all other officers of like grade in the United States. The act
also provided for the commissioning of contract physicians
in either the Regular Army or the Medical Reserve Corps,
depending upon their age.[2] This latter provision generated
the only serious opposition to the bill, with Representative

---

1. Leonard Wood, *Our Military History, Its Facts and Fallacies,*
(Chicago: Reilly and Britton, 1916), pp. 226–27.
2. On March 22, 1967, Brig. Gen. Hal C. Pattison, Chief of Military History wrote Maj. Gen. William J. Sutton, Chief, Army Reserve
that "although the National Defense Act of 1916 is viewed as providing
for the immediate ancestor of our Reserve system in its present form, it
is considered appropriate that 23 April 1908 be established as the official
birth date of the United States Army Reserve. The Act of Congress on
that date which created the Medical Reserve Corps, for the first time in
Army history, provided for the establishment of a reservoir of trained
officer personnel in a reserve status." Copy in OCAR Historical Files.

James R. Mann of Illinois predicting that it would allow contract surgeons to enter the Army and ultimately flow to the retired list after a short period of time. Mann's objections notwithstanding, the act passed the House 126 to 15, and the nation's first federal military reserve force was established.[3]

The first candidates for reserve commissions were certified on May 4, 1908, and by the end of the fiscal year on June 30, 160 contract physicians had been recommended for commissions in the Medical Reserve Corps. Their commissions would date from July 7, 1908. A year later, Surgeon General R. M. Reilly reported that "in order to build up the Reserve Corps with desirable material, a strong effort has been made to induce prominent physicians, surgeons, hygienists and laboratory workers to head it."[4] By June 30, 1909, 364 men had been commissioned in the Medical Reserve Corps, including 160 former contract physicians, and 184 such men were on active duty.[5]

In his 1909 report, Surgeon General George H. Torney spoke glowingly of his Medical Reserve Corps physicians, noting that "when it was necessary to assemble a board to investigate the important subject of inoculation for typhoid fever, it was possible to do so without going outside of the Medical Reserve Corps."[6] Torney stated that it would have been difficult to find a more qualified board anywhere. He also praised the Reserve doctors for aiding the Army in locating suitable physicians for commissions in the Army Medical Service.

---

3. The full text of Senate Bill 1424, as enacted, can be found on pages 66–69 of Part 1, Volume 35, *The Statutes at Large of the United States of America*. Representative Mann's voluminous objections are recorded on pages 3402–06 of Volume 42 of the *Congressional Record*.

4. R. M. O'Reilly, *Report of the Surgeon General, 1908* (Washington: War Department, 1908), pp. 131–32.

5. According to the *New York Times* of Nov. 30, 1908, the original 364 Medical Reserve Corps doctors included Dr. Roswell Park, the Buffalo, N.Y., surgeon who attended President McKinley after he was shot; Drs. Wyeth and Bryan, ex-Presidents of the American Medical Association; Dr. Souchin, a New Orleans, La., yellow fever expert; and Dr. Frank Billings, a respected surgeon with Johns Hopkins Hospital in Baltimore, Md. The *Times* also reported that the War Department commissioned Drs. William T. Bull and Andrew J. McCosh, "New York surgeons, both of whom are now critically ill in this city." Apparently, the standards for commissioning were somewhat vague.

6. *Report of the Surgeon General, 1909* (Washington: War Department, 1909), p. 173.

Table 2–1   Number of Physicians in the United States Army.

As of June 30 . . .	Medical Reserve Corps		Regular Army Medical Officers
	Not On Active Duty	On Active Duty	
1908	0*	0	301
1909	180	184	283
1910	245	175	345
1911	784	138	381
1912	990	115	414
1913	1,100	105	424
1914	1,163	91	426
1915	1,340	86	433
1916	1,757	146	443

*As of June 30, 1908, 160 surgeons had been recommended for appointment in the Medical Reserve Corps. Their commissions would date from July 7, 1908.

Source: Reports of the War Department (1908–1916).

By June 30, 1910, Torney was pleased to report that the "Medical Reserve Corps has now passed the experimental stage."[7] Within two years, the strength of the Medical Reserve Corps exceeded one thousand; and in 1913, Reserve officers manned the Army's garrisons to allow Regular Army physicians to deploy to the field. In July 1913, Reserve doctors provided medical care to aging Civil War veterans during their Gettysburg encampment, and Torney recommended placing Reserve physicians on active duty at maneuver camps.

In 1914, a number of Medical Reserve Corps officers were appointed as special professors to the Army Medical School to deliver lectures ranging from "prevention and control of infectious diseases" to "cardia arythmia and circulatory efficiency." The Medical Reserve Corps grew to 1,903 officers in 1916 and outnumbered Regular Army doctors four to one.

By virtue of the National Defense Act of 1916, the Medical Reserve Corps ceased to exist on June 3, 1917, when its members were commissioned in the Officers' Reserve Corps as members of the Medical Officer's Reserve Corps. The Act of 1916 also allowed the Surgeon General to appoint officers in the Veterinary Officers' Reserve Corps and

7. Report of the Surgeon General, 1910 (Washington: War Department, 1910), p. 456.

the Dental Officers' Reserve Corps. Together, these three corps contained 9,223 officers at the end of the 1917 fiscal year—a growth of twenty-five hundred percent in a decade.

While the officers of the Medical Reserve Corps were proving the value and desirability of a federal reserve force, a growing debate over the future of America's citizen-soldiers was beginning. In 1908, Congress had been intent upon clarifying the status of the National Guard and enacted legislation on May 27 to require the War Department to call the organized militia into service ahead of volunteer units when it was necessary to "execute the laws of the Union, suppress insurrection or repel invasion."[8] The Secretary of War was authorized to issue arms, equipment, clothing and military stores in general to the militia—provided that the United States retained title to the property.

When the Army General Staff realized that this act, which amended the Dick Act, required the War Department to use all militia, no matter how poorly organized, equipped or trained, before volunteer units, there was a strong desire to find another alternative reserve force.[9] This desire was expressed by John McAuley Palmer in his 1912 "Report on the Organization of the Land Forces of the United States."

ENTER JOHN MCAULEY PALMER

Palmer was the grandson of Maj. Gen. John M. Palmer, a volunteer Civil War officer who achieved high command with the Army of the Cumberland. A graduate of West Point, the younger Palmer was well acquainted with the capabilities of citizen-soldiers such as his grandfather. He was relatively uninfluenced by the anti-militia views of Emory Upton. Upton's *The Military Policy of the United States* had been posthumously published, and a distrust of the militia was very much in vogue among Regular Army officers in the early 1900s.[10]

---

8. Senate Bill 4316, enacted May 27, 1908, entitled "An Act to Further Amend the Act entitled 'An Act to Promote the Efficiency of the Militia of 1903,'" also divided the militia of the United States into the organized militia, known as the National Guard, and the Reserve Militia, which was otherwise undefined.

9. William H. Riker, *Soldiers of the States,* (Washington: Public Affairs Press, 1957), pp. 74–75.

10. Russell F. Weigley, *Towards an American Army, Military Thought from Washington to Marshall* (Westport, Conn.: Greenwood Press, 1962), pp. 228–29.

Palmer had for some time had the opinion that John C. Calhoun's idea of an expansible army "could have no congenial place in the American political system."[11] When Palmer assumed a peacetime Regular Army nucleus large enough to make a real foundation for effective expansion for war, he realized that the American people would be saddled with a prohibitively expensive standing Army. When he assumed a nucleus small enough to be acceptable to Congress, the expanded wartime force was insufficient for war on the European scale. This dilemma led Palmer to conclude that the only rational alternative was to rely upon the citizen-armies that had served Washington, Grant and Lee so well. He further reasoned that by organizing and training such armies in peacetime, these citizen-soldier armies would be preferable to any expansible army scheme.[12]

In the fall of 1911, Palmer was assigned to the War College Division of the new General Staff. Palmer's desire for a pre-trained reserve of citizen-soldiers coincided with the thoughts of Chief of Staff Leonard Wood. Indeed, Wood had written in his 1910 *Report of the Chief of Staff* that it was "imperatively necessary that steps should be taken to organize a proper reserve from which the regular and militia organizations can be properly filled with instructed men.[13] Palmer was thereupon given the task of drafting a major reorganization of the land forces of the United States. When Palmer was ready to outline his proposals, Wood arranged a meeting with Secretary of War Henry L. Stimson. The meeting took place during a long train ride to Fort Leavenworth, Kan., and Stimson and Wood listened to Palmer's ideas at great length.

Palmer proposed that American military policy should move away from the Regular Army as its central focus. Primary emphasis should be placed instead on "the citizen army and its relation to the permanent establishment." In Palmer's words, the "most important military problem is to devise means of preparing great armies of citizen soldiers to meet the emergency of modern war."[14] Stimson and Wood agreed with Palmer; and once the fundamental principle of a

---

11. John McAuley Palmer, *America in Arms*, (New Haven: Yale University Press, 1941), p. 135.

12. *Ibid.*, pp. 136–37.

13. *Report of the Chief of Staff, 1910*, as found in *War Department Reports, 1910* (Washington: War Department, 1910), Vol. I, p. 131.

14. I. B. Holley, Jr., *General John M. Palmer, Citizen-Soldiers, and the Army of A Democracy* (Westport, Conn.: Greenwood Press, 1982), pp. 200–04.

citizen reserve was agreed upon, Palmer was free to develop the details of the reorganization.[15]

Even though it was late in 1911, Palmer influenced the 1911 Report of the Secretary of War, which Stimson forwarded to the President on December 4. Stimson wrote that "it is absolutely imperative that provision should be made, by an adequate system of regular reserves, to fill up and maintain this first line of defense during the necessary time that must elapse while we are preparing and mobilizing our Militia and Volunteers."[16]

In the same report, Stimson stated that one of the main functions of a modern army is to train citizen-soldiers, who after training go back to their normal lives, ready to be called upon in an emergency.[17] Wood seconded Stimson by writing that "in view of the small size of the Regular Army and the small number of instructed militia, it is imperatively necessary that steps should be taken to organize a reserve of men . . . ."[18] Wood recommended a small monthly pay and 10-days annual maneuver or instruction with full pay for the members of this reserve. Wood also observed that 10 "Reserves" could be maintained for the cost of one Regular Army soldier—a ratio not very different from the cost of Reservists versus Regular Army soldiers in 1983.[19]

The Palmer plan, which was proposed to Congress in detail in 1912, organized the mobile land forces of the United States into three distinct parts. The first was a Regular Army ready for immediate use as an expeditionary force

---

15. When discussing his memoirs nearly 30 years later, Palmer summarized his beliefs thusly: "A government by the people must rest its defense upon Washington's army of the people and not upon Upton's expansible standing army. We must build strength into the democratic state without creating an exclusive samurai caste. We must have military power without militarism." (Letter of Palmer to Grenville Clark, Sept. 14, 1940.)

16. *Report of the Secretary of War, 1911* (Washington: War Department, 1911), pp. 22–23.

17. *Ibid.,* p. 21.

18. *Report of the Chief of Staff, 1911,* in *War Department Reports, 1911* (Washington: War Department, 1911), Vol. I, pp. 151–52.

19. A Reservist receives approximately one-sixth of the pay of an active-duty soldier, and lower operational and maintenance costs are likewise associated with Reserve units. A member of the Individual Ready Reserve (IRR) frequently receives only two weeks pay a year, or in many cases, no pay at all. Overall, the cost of maintaining the nearly 500,000 Reservists of the Ready Reserve is approximately one-tenth of that of maintaining a like number of men and women on active duty.

or for the first stages of a defensive war while the citizen-soldiery was being mobilized.

The second force was an army of citizen-soldiers organized into units and ready to reinforce the Regular Army in time of war. In 1912 this was the National Guard. Third was the army of volunteers, trained citizen-soldiers. Essentially, the 1912 plan was what the Army finally secured under the National Defense Act of 1920.[20]

The proponents of a federal reserve force were strengthened in February 1912 when Attorney General George W. Wickersham ruled that "the militia while in U.S. service might pursue an invading force beyond the U.S. boundary as part of repelling an invasion, but in general the militia cannot be employed outside of the United States."[21]

In arguing for an Army Reserve, Stimson pointed out that a reserve system was in effect in practically every nation of the world except the United States.[22] He pointed out that when the Spanish-American War broke out, many regiments were "greatly injured by the necessity of throwing into them a large number of perfectly raw recruits."[23] A trained federal reserve force of citizen-soldiers would prevent this problem, Stimson said.

In light of the Wickersham opinion, and persuaded by the exhortations of Stimson and Wood, Congress created an Army Reserve under provisions of Section 2 of the Army Appropriations Act of Aug. 24, 1912. This was accomplished by changing the term of Regular Army enlistment to seven years, with three or four years to be served with the colors and the balance to be a furlough to the Army Reserve.[24] This was the first provision for a federal reserve outside of the Medical Department.

Although pleased by the creation of the Army Reserve through the Act of 1912, Wood continued to press for a

---

20. Palmer, *America in Arms*, pp. 142–43.

21. Letter, Attorney General George W. Wickersham to Secretary of War Henry L. Stimson, Feb. 17, 1912.

22. According to the 1912 War Department *Annual Reports*, the United States had no Army Reserve, while the reserves of Great Britain stood at 215,000, and Japan counted one million reservists. The reserve strength of Italy was 1.5 million; Austria, 2.5 million; France, 3 million; Germany, 4.7 million; and Russia, 5.4 million.

23. *Report of the Secretary of War, 1912* (Washington: War Department, 1912), p. 20.

24. The portion of House Resolution 25531 pertaining to the new Army Reserve can be found on pages 590 and 591 of Part 1, Vol. 37, *Statutes at Large of the United States of America*.

more comprehensive federal reserve force. By August 31, 1913, the Army Reserve consisted of only eight men, and Wood observed that men would not enlist in the Army Reserve under present conditions. He sought pay for Reservists, noting that "we cannot secure valuable service for nothing."[25]

In his 1914 report to the President, Secretary of War Lindley M. Garrison stated that "present legislation with respect to a reserve has proven utterly useless for the purpose."[26] Noting that the Army Reserve had doubled to 16 men, Wood repeated his previous sentiments and asked for authority to commission 400 provisional lieutenants each year. These officers would serve one year in training with the Regular Army and then leave active duty to form a reserve of officers.

Wood's term as Army Chief of Staff ended in 1914, and he was assigned to command the First Military District at Governor's Island, NY. This reduction in responsibility gave him ample time for writing and speech-making. Wood wrote profusely for magazines, and his short books were eloquent and forceful in pleading for an Army Reserve. Wood also became involved in the Plattsburg camps and the Military Training Camps Association.

CIVILIAN TRAINING

As Chief of Staff, Wood had been successful in starting two experimental camps of military instruction for college students during their 1913 summer vacation. The camps had been the idea of Lt. Henry T. Bull, a cavalry officer detailed as professor of military science at Cornell University. Students paid their own transportation to the camps at Pacific Grove, Calif., and Gettysburg, Penn., and paid approximately $27.50 for uniforms and food.

Despite an arduous course of instruction, which began at 5:15 a.m., the 159 young men at the initial camps became so enthusiastic that officers occasionally had to order them to stop drill in order to swim or play ball. Later, 84 of these 159 received Reserve commissions and served in World War I.[27]

---

25. *Report of the Chief of Staff, 1913,* in *War Department Reports, 1913* (Washington: War Department, 1913), pp. 150–51.

26. *Reports of the Secretary of War, 1914* (Washington: War Department, 1914), p. 11.

27. John G. Clifford, *The Citizen Soldiers* (Lexington, Ky.: University Press of Kentucky, 1972), pp. 11–16.

The camps made a strong impression on several college presidents, including Henry Drinker of Lehigh University. Drinker accompanied his son to Gettysburg, and when the students formed the Society of the National Reserve Corps of the United States, Drinker was elected president.[28]

Drinker formed the Advisory Board of University Presidents for the National Reserve Corps and successfully rallied academic support for additional camps in 1914. Wood was able to arrange the detail of additional Army officers to instruct at the camps, and 667 students attended the second summer—again at their own expense.[29]

After the beginning of war in Europe on July 28, 1914, the General Staff began an update of the 1912 "Report on the Organization of the Land Forces in the United States" in order to overcome this country's military weakness. The result was the "Statement of a Proper Military Policy for the United States."

The statement recommended "more than doubling the size of the Regular Army, from 100,000 to 230,000; continued support of the Organized Militia; a Regular Army reserve; a reserve of trained citizen-soldiers; a reserve of officers; and a reserve of essential supplies."[30] To translate the statement into reality, Secretary Garrison devised his Continental Army proposal, which can be reduced to three main points:

1. A Regular Army large enough to meet immediate military needs while training other military forces.
2. A volunteer, trained federal reserve force—the Continental Army—to immediately augment the Regular Army in emergencies.
3. Retain the National Guard under state control, but with increased federal assistance.[31]

Garrison also proposed to recruit officer cadets from the National Guard for his Continental Army, but ruffled National Guard feathers when he said that "strictly speaking,

---

28. The constitution of the National Reserve Corps is found on page 587 of the Dec. 18, 1913, edition of *Leslie's Illustrated Weekly* as part of an article written by Wood entitled "How to Have a Bigger Army."

29. Clifford, *Citizen Soldiers*, pp. 18–24.

30. Marvin A. Kreidberg and Merton G. Henry, *History of Military Mobilization in the United States Army, 1775–1945* (Washington: Department of the Army, 1955), p. 190.

31. *Report of the Secretary of War, 1915* (Washington: War Department, 1915), pp. 22–27.

nothing less than Regular Army training makes an efficient soldier.[32] Garrison also irritated Guardsmen by writing the 1915 convention of the National Guard Association that Guard units would be "permitted" to transfer from the National Guard to the Continental Army. A speech by Assistant Secretary of War Henry Breckenridge to that same convention left many Guardsmen with the impression that the National Guard would no longer have any federal sanction, and its future would be left up to the states.

Meanwhile, stunned by the sinking of the *Lusitania* in May 1915, law partners Grenville Clark and Elihu Root, Jr., son of the former Secretary of War, determined to do something to demonstrate a firm national policy against Germany. Enlisting the aid of Theodore Roosevelt, Jr.,[33] they approached Wood with the idea of adapting the youth summer camps to camps for men in their twenties and thirties.

The general was supportive. If Clark and the others could sign up at least 100 professional and business men for the camps, Wood would provide the officers and equipment. When recruiting for the businessmen's camps went well, Wood was able to have the adult camp included under War Department General Order No. 38, June 22, 1915, which authorized that summer's college camps.

Approximately 1,200 men assembled at Plattsburg, NY, for the first businessmen's camp. Compressing the five-week student program into four weeks, the men started their day with 5:45 a.m. calisthenics, followed by drill until noon. After lunch, there was specialized instruction in the arms of the service—cavalry, signal, engineering. As with the student camps, the participants at Plattsburg tackled the training with great enthusiasm. Just as the students at Gettysburg organized at camp's end, the men at Plattsburg formed the First Training Regiment.

Determined that Plattsburg should not be a flash-in-the-pan, Clark worked with members of similar busi-

---

32. *Ibid.,* p. 35.
33. Theodore Roosevelt, Jr., went on to earn a commission before World War I. After a distinguished peace-time public service career, he was recalled to active duty in 1941. He served in the North African, Sicilian and Corsican landings and established a reputation for courage under fire. As a 57-year old brigadier general, he was the only general and the oldest man to go ashore in the first wave of the Normandy assault upon Utah Beach. He was the assistant division commander of the 4th Infantry Division.

nessmen's camps and with the Advisory Board of University Presidents of the National Reserve Corps to form the Military Training Camps Association of the United States (MTCA). The stated purpose of the MTCA was to encourage reasonable military training for citizens through federal training camps, and the group's efforts later played an important role in the "90-day-wonder" commissioning camps of World War I.[34]

In 1915, preparedness was a major issue in America; and the MTCA was an ideal apparatus for spreading the word on preparedness. The MTCA had a number of active committees staffed with well-known personalities, and the movement was national in scope. It was strongly influenced by ex-President Theodore Roosevelt and by Wood,[35] who saw his citizen-army gospel enhanced by the MTCA's enthusiasm for citizen's military training.[36]

In Lindley Garrison's mind, preparedness was his Continental Army plan. To the National Guard and Representative James Hay, Chairman of the House Military Affairs Committee, it was a stronger National Guard with increased federal support. This made for a collection of semi-allies with divergent interests operating under the general banner of increased preparedness.

While these divergent interests agreed that it was necessary to improve the national defense, it was impossible to reach a consensus on what should be done. In fact, in the opinion of historian Russell F. Weigley, the sweeping legislation of the 1916 National Defense Act could never have been achieved except for problems with Mexico.[37]

MEXICO

The United States had been involved in the internal affairs of Mexico following the 1911 overthrow of dictator Porfirio Diaz, the details of which are not relevant to this narrative. It is sufficient that displeasure with U.S. policies led peasant leader Francisco "Pancho" Villa to retaliate by raiding Columbus, New Mexico, on March 9, 1916. Within a week, the War Department sent 5,000 troops under Brig. Gen. John J. Pershing across the border in pursuit of Villa.

---

34. Clifford, *Citizen Soldiers*, pp. 116–17, 150.
35. Holley, *General John M. Palmer*, pp. 249–50.
36. Russell F. Weigley, *History of the United States Army* (New York: Macmillan Co., 1967), p. 343.
37. *Ibid.*, p. 347.

Villa made a mockery of the campaign, and the Mexican government demanded that Pershing be withdrawn. Villa continued to menace American towns, while war with Mexico seemed almost inevitable. On May 9 the War Department called out the Texas, New Mexico and Arizona National Guards, but this force did not appear to be enough.[38]

On May 17, because of the conditions along the border, all furloughs to the Army Reserve were suspended except for furloughs from the Coast Artillery.[39] On June 28, the War Department ordered the first mobilization of the Army Reserve. The military departments were directed to order Reservists to active duty for service with Regular Army regiments on the Mexican border, and approximately 3,000 Reservists answered the call.[40]

THE NATIONAL DEFENSE ACT OF 1916

Under pressure from events along the border, the Congress acted on compromise legislation proposed by Hay, which passed the Senate on May 17 and the House May 20. This was the comprehensive National Defense Act of 1916 that was signed into law by President Wilson on June 3, 1916.

More than 100 pages long, with 128 sections, the National Defense Act of 1916 defined the Army of the United States as the "Regular Army, the Volunteer Army, the Officers' Reserve Corps, the Enlisted Reserve Corps, the National Guard while in the service of the United States, and such other land forces as are now or may hereafter be authorized by law." As a military omnibus bill, it provided something for everyone.

38. *Ibid.*, p. 348; according to the 1917 *Report of the Adjutant General*, approximately 3,000 members of the Regular Army Reserve subsequently responded to a mobilization call of June 28, 1916, and were assigned to Regular Army units along the Mexico border. See page 193, *Report of the Adjutant General, 1917.*

39. Report of the Adjutant General, *War Department Reports, 1916* (Washington, DC: War Department, 1917), p. 255.

40. *Report of the Adjutant General, War Department Reports, 1917* (Washington: War Department, 1918), p. 193. In contrast to the official War Department reports, the July 7, 1916, *New York Times* reported on page 4 that the War Department was going to summon approximately 5,000 Reservists to the colors. According to The Adjutant General, this would have been impossible, since there were only 4,626 Reservists including the Coast Artillery. According to the National Guard Bureau, 158,664 National Guardsmen were also mobilized.

The National Guard received federal pay for drills,[41] which were set by the act at 48 per year. On the other hand, the carrot of federal pay was used to counterbalance the stick of federal recognition and standards for Guard officers, the authority of the President to prescribe the kind of units to be maintained by the states, and the requirements that enlistment qualifications for the Guard be the same as the Regular Army. Guardsmen were also required to take a dual oath to their State and the United States.

The Regular Army was authorized an increase to 175,000 men over a period of five years, and the number of general officers was increased. The Officers' Reserve Corps, the Enlisted Reserve Corps and the Reserve Officers Training Corps were also established statutorily. The comprehensive federal reserve force so ardently espoused by Root, Wood, Stimson and Garrison was finally authorized.

The MTCA had been instrumental in keeping a training camps provision intact during the legislative process that hammered out the National Defense Act of 1916. The lobbying of Clark and Drinker, with the assistance of Sen. Henry A. duPont of Delaware, resulted in the 16,000 men who took Plattsburg training in the summer of 1916 being the first to do so under federal statute.[42]

According to John G. Clifford in his book, *The Citizen Soldiers,* the 1916 camps were the product of hard work and cooperation between the MTCA and the War Department. The camps gave increased publicity to preparedness and the idea that citizens had a universal military obligation. These camps, called Regular Army Instruction Camps, augmented the country's trained military personnel as MTCA personnel, called Plattsburgers, flocked by the hundreds to join the new Officers' Reserve Corps (ORC) and Reserve Officers Training Corps (ROTC).[43]

By February 1917, approximately 500 Reserve Officers had been commissioned, in addition to nearly 2,000 in the still-separate Medical Reserve Corps. As United States intervention in World War I became more likely, the Army and the MTCA stepped up their recruiting efforts. As of March 1, 939 Reserve Officers had been commissioned and another 565 commissions were pending. The MTCA had 70,000 applicants for the 1917 Regular Instruction Camps. On April 1, 1917, the Regular Army, including the Philippine

41. Riker, *Soldiers of the States,* pp. 76–80.
42. Clifford, *Citizen Soldiers,* pp. 116–17.
43. *Ibid.,* pp. 152–53.

Scouts, had a strength of 133,111. There were 80,446 National Guardsmen in Federal service, plus 101,174 members of the Guard still in State service.[44]

WORLD WAR I

There was an obvious need for more Army officers following US entry into World War I on April 6, 1917, and the MTCA sent Secretary of War Newton D. Baker a telegram proposing to open the instruction camps as early as May to serve as a professional training ground for men being offered commissions in the ORC.

Baker agreed. The staggering task of recruiting 40,000 officer candidates in just three weeks began. The camps opened May 15 using the recently published *Plattsburg Manual*[45] as their basic text. Meanwhile, the commissioning process was accelerated, with 7,957 Reserve Officers appointed by May 15. These officers, as well as the new candidates, were required to attend the training camps in order to retain their commissions.[46]

Including officers transferred from the Medical Reserve Corps when it was merged with the ORC on June 3, 1917, the ORC on June 30, 1917, consisted of 21,543 officers.[47] It was with this nucleus of trained reserve officers and reserve enlisted men with specialized skills that the United States Army entered World War I.

The Enlisted Reserve Corps had been created by the National Defense Act of 1916 for the expressed purpose "of securing an additional reserve of enlisted men for military service with the Engineer, Signal and Quartermaster Corps and the Ordnance and Medical Departments of the Regular Army."[48] The purpose was to obtain a reserve of pretrained specialists who would augment the Regular Army upon call

---

44. Marvin A. Kriedberg and Merton G. Henry, *History of Military Mobilization in the United States Army, 1775–1945* (Washington: Department of the Army, 1955), p. 374.

45. *The Plattsburg Manual*, first published in March 1917 and indorsed by Wood, was designed to be a first textbook for those who desired an ORC commission. In 336 pages, it covered a wealth of military subjects from physical training to patrolling and trench warfare. It went through 10 printings in 14 months.

46. *Kriedberg, op. cit.*, pp. 224–225.

47. *Report of the Secretary of War, 1917* (Washington: War Department, 1917), pp. 193–94.

48. See Section 55, PL 64–85, 134 U.S.C. 195.

of the President; and this Enlisted Reserve Corps[49] was in addition to the Regular Army Reserve, which had been established in 1912 and continued under the 1916 act.[50]

Furloughs from the active Army to the Regular Army Reserve (RAR) were suspended on April 19, 1917, and virtually all members of the RAR were ordered back to active duty in May. Meanwhile, the Enlisted Reserve Corps was growing rapidly, reaching 35,000 men on June 30, 1917, and 55,000 by October 1 of the same year. According to the Adjutant General, nine Engineer regiments, were organized for railway work abroad, and 27 field Signal battalions, 12 telegraph battalions and six depot companies were formed from this Reserve.

In addition, the Enlisted Reserve Corps provided the men for 235 wagon companies, 106 auto-truck companies, 20 bakery companies and 24 pack-train companies, plus nearly 15,000 men who served in the Medical Department in World War I.[51] In all, approximately 80,000 Enlisted Reserve Corps or Regular Army Reservists served in World War I.[52]

The Officers' Reserve Corps provided a total of 89,476 officers during World War I,[53] of whom 57,307 were commissioned through the 90-day Officers' Training Camps. Included in the larger figure were 639 "colored" officers commissioned at Fort Des Moines, Iowa, in 1917. Two schools in Puerto Rico produced 433 officers.[54]

The Reserve Officers Training Corps produced 3,364 ORC officers, and 23,261 former enlisted men were commissioned through Officers' Training Schools operated by the

---

49. A particularly popular Enlisted Reserve Corps option was in the Aviation Section, Signal Enlisted Reserve Corps. A number of the Army's early aviators came out of this corps including Edward V. "Eddie" Rickenbacker, who won the Medal of Honor and the Distinguished Service Cross with six Oak Leaf Clusters as a World War I flying ace. The Enlisted Reserve Corps was also a holding status for potential officers with special skills such as medical students.

50. The Regular Army Reserve was never a large force. This body of soldiers furloughed from the Regular Army stood at 4,648 on June 30, 1916, and grew to 8,355 before furloughs were suspended on April 19, 1917.

51. *Report of the Secretary of War, 1917.*

52. "Report of the Adjutant General," in *War Department Annual Reports, 1919* (Washington: War Department, 1919), Vol. I, pp. 500–01.

53. *Ibid.*

54. *Report of the Chief of Staff, 1919,* in *War Department Annual Reports, 1919* (Washington: War Department, 1919), pp. 299–301.

various corps and divisions before all distinctions between components were ended on August 7, 1918. After that date, the appellations "Regular Army," "Officers' Reserve Corps," "National Guard," and "National Army" were dropped and all commissions were granted in the Army of the United States.

The American Expeditionary Force (AEF) commander in Europe was General John J. Pershing, a Regular Army man who had previously commanded the US forces on the Mexican border. Pershing was greatly concerned about the short period of training that the American draftees and volunteers received, and he devoted many months to training the men who reached Europe in 1917 and early 1918.[55] Pershing's insistence on additional training was vindicated, for American units gave a good account of themselves in places like St. Mihiel and the Meuse-Argonne,[56] and Pershing himself was apparently convinced that a large standing army was unnecessary in time of peace.

As in subsequent wars, the divisions of World War I did not remain pure Regular Army, National Army or National Guard divisions even prior to August 7. Officers of all components and men from the Enlisted Reserve Corps served in every division, making the Army Reserve's contribution to World War I a contribution to the total war effort.[57]

---

55. Weigley, *History of the United States Army,* p. 372.

56. Charles B. MacDonald, "World War I: The U.S. Army Overseas," in Maurice Matloff (Gen. Ed.), *American Military History* (Washington: Office of the Chief of Military History, United States Army, 1969), pp. 396–403.

57. *Report of the Chief of Staff, 1919,* p. 280.

3

Between the World Wars 1919–1939

Demobilization proceeded rapidly after the war, and by June 30, 1919, 2,608,218 enlisted men and 128,436 officers had been discharged. Six months later the US Army consisted of only 130,000 Regular troops, about the same number as in April 1917.[1] There were no special plans for strengthening the reserve forces of the Army, and in fact Army Chief of Staff Peyton C. March proposed to Congress in 1919 a plan for an expanded Regular Army of over 500,000 men, filled out in time of war by a horde of conscripts backed up by the National Guard.[2]

Congress was in no mood, however, to provide for such a substantial increase in the standing army, and both houses resisted the blandishments of the War Department. Congress sought a reasonable alternative to March's proposal, and in October 1919 it found a man who was willing to offer such. Colonel John McAuley Palmer had been one of Pershing's proteges in the AEF, and he had returned to Washington after the war as a member of the War Plans Division of the General Staff. Palmer's experience in France had strengthened his existing belief in the values of the citizen-soldier, and when Senator James J. Wadsworth invited him to testify before the Committee on Military Affairs, Palmer was ready to offer his opinions.[3]

---

1. Russell F. Weigley, *History of the United States Army* (New York and London: Macmillan Publishing Co., Inc. and Collier Macmillan Publishers, 1967), p. 396.
2. *Ibid.* pp. 396–97.
3. Jonathan M. House, "John McAuley Palmer and the Reserve

By the end of Palmer's two days as an expert witness, Sen. Wadsworth was convinced that the outspoken colonel—who had castigated the proposals of Chief of Staff March—was just the man to work on a Senate proposal for amending the National Defense Act of 1916. Palmer was thereupon loaned to the Committee, and he worked for eight months on the project. After much compromising with the House of Representatives, which had developed its own bill, many of Palmer's ideas (except his plans for universal military training) were enacted into law in 1920.

Usually called the National Defense Act of 1920,[4] this piece of legislation was far-reaching in its impact on the organization of the United States Army. The Army was now defined as consisting of the Regular Army, the National Guard, and the Organized Reserves; and the entire country was divided into corps areas. In each corps was to be at least one division of Organized Reserve troops. The Regular Army reserve was abolished by the 1920 statute, and its members were relieved of further military obligations.[5]

Of primary interest to reservists were a re-statement of the 1916 Defense Act provisions creating the Officers' Reserve Corps, the Reserve Officers' Training Corps, and the Enlisted Reserve Corps and the statutory regulation of the Citizens' Military Training Camps that had developed out of the pre-war Plattsburg movement.[6] Because of the small inter-war size of the Enlisted Reserve Corps, this chapter is restricted almost totally to the Officers' Reserve Corps.

On July 21, 1921, General Pershing succeeded General March as Chief of Staff of the Army, and under him the reserves received greater attention than ever before.[7] The instrument of this attention was none other than Brig. Gen. John McA. Palmer, who was a member of Pershing's personal staff. During Pershing's tenure as Chief of Staff, wrote Palmer, "my principal duty was to advise him in questions of policy relating to reserve and other 'citizen army' affairs." He acted purely in an advisory capacity, said Palmer, and when his advice "pointed to administrative action, he [General Pershing] ordered the proper agency of the War Department to take that action."[8]

Components," *Parameters: Journal of the US Army War College,* Vol. XII (September 1982), pp. 14–15.

4. Public Law 66–242.
5. *Ibid.,* Secs. 3, 30.
6. *Ibid.,* Secs. 37, 40, 47 and 55.
7. Weigley, *History of the United States Army,* p. 560.
8. Letter, John McA. Palmer to Col. E. S. Hartshorn, Executive for

The problems of the Army's Organized Reserve forces after World War I were numerous, even after passage of the National Defense Act of 1920. Lack of an institution for providing guidance at the Army Staff level, poor opportunities for training, and—given these two problems—an unrealistic view of mobilization were endemic. The Army Staff did not have any ready solution in any of these areas, but Chief of Staff Pershing decided that the first priority was to insure that someone at the Army Staff level would have a continuing responsibility for reserve affairs after he and Gen. Palmer were gone.

ESTABLISHMENT OF A RESERVE OFFICE

In a March 1, 1923, memorandum, Pershing directed the Deputy Chief of Staff to study the question of "establishing an agency in the War Department whose express function will be to handle questions pertaining to the Reserves, that is, an agency to which reserve officers seeking information or with recommendations to make, or any business relating to the reserves could go and receive a cordial welcome and thoughtful consideration. I think no such agency now exists in the department."[9]

As a result of Pershing's memorandum, a Reserve Officers' Section was established on June 12, 1923, under the Assistant Chief of Staff, G–2. Maj. C. F. Thompson was given temporary responsibility for the section, as an additional duty. Thompson's tenure, however, lasted only until July 2, at which time he was succeeded by Maj. Walter O. Boswell.[10]

The position of "Chief of the Reserve Section, G–2" did not accord enough importance to the role of the Officers' Reserve Corps during the inter-war period.[11] In March 1927,

Reserve Affairs, July 1, 1935, in National Archives, Record Group 319 (Army Staff), Entry #343 (Records for Reserve and ROTC Affairs), Box 100. Hereinafter cited by RG #, Entry #, and Box #.

9. Memorandum, General John J. Pershing to Deputy Chief of Staff, March 1, 1923, RG 319, Entry 343, Box 97.

10. Memorandum, H. C. McCormick to Col. E. S. Hartshorn, June 27, 1935, RG 319, Entry 343, Box 97. Major Thompson returned later as Brig. Gen. Thompson and served as Executive for Reserve Affairs, September 16, 1938–June 9, 1940. A complete listing of the Chiefs of the Army Reserve—by whatever title they were known—is in Appendix A.

11. The Enlisted Reserve Corps, created by the National Defense Act of 1920, was of very minor importance between World Wars I and II. It consisted of only 6000 men in 1928, and by 1936 its ranks num-

therefore, Colonel David L. Stone was transferred to the Army Chief of Staff's Office from the Office of the Assistant Secretary of War and was assigned as "Executive for Reserve Affairs."[12] This reporting relationship lasted only ten days, for on March 15, 1927, The Adjutant General suspended "until further notice" the transfer of the position to the Chief of Staff's Office.[13] Col. Stone's successor, Col. (later Brigadier General) Charles D. Herron, took over the position in May 1930, and he, too, reported to the Assistant Secretary of War. In November 1930, however, Col. Herron was transferred to the Office of the Chief of Staff, where the status of the Executive for Reserve Affairs was "analogous to that of the Legislation Branch." Col. Herron was soon informed that the office, which as late as September 1936 consisted only of the Executive and a secretary, would "be an adjunct to, and will function directly under, the Deputy Chief of Staff."[14]

The Office of the Executive for Reserve Affairs remained at this small staffing level until April 16, 1941, when it was allocated two additional officer positions: a lieutenant colonel and a captain. The title was officially changed at almost the same time to the "Office of the Executive for Reserve and ROTC Affairs," a title that was used until 1954.[15]

---

bered less than 4000. "Organization of the Army, 1928," RG 319, Entry 343, Box 97; "Strength of the O.R.C. and E.R.C., June 30, 1936," RG 319, Entry 343, Box 100.

12. Special Orders No. 53, Par. 24, March 5, 1927, cited in "Digest of War Department Policies," Subject: "Supervision of Reserve Affairs," November 7, 1930, RG 319, Entry 343, Box 98.

13. Letter from TAG, March 15, 1927, cited in "Digest of War Department Policies," Subject: "Supervision of Reserve Affairs," November 7, 1939, RG 319, Entry 343, Box 98.

14. "Digest of War Department Policies," Subject: "Supervision of Reserve Affairs," November 7, 1930, RG 319, Entry 343, Box 98; Memorandum, Gen. C. P. Summerall to The Adjutant General, November 1, 1930, Subject: "Executive for Reserve Affairs," RG 319, Entry 343, Box 98; Memorandum, Brig. Gen. Edwin S. Hartshorn to Mr. Murray, Investigator, Civil Service Commission, September 8, 1936, RG 319, Entry 343, Box 100; Memorandum, Lt. Col. Clement H. Wright, Secretary of the General Staff, to Col. Charles D. Herron, Executive for Reserve Affairs, November 7, 1930, RG 319, Entry 343, Box 98.

15. Letter, TAG to Executive for Reserve Affairs, April 16, 1941, Subject: "Allotment of Additional Officers to the Office, Chief of Staff, War Department Overhead," RG 319, Entry 343, Box 104; Order of the Secretary of War, June 16, 1941, reported in TAG letter, AG 008 ORC (6–11–41), RG 319, Entry 343, Box 104.

The head of the Reserve office during the inter-war period had no direct authority over anyone except his own clerk. Brig. Gen. Palmer, whose position was purely unofficial, had described his role as "solely . . . advisory," and this was the pattern for the men who were later given the title of "Reserve Executive." In 1936, for example, Brig. Gen. E. S. Hartshorn informed an investigator for the Civil Service Commission that "The Chief of Staff retains to himself the supervision and control of the Reserve Component of the Army of the United States. The Executive for Reserve Affairs is the assistant to the Chief of Staff and his immediate adviser in all matters relating to the administration of the Reserve Component. It is the duty of the Executive for Reserve Affairs to maintain contact with the personnel of the Officers' Reserve Corps and, speaking for the Chief of Staff, to render decisions upon such matters as are delegated to him by the Chief of Staff. All instructions issued by the Office of the Executive for Reserve Affairs are given in the name of the Chief of Staff."[16] Though his authority was not very great, the presence of a general officer whose full-time job was that of looking after the interests of Reservists in the Army meant that Gen. Pershing had at least partially succeeded. The Officers' Reserve Corps, the Reserve Officers' Training Corps and the Enlisted Reserve Corps finally had a spokesman, and they would need that and more during the coming year.

BUILDING THE ORC

National defense policy during the years between World Wars I and II was that of maintaining a relatively small Regular Army, supplemented by a much larger force of trained reservists. Philosophically, this was what the nation desired; fiscally, however, it was not prepared to support even this modest level of military activity.

"During the past year," wrote Secretary of War John W. Weeks in 1923, "I have heard a few criticisms of our defensive measures, on the basis of their cost. It is apparently a matter of astonishment for some of our citizens to discover that national defense consumes an appreciable part of the Federal Budget." During Fiscal Year 1923, continued Weeks, the War Department appropriation was

---

16. Memorandum, Brig. Gen. E. S. Hartshorn, Executive for Reserve Affairs, to Mr. Murray, Investigator for the Civil Service Commission, September 8, 1936, RG 319, Entry 343, Box 100.

$340,884,122, of which $256,415,470 was for "military purposes. These are tremendous sums," he wrote, "but ours is a great nation. The total Federal Budget for this period was over $4,000,000,000. The War and Navy Departments consumed, roughly, 14 percent of the total Federal Budget, and purely military activities 6 percent . . . . The per capita cost is slightly more than $2 annually."[17]

There were two major interrelated problems for the Officers' Reserve Corps during the inter-war years: first, increasing the size of the ORC and second, providing adequate training opportunities for its members. Officers could be commissioned through ROTC and the Citizens' Military Training Camps (CMTC), but unless regular opportunities for training were provided, it would be difficult to sustain motivation, effectiveness, and even membership. Fiscal constraints, however, were a real problem.

World War I had created a large pool of combat veterans from which members of the ORC could be obtained. During the fiscal year that ended on June 30, 1920, there were a total of 35,060 new appointments to the Corps, some 83 percent of which were in the rank of captain and below. Slightly over 12,400 officers left the ORC during the year, so the Officers' Reserve Corps ended FY 1920 with a strength of 68,232.[18] "By means of expert instruction in time of peace," wrote the Secretary of War in 1926, "the Reserve Officers' Training Corps is gradually building up a most valuable complement of junior officers . . . . Without this source of replacement the Officers' Reserve Corps . . . would become ineffective."[19] Indeed, the ROTC was the largest source of new officers for the ORC. Table 3–1 shows the gains from ROTC for the years 1920 through 1937 and indicates for the years 1931–37 the accumulated losses through resignations, dismissals, and other causes. As of 1937· the Army had a goal of 120,000 active members of the Officers' Reserve Corps. The average annual increase in ORC strength was 11,633, of which 6535 came from ROTC. The second largest source of new ORC members was

17. "Report of the Secretary of War to the President, 1923," in *Annual Reports, War Department, Fiscal Year Ended June 30, 1923* (Washington: GPO, 1923), pp. 2–3.

18. "Report of the Adjutant General, 1920" in *War Department Annual Reports, 1920* (Washington: GPO, 1921), p. 257.

19. "Report of the Secretary of War to the President, 1926" in *Annual Reports, War Department, Fiscal Year Ended June 30, 1926* (Washington: GPO, 1926), p. 55.

Table 3–1   ROTC Appointments in the ORC, 1920–1937.[20]

Fiscal Year	# Appointments	Accumulated Total	Accumulated Loss
1920	135	945	
1921	811	2,977	
1922	2,031	5,851	
1924	3,317	9,168	
1925	4,153	13,321	
1926	4,842	18,163	
1927	5,018	23,181	
1928	5,685	28,866	
1929	5,752	34,618	
1930	6,514	41,132	
1931	5,989	47,121	12,935
1932	6,530	53,651	16,935
1933	6,770	60,421	20,179
1934	6,347	66,768	23,649
1935	6,780	73,548	27,410
1936	5,722	79,270	31,927
1937	5,704	84,974	36,601

direct commissioning of civilians, and the third largest source was the Citizens' Military Training Camps.[21]

The CMTC's had grown out of the pre-World War I "Plattsburg idea" promoted by Army Chief of Staff Leonard Wood. The camps were given statutory authority in the National Defense Act of 1920, and they enjoyed the patronage and support of influential members of the political and social hierarchy through the Military Training Camps Association.[22] The CMTC provided a certain amount of military training to the young men who participated, but they consumed a disproportionate share of the War Department's Reserve Officer procurement funds. Table 3–2 compares the appropriations and officer production for the ROTC and the CMTC for the fiscal years from 1925 through 1928.

20. "Analysis of Gains and Losses in ROTC Appointees Since 1920," found in RG 319, Entry 343, Box 102.

21. Memorandum, Lt. Col. J. H. Woodberry, Chief, Statistics Branch, Army General Staff, to Brig. Gen. E. S. Hartshorn, Executive for Reserve Affairs, February 24, 1927, Subject: "Reserve Officer Objective," RG 319, Entry 343, Box 101.

22. Lt. Col. R. A. Hill, "Reserve Policies and National Defense," *Infantry Journal,* XLII (January–February 1935), p. 61; See also Ralph Barton Perry, *The Plattsburg Movement* (New York: Dutton, 1921) and John G. Clifford, *The Citizen Soldiers: The Plattsburg Training Camp Movement, 1913–1920* (Lexington: University Press of Kentucky, 1972).

Table 3–2 ROTC and CMTC, FY's 1925–1928.[23]

	1925		1926		1927		1928		Total	
	$	#	$	#	$	#	$	#	$	#
ROTC	3.8	4153	3.8	4842	3.9	5018	2.6	5685	14.1	19,698
CMTC	2.3	487	2.8	71	2.8	59	2.8	24	10.7	641

*All dollar figures are in millions; # refers to number commissioned.

Regardless of the source from which the commissions came, the ORC grew too slowly, for projections in 1937 indicated that the Army would not meet its ORC strength objective until sometime in 1944. There was some doubt, moreover, that the training received by this group of officers would prepare them for their wartime roles, because training, indeed, was the Achilles heel of the ORC during the inter-war period.[24]

TRAINING THE ORC

The lessons of World War I, as assimilated by the Army General Staff and the Congress, did not include the necessity for extensive training for members of the Officers' Reserve Corps. From 1920–1940 ORC members were typically under-trained; what training they did receive generally fell into five categories: active duty training with the Regular army, active duty training with Citizens' Military Training Camps, active duty with the Civilian Conservation Corps, inactive duty training with a Reserve unit, and correspondence courses. Many Reservists benefited from several of these methods of training, but few people would maintain that the ORC was ever the recipient of enough training during the inter-war years.

Members of the ORC were lucky if they received a two week active duty training tour every four or five years during the 1920's. Table 3–3 shows the number of individuals

23. Figures are taken from "Reports of the Secretary of War" for Fiscal Years 1925–28 and from "Analysis of Gains and Losses in ROTC. Appointees since 1920," RG 319, Entry 343, Box 102.

24. Memorandum, Lt. Col. J. H. Woodberry, Chief, Statistics Branch, Army General Staff, to Brig. Gen. E. S. Hartshorn, Executive for Reserve Affairs, Subject: "Reserve Officer Objective," RG 319, Entry 343, Box 101. It should be pointed out that producing Reserve officers was not the primary purpose of the CMTC "Instilling citizenship" was its paramount objective.

Table 3–3   Active Duty Training (15 Days or Less) of ORC Members, 1924–1930.[25]

Fiscal Year	# Trained	# Days	Cost of Training (Per Capita)
1924	7,926	15	(*)
1925	10,859	15	(*)
1926	14,883	15	$143.83
1927	16,173	15	$141.27
1928	16,789	14	$123.94
1929	19,608	14	$126.75
1930	21,270	14	$121.89

*Unknown.

who received such training, and the per capita cost of the training.

Table 3–3 does not, however, tell the entire story. In FY 1930, for example, 1,123 Reserve Officers received active duty training in excess of 15 days. The problem from the standpoint of readiness, however, was that there were 79,285 active Reserve Officers at the time, meaning that slightly over 28 percent of the ORC was able to train during that fiscal year.[26]

A member of the 306th Infantry Regiment, 77th Division, recalled that the officers in his unit did not have two weeks of annual training each year. "We went most years," he stated, "to either Fort Dix [New Jersey], or Plattsburg [New York]. Our unit didn't have any vehicles, so we carpooled to camp, or got there on our own. When we got there, they had to issue equipment to us, like rifles and machine guns, because we didn't have anything of our own."[27]

Another ORC member in Chicago remembered monthly meetings during the 1920's. "We had RA [Regular Army] instructors, and we went on occasional field trips. I went to Carlisle Barracks [Pennsylvania], once and spent most of that time studying general military subjects. I

25. Memorandum, Lt. Col. Karl Truesdell, Chief, Budget and Legislative Planning Branch, Army General Staff, to Col. C. D. Herron, Executive for Reserve Affairs, August 14, 1931, RG 319, Entry 343, Box 98.

26. "Report of the Secretary of War to the President, 1930," in *Annual Reports, War Department, Fiscal Year Ended June 30, 1930* (Washington: GPO, 1930), pp. 317, 6.

27. Interview of Capt. Kenneth Carson (USAR—Ret.) by Maj. James T. Currie, April 1, 1983. Notes in OCAR Historical File.

didn't get any pay except for those two weeks." Shortly before World War II, this particular ORC member became commander of a Training Unit of Sanitary Reserve Officers. "We were active, then," he said. "We had monthly dinner meetings, followed by lectures, illustrations, and slide shows. We studied water supply treatment, waste treatment, and field sanitation."

A third ORC Member recalled that "Prior to World War II, reserve training was rather hit or miss, at least in the area of Minneapolis . . . . [We had] space in the Wesley Temple, a church-owned office building. Each fall a schedule of classes was drawn up—September through May—and officers volunteered to instruct one or more sessions. Some subjects were required, and some dates were open for the instructor to pick his own topic. Some officers came well-prepared and gave excellent presentations. Some officers came with no preparation—they spoke 'off the cuff' with no outlines or notes, relying on experience, and these sessions were poor and uninteresting."[28]

Limited funds for Reserve training and the limited number of Regular Army officers available for duty in the CMTC convinced the War Department to use Organized Reserve officers as instructors in the Camps. The individual Organized Reservists showed a high level of competence, and in 1928 the War Department General Staff decided to use some Organized Reserve units to assist with CMTC training.

The Organized Reserve units performed well during the 1928 training year, and in December 1928 Secretary of War Dwight F. Davis directed that Organized Reserve units be used in at least one camp in each of the nine Corps areas. "Reserve organizations assigned to this work," stated Davis, "should be those which are, in the judgement of the Corps Area Commander, best qualified. It should be the objective of Corps Area Commanders to qualify all Reserve units for this work to the end that they may become competent to perform this type of training."[29]

The public reaction was immediate—and unfavorable. The Hearst newspapers editorialized against the use of Orga-

28. Interview of Col. A. S. Behrman, (USAR-Ret.) by Maj. James T. Currie, April 11, 1983. Notes in OCAR Historical File; Letter, Col. Stan W. Carlson (USAR-Ret.) to Maj. Dick Crossland, July 4, 1983, OCAR Historical File.

29. Letter, TAG to All Corps Area Commanders, February 9, 1929, Subject: "Training Reserve Regiments through the use of C.M.T.C." RG 319, Entry 343, Box 98.

nized Reserve units at the Camps, and Horace C. Stebbins, a wealthy textile merchant and leader in the Military Training Camps Association, sent a protesting telegram to the Secretary of War. On February 18, 1929, Charles B. Pike, Chief Civilian Aide to War Secretary Davis, forwarded copies of letters protesting the use of Organized Reserve officers in the CMTC.[30] The underlying reason for the protest against the Reserve officers probably was less with doubts of their effectiveness than with a perception that the prestige of the CMTC was diminished by not having a cadre of Regular Army personnel only.

The protests were to no avail, however, and the Army continued to use Organized Reserve officers to train the young men of the CMTC. Considering the small number of men who received their commissions through the Camps, the only way to justify Army expenditures on the CMTC is that the men of the ORC received valuable leadership experience.

The Citizens' Military Training Camps continued to function during the 1930's, and the ORC received just over 4700 new lieutenants from the Camps from 1929 through 1940.[31] As a source of strength for the ORC, the Citizens' Military Training Camps were not terribly important; as a way of providing training for the Reserves, the CMTC was rapidly eclipsed by the Civilian Conservation Corps (CCC).

The New Deal of President Franklin D. Roosevelt began on March 20, 1933, and one of Roosevelt's innovative ways of giving jobs to unemployed men was the Civilian Conservation Corps. The CCC was established almost immediately after FDR took office, and the Army was initially charged only with immunizing the enrollees, issuing them clothing and equipment, and organizing them into companies of 200 men each. The Departments of Interior and Agriculture were given control of all other functions, including that of commanding the camps.[32]

---

30. Telegram, Assistant Secretary of War Charles B. Robbins to Horace C. Stebbins, February 11, 1929 and Letter, Charles B. Pilse to Dwight F. Davis, February 18, 1929, both in RG 319, Entry 343, Box 97; *New York Times,* June 3, 1947, p. 25.

31. Reports of the Secretary of War, 1934–41.

32. "Report of the Secretary of War, 1933," in *Annual Reports, War Department, Fiscal Year Ended June 30, 1933* (Washington: GPO, 1933), p. 4. A recent article on the subject is Terence J. Smith (Col., USAR-Ret.), "The Army's Role in the success of the CCC," *The Retired Officer* (July 1983), pp. 30–34.

The Army handled its role without difficulty, and on April 10, 1933, the President directed the Army to assume "complete and permanent control" of the CCC. To supplement available Regular Army personnel, the President authorized members of the ORC to work in the CCC Camps.

By July 1, 1933, there were a total of 1315 camps in operation. "With few exceptions," stated Secretary of War George H. Dern, "each camp comprised 2 Regular officers, 1 Reserve officer, 4 enlisted men of the Regular Army, and about 200 men of the Civilian Conservation Corps." By the end of the fiscal year a total of 1774 ORC members were on CCC duty, a number that would swell significantly in the next few years.[33]

Thousands of members of the ORC were unemployed during the Great Depression years, and many of these men leaped at the chance for active duty with the CCC. The War Department regarded the CCC as an opportunity for the Reservists to receive some needed training in "practical leadership, "but the main benefit of using the ORC members was that the Regular Army officers could go back to their previous military assignments.[34]

The replacement of Regular Army officers with Organized Reservists continued apace, and by the end of fiscal year 1934 the number of Regulars on duty in the CCC camps had dwindled to 498, while the number of Reservists had risen to 5,035.[35] The number of Officers' Reserve Corps members had reached 5,853 by September 30, 1934, a figure that included 1120 medical officers and 164 chaplains.[36]

A further incentive to the use of ORC members in the CCC Camps was provided by the camp enrollees themselves. The CCC was not intended to be a military experience, and the Regular Army CCC camp commanders were often regarded by the enrollees as "too military" in their attitudes. Relations with the enrollees improved greatly, wrote one student of the CCC experience, once Organized Reservists were placed in command of the camps.[37]

Black ORC members, too, shared the opportunity presented by the CCC, which was racially segregated. There were separate black and white encampments (except for a few camps in California), and the Army initially assigned

---

33. "Report of the Secretary of War, 1933," p. 6.
34. *Ibid.*, p. 10.
35. "Report of the Secretary of War, 1934," p. 197.
36. "CCC Facts," RG 319, Entry 343, Box 99.
37. John A. Salmond, *The Civilian Conservation Corps, 1933–1945: A New Deal Case Study* (Durham, N.C.: Duke University, 1967), p. 86.

white Regular Army officers as commanders of the all-black camps. This policy changed in 1934, however, and black ORC members thereafter commanded the black CCC camps. This policy was especially encouraged by President Roosevelt until after the 1936 election, following which he apparently lost interest in the matter.[38]

The War Department continued to regard CCC duty as a valuable training experience for the officers in the ORC, and in 1937 it proposed an 18-month limit on the length of a CCC tour, so that more ORC members could benefit from the experience. The outcry from the ORC members, who had come to regard their CCC jobs as permanent, was vociferous, and the War Department quickly backed down on its idea.[39]

Overall, the CCC experience was valuable for the ORC, members of which served on active duty with the camps until December 31, 1939. By that date, "pursuant to Executive directive," all of the ORC members were placed in a civilian status.[40] The total number of Corps members who enjoyed active duty with the CCC was reportedly in excess of 30,000,[41] and it is probable that for many of these men their interest in the Officers' Reserve Corps and their determination to maintain their Reserve status were enhanced by the experience. Given the paucity of incentives for Organized Reserve members during the inter-war period, this was no small accomplishment.

Members of the ORC could not count on two weeks of active duty each year, as could members of the National Guard, and there was no pay at all for inactive duty drills. As was indicated in Table 3–3, the number of Reservists who were given two weeks of active duty training each year varied from under 8,000 in 1924 to over 21,000 in 1930. The strength of the active Reserve grew from 62,000 in the earlier year to 80,000 in the latter, meaning that by 1930 the "average" Reservist had a 1 in 4 chance of getting active duty training in a given year.[42]

---

38. *Ibid.*, p. 190.

39. *Ibid.*, p. 172.

40. "Report of the Secretary of War to the President, 1940," in *Annual Reports, War Department, Fiscal Year Ended June 30, 1940* (Washington: GPO, 1940), p. 66.

41. "How Far We Have Accomplished Our Objectives," in RG 319, Entry 343, Box 101. Although the figure of 30,000 ORC members is given, this seems awfully high.

42. Reports of the Secretary of War for 1924 and 1931.

In actuality, however, the odds were not really as favorable as 1 in 4, because some officers were given training almost every year, to the detriment of others who were forced to wait seven or eight years between tours. Harry S. Truman, for example, a member of the Field Artillery, Officers' Reserve Corps, performed active duty training on ten occasions between 1920 and 1933.[43] Truman was not unique, either, for Secretary of War Patrick J. Hurley reported that during FY 1928, 16 percent of all Reserve officers placed on active duty for training were on their third consecutive tour; during FY 1929 the figure rose to almost 23 percent; and for FY 1930 the figure was 34 percent. Hurley thereupon ordered "that the number of Reserve officers who have been placed on active duty year after year be materially reduced and that effort be made to expend available funds upon Reserve Officers who have had active duty training less recently. A minimum of Reserve officers should be placed on active duty for more than two consecutive years, and where this policy is not adhered to, Corps Area Commanders should be sure that the interests of the Service are being thoroughly considered."[44]

The problem continued, however. As Col. Charles D. Herron, Executive for Reserve Affairs, explained almost a year later, "The argument is between those who believe in a Reserve Corps with a few highly trained officers and a majority practically untrained, as opposed to those who believe that all should have some training. The War Department," stated Herron, "takes the latter stand." The "principal restrictions" in effect at the time, said Herron, were as follows:

"(a) Not more than 10% of the trainees will be field grade officers.

"(b) Not more than 20% will be staff.

"(c) Officers of organizations ordered to unit training are given preference over officers of those not ordered to unit training.

"(d) Officers who have prepared themselves for active duty during the winter through inactive training have preference.

---

43. "Statement of Military Service of Harry S. Truman, 0 129 869," National Archives and Records Service, National Personnel Records Center (Military Personnel Records), St. Louis, Mo.

44. Letter, TAG to Corps Area Commanders, Department Commanders, and Chiefs of Arms and Services, January 10, 1931, Subject: "Training of Organized Reserves," RG 319, Entry 343, Box 98.

"(e) Only key men (regimental commanders, etc.) are placed on duty for more than two consecutive years."[45]

Congressional leaders too, displayed a keen interest in the status of ORC training, though the Congress never apparently considered appropriating enough money to allow yearly training for all ORC members. On April 20, 1934, Sen. Royal S. Copeland and Rep. Ross A. Collins, Chairs of the Senate and House Appropriations Conferees, respectively, sent to the Secretary of War a letter explaining the conference committee's intentions. Trainees, wrote the Congressional leaders, should be a maximum of 45 years old. Ninety percent of them should be company grade officers, and 90 percent should serve in the combat arms. They almost wrote these provisions into the Military Appropriations Bill, said the authors of the letter, but they finally decided against placing an "unconditional age restriction" on Reserve training.[46]

Secretary of War George H. Dern's response, which was prepared by Reserve Executive Herron and revised by a General Staff Major named Eisenhower, informed Copeland and Collins that the War Department's policy in many cases was almost identical to what they were suggesting. Indeed, the policies expressed in Dern's response do not appear to be much different from those enunciated by Col. Herron over two years earlier.[47]

The suggestion that 90 percent of all trainees be combat arms officers, however, rather than the 80 percent specified by War Department policy, met with resistance from the Secretary. "With an appropriation for an annual quota of 20,000, the average staff officer [is] trained once in six years. With adoption of a 90 percent policy and a 16,500 quota, training would occur only once in fifteen years. This means that the trained Reserve staff officer, indispensable to prompt mobilization, would cease to exist." Because of the inadequacy of funds, concluded Dern, "training of the Officers' Reserve Corps has never been carried out on a scale

---

45. Memorandum, Col. Charles D. Herron to Chief of Staff Douglas MacArthur, December 10, 1931, Subject: "Active Duty Training for Reserve Officers," RG 319, Entry 343, Box 98.

46. Letter, Sen. Royal S. Copeland and Rep. Ross A. Collins to Secretary of War George H. Dern, April 20, 1934, RG 319, Entry 343, Box 99.

47. Letter, Secretary of War George H. Dern to Sen. Royal S. Copeland, April 30, 1934 (with pencilled notations indicating authorship), RG 319, Entry 343, Box 99. An identical letter was sent to Rep. Collins.

sufficient to insure requisite efficiency. Aside from inactive instruction, each combat officer should be required to undergo two weeks' training annually, while others should be called out sufficiently often to insure their familiarity with assigned duties. This is the standard that has been fixed by law for the National Guard, and should apply with equal force to the Officers' Reserve Corps."[48]

The number of Reservists who received two weeks of training rose steadily from a low of 14 percent in 1934 to over 30 percent as mobilization neared in 1940, as can be seen in Table 3–4.

Table 3–4   Active Duty Training (14 Days or Less) of ORC Members 1931–1940.[49]

Fiscal Year	# Trained	# Active ORC*	% Trained
1931	20,998	80,399	26
1932	21,527	83,808	26
1933	20,948	86,338	24
1934	11,944	88,107	14
1935	16,785	91,955	18
1936	22,175	95,619	23
1937	22,595	96,545	23
1938	26,089	100,116	26
1939	30,705	104,575	29
1940	31,741	104,228	30

*Includes only those eligible for active duty.

Increasing the number and percentage of ORC members who received two weeks of training each year was only one of the readiness questions facing the War Department during the years prior to World War II. The National Guard had received in the National Defense Act of 1916 a guarantee of Federal pay for 48 drill periods per year for each member, but there was no comparable compensation provision for the members of the Officers' Reserve Corps. "We met once a week," during the 1930's recalled an ORC member of the 306th Infantry Regiment, 77th Division, "and it seems to me that all we ever did was disassemble, clean, and reassemble our machine guns. I did this every week for nine years in a non-pay status."[50] By 1937, mem-

48. *Ibid.*
49. Compiled from "Reports of the Secretary of War" for the fiscal years 1931–1940.
50. Interview of Col. Milton Barall, (USAR-Ret.), by Maj. James T. Currie, February 4, 1983. Notes in OCAR Historical Files.

bers of the ORC, through their lobbying group, the Reserve Officers Association, mounted a campaign to receive pay for inactive duty training (IADT).

H. R. 9503, a bill "To amend the National Defense Act of June 30, 1916, as amended, with respect to the pay and allowances of certain Reserve Officers," was the legislative means through which the inactive duty training change was proposed. The measure contained a $75 per year maxiimum on the amount of drill pay a member could receive,[51] but the Department of War opposed even this modest proposal. Secretary of War Harry H. Woodring spoke out vigorously against the bill, though he admitted that National Guard officers received pay for inactive duty training. The comparison with the Guard, said Woodring, was "in no sense complete," because the National Guard officers "are required to perform definitely prescribed duties such as armory drills, field exercises, target practice, etc." Why similar duties could not have been required of ORC members as a precondition of receiving IADT pay, the Secretary did not indicate.

Woodring's final argument against IADT pay for the Reservists was a disingenuous statement that the members of the ORC themselves opposed this bill because they maintained their "amateur standing" as a "cherished possession."[52] This specious line of reasoning was repeated from time to time by the War Department, but the issue would not die.

A bill calling for IADT pay and allowances for uniforms and equipment was introduced into the Seventy-Sixth Congress, and it, too, was opposed by the War Department. By the time the bill reached FDR's desk, the IADT provision had been taken out, but Roosevelt vetoed the measure anyway.[53] The level of frustration continued to rise among ORC members, and in March 1940, Col. Edward S. Bres, National President of the Reserve Officers Association, sought to find out why the War Department continued to oppose drill pay for Organized Reservists. Col. Bres was unable to get an official answer to his question, but Brig. Gen. Charles F. Thompson, Executive for Reserve Affairs, told him unofficially that it would simply cost too much—

---

51. Copy of H. R. 9503 in RG 319, Entry 343, Box 101.

52. Statement of Secretary of War Harry F. Woodring, April 25, 1937, RG 319, Entry 343, Box 101.

53. Message to Congress, August 1, 1939, RG 319, Entry 343, Box 102.

$5 million per year. Furthermore, wrote Thompson, ORC members in the Judge Advocate General, Chaplain, and Medical branches gained their commissions because of their professional qualifications. "It would be of questionable propriety," stated Thompson, "to provide an annual retainer fee . . . " to such officers. Furthermore, said the Reserve Executive, "Many Reserve Officers are concerned with possible detraction from the unselfishness and patriotic motives which heretofore have typified the ORC."[54] The ROA's reaction to Thompson's letter is unknown.

Correspondence courses were an important means of ORC training during the years between the two World Wars. Such courses began in fiscal year 1921, stated Secretary of War John W. Weeks, "to supplement the limited appropriation for the training of the Organized Reserve." Through these courses, wrote Weeks, it was hoped that "much instruction can be given to officers and candidates in the National Guard and Organized Reserve, at the same time meeting the demand for economy in cases when field training is not absolutely necessary."[55]

By 1931 the Secretary of War was able to report that "extension courses continue to be the least expensive means . . . for the dissemination of military knowledge," with a cost per student of approximately $1.85 per year. Table 3–5 shows enrollment data for the years 1923–1931.

Table 3–5 Extension Course Enrollment, 1923–1931.[56]

Year	ORC	ERC	Total Organized Reserves
1923	10,719	613	11,332
1924	10,696	523	11,219
1925	15,939	538	16,477
1926	18,492	639	19,131
1927	22,446	913	23,359
1928	24,204	1,216	25,420
1929	26,356	1,037	27,393
1930	24,120	1,222	25,342
1931	27,505	1,596	29,101

54. Letter, Brig. Gen. Charles F. Thompson to Col. Edward S. Bres, March 11, 1940, RG 319, Entry 343, Box 103. The debate over IADT pay for Reservists did not end until the enactment of Public Law 80–460 on March 25, 1948.
55. "Report of the Secretary of War to the President, 1921," in *Annual Reports, War Department, Fiscal Year Ended June 30, 1921* (Washington: GPO, 1921), p. 26.
56. "Report of the Secretary of War to the President 1931," in

By March 31, 1940, ORC enrollment in extension courses totaled 63,675, while Enlisted Reservists involved in the courses numbered 1,056. The cost per student had dropped to $1.52 per year, and 66,675 students—a figure that includes more than just the Organized Reservists—completed a total of 168,887 subcourses during the year. Mobilization of Organized Reservists and National Guardsmen soon cut into extension course enrollments, but the Army had found a way to keep a sizable number of Reservists active and interested at a very low cost.[57] There were not, however, very many other things the War Department did to reward and encourage the members of the ORC during this period, but two actions do stand out.

REWARDING MEMBERSHIP

By 1932, reported the Secretary of War, "the march of time has so changed the character of the Officers' Reserve Corps that an organization which was in the beginning made up entirely of World War officers has now but one-third of that class." The new officers coming in, reported the Secretary, were almost exclusively the product of the ROTC and CMTC.[58] The need to give additional training to these new officers was obvious, and the Army's way of accomplishing such has already been discussed. What the Army did not anticipate, however, was that these non-war veterans would soon ask for medals and ribbons to dress up their uniforms and reward their service in the ORC.

The Reserve Officers Association first broached the idea to Brig. Gen. Charles D. Herron, Executive for Reserve Affairs, in December 1934. Lt. Col. Frank E. Lowe, ROA President, suggested a ribbon denoting five years of service as a Reserve Officer. Herron was not in favor of the idea, believing that only war-time service should be honored in this manner, but he told Lowe that he would look into the suggestion. Herron's official response was that the War Department did not favor the proposal.[59]

Annual Reports, War Department, Fiscal Year Ended June 30, 1931 (Washington: GPO, 1931), pp. 223–24.

57. "Report of the Secretary of War to the President, 1940," in *Annual Reports, War Department, Fiscal Year Ended June 30, 1940* (Washington: GPO, 1940), p. 64.

58. "Report of the Secretary of War to the President, 1932," in *Annual Reports, War Department, Fiscal Year Ended June 30, 1932* (Washington: GPO, 1932), p. 7.

59. Letter, Brig. Gen. Charles D. Herron to Lt. Col. Frank E. Lowe, January 26, 1935, RG 319, Entry 343, Box 99.

By August 13, 1935, however, the War Department had changed its mind, and on that date it authorized members of the Officers' Reserve Corps to wear as part of their uniform a new "Minute Man" badge. The design was a drawing of Captain John Parker (the Minute Man) superimposed on an eagle and bearing the inscription "Officers' Reserve Corps." A bar showing length of service—five years, ten years, etc.—was to be worn suspended from the badge. ORC members who had received "certificates of capacity" would receive a badge with a red background. The number of ORC members who received this award is unknown, but apparently the ROA was satisfied.[60]

Of considerably more substance and importance to the inter-war Reservists was the passage of Public Law 74–67 on June 15, 1936. This act extended certain benefits to members of the Organized Reserve, National Guard, ROTC and CMTC who were injured in line of duty while undergoing military training. If injured under these circumstances the member was entitled to medical and surgical care, hospitalization, transportation, and pay and benefits during treatment. If the ultimate misfortune occurred, the Army would pay burial expenses.[61]

PREPARING FOR MOBILIZATION

All of the recruitment, training, rewards, and benefits given members of the Officers' Reserve Corps was designed to reach one end: preparation and retention of a trained group of Army officers who could assume leadership roles during any future mobilization and war.

Army planners during the early 1920's envisioned an initial mobilization of 66 divisions: 11 Regular Army, 22 National Guard, and 33 Organized Reserves.[62] By the close of fiscal year 1924, the 27 Organized Reserve infantry divisions were at 73.9 percent of their authorized officer

---

60. War Department Immediate Release, "Badge for Reserve Officers," August 16, 1935, RG 319, Entry 343, Box 100. Active Reservists are eligible today for both the Army Reserve Components Achievement Medal and the Armed Forces Reserve Medal; the "Minute Man" Badge is no longer awarded. See Army Regulation 672–5–1.

61. Cited in "Report of the Chief of Staff, 1936," in *Annual Reports, War Department, Fiscal Year Ended June 30, 1936* (Washington: GPO, 1936), p. 40.

62. Marvin A. Kreidberg and Merton G. Henry, *History of Military Mobilization in the United States Army, 1775–1945* (Washington: GPO, 1955), pp. 401–402.

strength, and the 6 Organized Reserve cavalry divisions had reached 83.5 percent of their officer strength.[63] Because of the insignificant number of enlisted Reservists, however, these divisions were never more than cadre units during the inter-war period.

By 1933 the Secretary of War reported that there would be 80,000 officer vacancies "in the early weeks of an emergency" in existing Regular Army and National Guard units. Seventy thousand of these vacancies, stated the Secretary, would be filled by Reserve officers, and additional Reservists would be needed for "Reserve units that might be called to the colors during the subsequent stages of a mobilization."[64] By mid-1936 the number of active, eligible members of the Officers' Reserve Corps had reached 95,619, but activation of the first Reserve units was not anticipated until M + 60.[65]

The number of Reserve officers, as has been indicated earlier, grew slowly during the inter-war years, but Organized Reserve units themselves remained only skeletons, having few enlisted personnel and only minimal equipment. The individual members of the ORC were destined to play a major role in any mobilization, but there was some doubt that Organized Reserve units would ever be activated as such.[66] In an article prepared in mid-1939, as threats of war loomed in Europe and war actually raged in the Far East, the Army's Assistant Chief of Staff for Plans and Operations (G–3) wrote that "Many units of the Organized Reserves— most of them in fact—are of late mobilization priority. But the Officers' Reserve Corps is quite another matter." Members of the ORC, stated the ACS/G–3 in a remarkably accurate prediction, would become "inextricably mingled" with

---

63. "Report of the Secretary of War to the President, 1924," in *Annual Reports, War Department, Fiscal Year Ended June 30, 1924* (Washington: GPO, 1924), p. 10.

64. "Report of the Secretary of War to the President, 1933," in *Annual Reports, War Department, Fiscal Year Ending June 30, 1933* (Washington: GPO, 1933), p. 14.

65. "Report of the Secretary of War to the President, 1936," in *Annual Reports, War Department, Fiscal Year Ending June 30, 1936* (Washington: GPO, 1936), p. 72; memorandum, Brig. Gen. John H. Hester to ACS/G–3, November 7, 1940, Subject: "Source of Units for Activation," RG 319, Entry 343, Box 103.

66. The cadre units of the Organized Reserve Corps were not in the Initial Protective Force listed in the Protective Mobilization Plan (PMP). For a discussion of the PMP see Kreidberg and Henry, *History of Military Mobilization,* pp. 476–92.

Regular Army and National Guard personnel in RA and NG units.[67]

As the 1930's drew to a close, it became more and more apparent that the Army would soon be placed into the position of testing its carefully-developed mobilization planning. The question was whether the ORC would be ready, and in enough numbers.

67. Article, untitled, prepared by ACS/G–3, June 20, 1939, in RG 319, Entry 343, Box 102.

Drs. Charles H. (left) and William J. (right) Mayo were among the many prominent physicians who joined the Officers' Reserve Corps. They both achieved the rank of Brigadier General after the First World War. (Photo courtesy of the Mayo Clinic, Rochester, Minnesota)

Members of the 80th Infantry Division receive bayonet training from a British NCO at Boque Maison, France, April 1918. The 80th Division today is an Army Reserve Training Division headquartered in Richmond, Virginia. (Photo courtesy of the National Archives)

Captain Edward V. "Eddie" Rickenbacker was one of the most decorated American flyers during WW I. Rickenbacker joined the Signal Enlisted Reserve Corps on May 25, 1917, and was commissioned a First Lieutenant, Signal Officers' Reserve Corps, on October 4, 1917. Rickenbacker received the Medal of Honor, the Distinguished Service Cross with six Oak Leaf Clusters, the French Legion of Honor, and two Croix de Guerre with Palm. He was appointed a Colonel in the Officers' Reserve Corps in June 1929. (Photo courtesy of the Fort Meade, Maryland Museum)

Prior to August 7, 1918, when the distinctions between "Regular Army," "National Guard," and "National Army" were discontinued, Army Reserve officers wore "USR" collar insignia, rather than just "US." The Reserve insignia shows clearly on this identification pass photo of Captain James S. Smyser, ORC. (U.S. Army photo)

Company A, 306th Machine Gun Battalion, 77th Infantry Division, trains with the Vickers gun in France, May 1918. The 77th Division was formed from citizen-soldiers in the New York City area. The 77th U.S. Army Reserve Command, Flushing, NY, is today the inheritor of the 77th Division's heritage. (Photo courtesy of the National Archives)

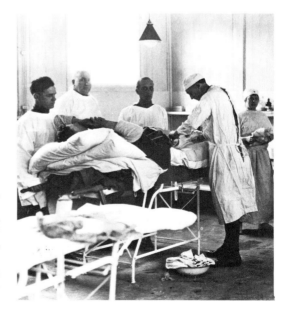

Surgeons attend to shrapnel wounds at Base Hospital No. 6, Sebastopol, France, May 1918. More than 15,000 members of the Enlisted Reserve Corps served in medical units during WW I, and medical officers of the Officer's Reserve Corps numbered 29,299 on November 11, 1918. The number of Regular Army medical officers on that date was 920. (Photo courtesy of the National Archives)

Soldiers from the 78th Division's 305th Machine Gun Battalion fire at German positions near St. Juvin, Ardennes, France, November 1, 1918—just ten days before the Armistice. Today's 78th Division is an Army Reserve Training Division headquartered at Camp Kilmer, NJ. (Photo courtesy of the National Archives)

American Coast Artillerymen pound the German lines opposite Baleycourt Woods, Meuse, France, September 1918. (Signal Corps photograph)

Harry S. Truman was an Army Reservist. Following his active service in the Army during World War I, Truman joined the Organized Reserve Corps and rose to the rank of Colonel as Commander of the 379th Artillery (horse drawn). He also founded the Kansas City, Missouri, chapter of the Reserve Officers Association. Truman's request for active duty at the beginning of World War II was turned down by Army Chief of Staff George C. Marshall, who felt that Truman could be of more use in the U.S. Senate. After stepping down as Commander-in-Chief, Truman retired from the Army Reserve and began drawing his retirement pay of $111.92 per month. (Photo courtesy of the Truman Library, Independence, Missouri)

Charles A. Lindbergh was one of many Army Reservists awarded the Medal of Honor. On December 14, 1927, Congress awarded the medal to Lindbergh for his heroic solo crossing of the Atlantic Ocean. (Photo courtesy of the National Archives)

Drill, chemical mortar, column of squads. These members of the ORC are shown at their training site, Edgewood Arsenal, Maryland, on July 23, 1931. The mortars may well have been a loan from the active Army, since Organized Reserve units had very little equipment of their own. (Signal Corps Photo)

Members of the ORC performed important duty as Commanders of Civilian Conservation Corps camps during the Depression. Some 30,000 ORC members received valuable leadership training through service in the camps. Here, the Commander of the CCC camp in Lassen National Forest (Calif.), presents a meritorious flag to the enrollees with the cleanest barracks. (Photo courtesy US Forest Service)

Training opportunities were limited, and equipment was often primitive for Organized Reserve units during the period between World Wars I and II. ORC members and units trained with the Regular Army whenever possible. Shown is a coordinated infantry-tank assault at Pine Camp, NY, August 1935. (National Archives photo)

Organized Reserve units between the two World Wars usually consisted only of officers. Pictures here is the entire 61st Battalion, 100th Infantry Division during its annual training at Fort Knox, Ky., in July 1934. The battalion commander was Lt. Col. D. Y. Dunn, bottom row, third from left. (Photo courtesy of D.Y. Dunn)

Most members of the Officers' Reserve Corps were called to active duty even before Pearl Harbor, December 7, 1941, and began an intensive training program with Regular Army and National Guard units. Shown here are the 2nd Army maneuvers in Arkansas, September 1941. (Signal Corps photo)

4

Mobilization and War 1940–1945

Hitler's invasion of Poland began on September 1, 1939, and a week later President Roosevelt authorized a 17,000-man increase in the Regular Army, to bring it up to a total of 227,000 men. The Army General Staff did not believe this strength level would suffice for very long, and it began to plan for a Regular Army of, successively, 242,000, 280,000, and 330,000 men. As the Regular Army increased in strength, it became necessary to bring more Organized Reserve officers onto active duty to supplement the 14,000 Regular Officers.[1]

Isolationist sentiment in the Congress was still a powerful force, however, even after the German invasion and conquest of Poland. Throughout the last months of 1939 and on into 1940, there was a marked Congressional reluctance to acknowledge the worsening situation in Europe by appropriating enough funds to modernize the Army and significantly increase its state of readiness. The ORC received very little attention from the Army's planners, and by the time war resumed in Europe the Organized Reserves were little better prepared than they had been a year earlier.[2]

The pace of war in Europe quickened on April 9, 1940, when Germany invaded Denmark and Norway, followed the next day by the NAZI invasion of the

---

1. Marvin A. Kriedberg and Merton G. Henry, *History of Military Mobilization in the United States Army, 1775–1945* (Washington: GPO, 1955), pp. 536–66.
2. Mark S. Watson, *United States Army in World War II, The War Department, Chief of Staff: Prewar Plans and Preparations* (Washington: US Army, 1950), pp. 164–65.

Netherlands, Belgium, and Luxembourg. By June 22 all of these countries, plus France, had fallen before the German onslaught, and public and Congressional opinion in the United States had swung decidedly in the direction of greater defense preparedness.[3]

CALLING-UP THE ORC

War Department planners soon began to realize that there might be a mobilization without an M-day. The Regular Army was gradually expanded, and on August 27, 1940, the 76th Congress, by joint resolution, gave to the President the authority to call the Organized Reserve (officers and enlisted men) and the National Guard to active federal service for a period of twelve months.[4]

The Officers' Reserve Corps consisted in mid-1940 of some 104,228 members who were eligible for active duty, while the ERC consisted of only 3233 men.[5] In a memorandum of September 5, 1940, The Adjutant General directed Corps Commanders to establish rosters for ordering ORC members to active duty, based upon the following priorities:

1. The extent of deferment proposed by the officer and the reasons therefor;
2. The officer's personal obligation to his dependents;
3. The officer's professional attainments and value to the service, together with his age and physical condition;
4. The need for the officer's service in the community as a civilian.

These rosters were confidential, and separate rosters were to be established for medical officers.[6]

The first peace-time conscription in this country's history passed the Congress on September 16, 1940, and draftees began entering the Army in large numbers by the following January. As Kreidberg and Henry expressed it, "The immediate need for large numbers of additional officers was filled by extending the active duty tours of capable Reserve officers already in the service and by calling still more Re-

---

3. Kreidberg and Henry, *History of Military Mobilization* p. 570.

4. *Ibid.,* pp. 575, 579–80.

5. "Report of the Secretary of War to the President, 1940," *Annual Report, War Department, Fiscal Year Ended June 30, 1940* (Washington: GPO, 1940) p. 95.

6. Memorandum, TAG to Corps Commanders, September 5, 1940, in RG 319, Entry 343, Box 103.

serve officers to active duty." On June 30, 1940, there had been only 2,710 Reserve officers on active duty; by May 15, 1941, there were over 46,000.[7]

Not all ORC members who wanted active duty in 1941, however, were able to obtain such, for field grade officers who were "somewhat old for the grades they hold" were being turned down for active duty by the War Department. This policy drew a sharp protest from Morris Sheppard, Chairman of the Senate Committee on Military Affairs, but Under Secretary of War Robert P. Patterson assured the Senator that "in the event of any enlargement of our present program this age restriction would almost certainly be lifted."[8] Problems of active duty for field grade officers did not end even after Pearl Harbor, but ORC company grade officers never experienced such difficulty. By June 30, 1941, the number of ORC members on extended active duty had reached a total of 57,309, and on that same date more than 90 percent of the company grade officers on duty with the Regular Army were Organized Reservists.[9]

ORC unit members, naturally enough, were more than a little curious about their fate. National Guard units, which contained both officers and enlisted men, had begun entering active federal service in September 1940, but no mention had yet been made of the units of the ORC, skeletal though they were. Brig. Gen. Frank E. Lowe, Executive for Reserve and ROTC Affairs, was on the receiving end of a constant stream of inquiries from members of the ORC, and on July 30, 1941, he asked the ACS/G–3 for a statement as to the War Department's policy on Reserve unit mobilization. The reply from Brig. Gen. Harry L. Twaddle

7. Kreidberg and Henry, *History of Military Mobilization,* p. 605. The Army had a total active strength of 1,320,500 on May 15, including 14,000 RA officers, 20,500 NG officers, and 46,000 ORC officers on active duty. War Department Press Release, May 15, 1941, in RG 319, Entry 343, Box 104.

8. Letter, Under Secretary of War Robert P. Patterson to Senator Morris Sheppard, June 9, 1941, RG 315, Entry 343, Box 104. Commissioned officers are divided into "Company Grade" (lieutenants and captains), "Field Grade" (majors, lieutenant colonels, and colonels) and "General Officers."

9. "Report of the Secretary of War, 1941," p. 95; War Department Study, October 20, 1942, entitled "The Organized Reserve in the War," RG 319, Entry 343, Box 106. Two weeks earlier the percentage of ORC members on active duty, by rank, had been as follows: Col.—31%, Maj.—49%; Capt.—60%, 1Lt.—49%, 2Lt.—43%. Memorandum, Brig. Gen. Harry L. Twaddle, ACS/G–3, to Executive for Reserve and ROTC Affairs, June 19, 1941, RG 319, Entry 343, Box 104.

was unequivocal: "Present plans do not contemplate the mobilization of Organized Reserve units prior to the Declaration by Congress of a national emergency and an attendant authorization for a material augmentation of the Army."[10] The scenario contemplated by Twaddle, however, never did occur, for as a War Department study described it, "The nature of the pre-war mobilization—a state neither of war nor of peace—made it impracticable to activate the units of the Organized Reserve . . . ."[11] Individual Organized Reservists, however, continued to be called to active duty, and the pre-war ORC units themselves, stated Brig. Gen. Edward S. Bres, "were completely disintegrated."[12]

Active duty training tours of 14, 21, and 28 days were largely eliminated during 1941 because there were many opportunities for longer training on an extended active duty basis. Field grade officers were not in as great demand by the regular components, however, as were those of company grade, and in March 1941, the War Department announced plans to give 28-day training tours to 50 colonels, 200 lieutenants colonels, and 250 majors. These officers were attached to Regular Army and National Guard divisions for training.[13]

There were many Organized Reserve officers, however, who received neither orders to active duty nor opportunities for training, and many of them wrote to the Executive for Reserve and ROTC Affairs with their complaints. Brig. Gen. Lowe forwarded these concerns to the Chief of Staff of the Army in early November 1941 and emphasized his opinion that "*first* priority should be given to combat training of all Promotion List Reserve Officers who are eligible, available, and physically qualified for not less than thirty months service with troops . . . ." Lowe's memorandum was never directly answered, however, because by the time it had made its way through the Army's bureaucracy and received a recommendation from the ACS/G–1, the date was December 17, 1941. "In view of the proposed augmentation of the army and the probability that all available Reserve officers

---

10. Memorandum, Brig. Harry L. Twaddle, ACS/–3, to Brig. Gen. Frank E. Lowe, August 16, 1941, RG 319, Entry 343, Box 104.

11. "The Organized Reserve in the War," RG 319, Entry 343, Box 106.

12. Memorandum, Brig. Gen. Edward S. Bres, Executive for Reserve and ROTC Affairs, to ACS/G–3, Subject: "Mobilization Plan," RG 319, Entry 342, Box 9.

13. War Department Press Release, "500 Reserve Field Officers to be Given 28 Days Training," RG 319, Entry 343, Box 104.

will be called to duty within the next few months," wrote Brig. Gen. Wade H. Haislip, "it is believed that no action is necessary on this paper."[14]

By December 1941 over 80,000 ORC members were on active Army duty, and on December 13 Congress removed the pre-war prohibition that restricted the geographical area in which Reservists could be used.[15] On February 6, 1942, President Roosevelt ordered into "active military service of the United States, effective on dates to be hereafter announced by the Secretary of War, for the duration of the present war and for six months after the termination thereof, . . . each of the organizations and units and all of the personnel of the Organized Reserves not already in such service."[16]

President Roosevelt's Executive Order, together with the fact that the Order of Battle list for World War II contains numerous units that were in the Organized Reserve, has led some people to give the Organized Reserve credit for furnishing 26 infantry divisions during the war.[17] This credit is in error, however. "When the decision was taken to activate the divisions and other units of the Organized Reserve early in 1942," explained the War Department, "few of the Reserve officers originally assigned to these units were available for duty with them. Consequently, the units as activated bore small resemblance to those of peacetime . . . ."[18] It would be misleading, then, to allege that Organized Reserve units served during World War II. While it is true that Organized Reserve infantry divisions like the 77th, 79th, 81st, 83d, 90th, 94th, 102d, and others were activated in 1942, very few of the pre-war members of these divisions were available for assignment to them by that time. As a 1965 study of the Army's force structure put it, "The OR divisions of World War II were not reserve divisions in any real sense of the word." This is not to say, of course, that

14. Memorandum, Brig. Gen. Frank E. Lowe, Executive for Reserve and ROTC Affairs, to Chief of Staff, November 4, 1941, Subject: "Extended Active Duty for Reserve Officers," and memorandum, Brig. Gen. Wade H. Haislip, ACS/G–1 to Chief of Staff, December 17, 1941, same subject, both in RG 319, Entry 343, Box 104.

15. "The Organized Reserve in the War," RG 319, Entry 343, Box 106; Public Law 77–338, December 13, 1941.

16. Executive Order No. 9049, February 6, 1942.

17. *Order of Battle, United States Army, World War II, European Theater of Operations, Divisions* (Paris, 1945), p. 571.

18. "The Organized Reserve in the War," RG 319, Entry 343, Box 106.

the Organized Reserve was unimportant during the WW II mobilization. As Chief of Staff George C. Marshall put it in 1941, "The procurement of suitable officer personnel was fortunately solved by the fact that during the lean, post-war years over 100,000 Reserve officers had been continuously trained . . . . These Reserve officers constituted the principal available asset which we possessed at this time. Without their assistance the program could not have been carried out except in a superficial manner, as is evidenced by the fact that today they [Reserve officers] constitute 75% to 90% of the officer strength with Regular Army units."[19]

Even after Pearl Harbor, individual members of the ORC were not always ordered to active duty, even when they requested such. Col. W. R. Frost, the Acting Executive for Reserve and ROTC Affairs, told Col. Porter P. Wiggins in an "informal memorandum" that the chances were "very remote indeed" that any Reserve officers over the age of sixty would be ordered to active duty. "Only in rare cases," wrote Frost, "has an exception been made to [this] . . . policy."[20] By May 1942, the War Department sought to order to active duty all colonels under 53 years old and lieutenant colonels under 51 years old who were physically qualified and who desired active duty.[21]

By the end of 1942 there were over 140,000 Reserve officers on active Army duty, while 12,100 ORC members had not received such orders.[22] Of these Reserve officers who had not been placed on active duty, 1,214 were medical students or interns and 422 were deferred for other academic reasons; 878 were Air Corps Reservists, and 2284 were de-

---

19. See compilation by R. L. Thompson, February 16, 1962, in *Reserve Components History, 1916 to present*, in Center of Military History files; see also memorandum, TAG to Commanding Generals, All Armies, Army Corps and Corps Areas, June 9, 1942, Subject: "Ordering into Active Service Certain Organized Reserve Divisions During August and September, 1942," in AG 320.2 (5–26–42), copy in CMH files. Office, Chief of Military History, Department of the Army, *Historical Resume, Division Force Structure, Active and Reserve, 1935–1963*, copy in CMH Files. *Report on the Army, July 1, 1939 to June 30, 1943, Biennial Reports of General George C. Marshall, Chief of Staff of the United States Army to the Secretary of War* (Washington: *The Infantry Journal*, 1943), pp. 11–12.

20. Letter, Col. W. R. Frost to Col. Porter P. Wiggins, March 26, 1942, RG 319. Entry 343, Box 105.

21. Memorandum, Brig. Gen. J. H. Hilldring, ACS/G–1 to Brig. Gen. Frank E Lowe, May 14, 1942, Subject: "Bringing Reserve Officers to Active Duty," RG 319, Entry 343, Box 105.

22. "The Organized Reserve in the War," RG 319, Entry 343, Box 106.

ferred because of their status with the Veteran's Administration or various branches of the Army. In addition, 92 ORC members had not been called to duty "due to request of G–2;" 46 were "not ordered due to nationality"—"Japs;" 35 were "Congressmen, Judges, Senators, etc.;" and 268 were not available because they were in enemy territory. Other categories included 29 "Colored officers," 7 brigadier generals, 174 colonels, and 427 lieutenant colonels for whom no vacancy could be found. A total of 3,741 Reservists were 59 years old or older, 1962 had over 15 years of service and were considered permanently physically disqualified, and 513 others fit into such categories as "Deferred by Directive G–1," "No Vacancy-Veterinary," and "Resignation Pending."[23]

The war-time files of the Executive for Reserve and ROTC Affairs contain numerous letters from Reserve officers—particularly colonels—who were literally begging for active duty assignments. Many of these men had served fifteen or more years in the ORC, had participated actively in every training opportunity that presented itself, and had been promoted to such a high level that the Army no longer had a place for them on active duty, even in war-time. It was embarrassing, said these officers, to have to explain to their neighbors that they had done everything in their power to get into the active Army. The accusing stares from their fellow citizens were almost more than they could bear, and any attempt by them to justify the Army's policy toward high-ranking Reserve officers only made matters worse.

Brig. Gen. Edward W. Smith, Executive for Reserve and ROTC Affairs, explained the War Department's policy in this area to Col. Philip S. VanCise, an Organized Reservist from Denver who had attempted without success to get active duty orders:

It has been a problem with the War Department to place on duty all of our high-ranking Reserve officers. As you probably know,

23. List signed by Col. H. N. Sumner, Chief, Appointment and Induction Branch, TAGO, December 17, 1942, RG 319, Entry 343, Box 105. According to Maj. Gen. Harry Vaughan, one ORC member whose request for active duty was not granted was Colonel (Senator) Harry S. Truman, commander, 379th Field Artillery Regiment (horse-drawn). When Truman went to Chief of Staff George Marshall and requested active duty, Marshall told him he was too old and said he would be of more value in the Senate The story is recounted in John T. Carlton and John F. Slinkman, *The ROA Story: A Chronicle of the First 60 Years of the Reserve Officers Association of the United States* (Washington: ROA, 1982), pp. 141–42.

the age-in-grade of full colonels is 55 but very few colonels who have passed their fiftieth birthday, either Regular or Reserve, are used with troops for overseas duty. Therefore, officers who have passed their fiftieth birthday are not primarily considered for troop duty but are considered for administrative work. Each Service Command is allotted a certain number of officers of each grade. Naturally, their allotment of full colonels is rather limited and many times the services of these officers cannot be utilized because of the fact that there is no vacancy in their grade existing in the Service Command.[24]

Brig. Gen. Smith went on to say that The Adjutant General's Office was doing its best to put Reserve officers on active duty and that TAGO was "hopeful for results." This effort, reported Smith, was limited to officers who had not reached their fifty-ninth birthday.[25] The effort to put Reserve officers on active duty never met with total success, however, and as late as mid-December 1944 there were almost as many non-active duty Organized Reservists—11,386—as there had been two years earlier.[26] The number of active duty Organized Reserve officers continued to increase throughout the war, reaching a peak of almost 200,000 early in 1945,[27] and ORC members were well-represented in Regular Army and National Guard combat units.

A War Department analysis of officers in an unidentified Regular Army infantry division overseas showed that as of March 31, 1944, the percentage of Organized Reserve officers by rank was as follows:

Colonel—0%
Lieutenant Colonel—42.9%
Major—95.9%
Captain—83.8%
First Lieutenant—56.3%
Second Lieutenant—10.9%

In addition, 62.5 percent of the battalion commanders, 84.5 percent of the company commanders, and 30.3 percent

24. Letter, Brig. Gen. Edward W. Smith to Col. Philip S. Van Cise, January 1, 1943, RG 319, Entry 343, Box 105.

25. *Ibid.*

26. "Reserve and Deferred AUS Officers not on Active Duty," December 15, 1944, RG 319, Entry 343, Box 112. It should be pointed out that the number of Reserve Officers had increased by more than 50 percent during that time. See memorandum, Col. C. M. Boyer to Brig. Gen. Edward W. Smith, October 2, 1944, Subject: "Strength of Reserve Officers as of 31 July 1944," RG 319, Entry 343, Box 112.

27. Letter (drafted, but unsent), Brig. Gen. Edward W. Smith to Cedric Foster, no date, but probably April 1945, RG 319, Entry 343, Box 112.

of the platoon leaders in this particular division were Organized Reserve officers.[28]

In a more extensive study a few months later, the War Department examined the 1st, 4th, and 90th Infantry Division, the 1st and 2d Armored Divisions, and the 29th, 34th and 37th Infantry Divisions (National Guard). The percentage of ORC members of each rank was as given in Table 4–1.

Table 4–1   Percentage of Organized Reservists in Officer Cadres.[29]

1st, 4th, 90th Infantry Divisions 1st and 2d Armored Divisions		29th, 34th, 37th Infantry Divisions (NG)	
BG	12.5%	BG	0
COL	0	COL	0
LTC	52.0%	LTC	21.5%
MAJ	82.5%	MAJ	56.6%
CPT	70.0%	CPT	45.7%
1LT	26.1%	1LT	16.0%
2LT	9.3%	2LT	8.9%
Total	37.4%	Total	22.2%

The number of Organized Reservists who were decorated for heroism is unknown, but it is certain that ORC members were in the forefront of combat activity. From September 1, 1943, to May 31, 1944, 28.7 percent of the officers in the active Army were ORC members. During this same period, ORC officers constituted 52.4% of the officers killed-in-action, 27.7% of those missing-in-action, and 27.4% of officers captured by the enemy.[30]

Reserve officer strength was concentrated in the middle ranks—captain, major and lieutenant colonel—but there were a number of Organized Reservists who achieved general officer rank during the war. As of June 30, 1943, there were 1,065 general officers in the Army. Of these, a total of 18 were from the Officers' Reserve Corps. One Organized Reservist who achieved three-star rank in 1944 was James H. Doolittle, while another well-known ORC general was Maj. Gen. William J. "Wild Bill" Donovan of the Office of Strategic Services—the forerunner of the CIA. Brig. Gen. The-

28. "Chart 3—Infantry Division," RG 319, Entry 342, Box 6.

29. "Composition of Officer Strength," RG 319, Entry 324, Box 9.

30. "Chart 4—Proportion of All Officer Battle Casualties Suffered by Reserve Officers, 1 September 1943–31 May 1944," RG 319, Entry 342, Box 6.

odore Roosevelt, Jr., an ORC member, received a Medal of Honor for his actions in the first assault wave on D-Day as Assistant Commander of the 4th Infantry Division.[31]

INCREASING THE CORPS

In addition to its general officers, the ORC numbered, at its peak in 1945, about 200,000 commissioned officers of lower grades. Almost 100,000 of these individuals had been commissioned in the Reserves after the beginning of the war, mostly through ROTC, Air Corps Cadet School, or by direct appointment from civilian life. This last category had never been a large source of ORC members, because the Army resisted attempts to commission civilians with little or no military training. There had always been a certain number of individuals, however, particularly in the fields of medicine and religion, who received such direct commissions. The Army's desire to avoid politicization of the commissioning process within the ORC was emphasized in a letter that Brig. Gen. Charles D. Herron, Executive for Reserve Affairs, sent to the Reserve Officers Association almost nine years before Pearl Harbor:

There are undoubtedly many prominent citizens whose appointments in the Officers' Reserve Corps would conduce to the cause of preparedness . . . .But [this] . . . course has the very great disadvantage that in the event of war many of the holders of such commissions would demand, often with great political influence, employment commensurate with their rank. This could only be obtained by wresting such employment from active officers of demonstrated qualifications.[32]

This policy was generally observed until the immediate pre-war period, when many prominent civilians sought Reserve commissions. Secretary of War Henry L. Stimson

---

31. *Biennial Report of the Chief of Staff of the United States Army, July 1, 1941 to June 30, 1943 to the Secretary of War* (Washington: *Infantry Journal*, 1943), p. 111; "General Officer Appointments in the Organized Reserve," *The Officer*, June 1947, *pp. 16–17, 22;* Gordon A. Harrison, *United States in World War II; The European Theater of Operations; Cross-Channel Attack* (Washington: Office of the Chief of Military History, Department of the Army, 1951), p. 304n; Omar N. Bradley (Gen. of the Army) and Clay Blair, *A General's Life: An Autobiography* (New York: Simon and Schuster, 1983), pp. 347–48.

32. Letter, Brig. Gen. Charles D. Herron to Maj. Bennett A. Molter, March 15, 1983, RG 319, Entry 343, Box 99.

thereupon set forth in writing the three criteria that would be applied when considering such requests:

1. No ORC Commission would be given to men who were subject to the draft unless they had completed Army courses leading to a commission;
2. "All political or personal considerations should be rigidly excluded;"
3. A commission was to be given only where the individual had special qualifications required for a particular branch of the service.[33]

Under War Department regulations, officers in the ORC were commissioned for five-year terms. If a Reservist wanted to continue as an active member of the ORC, he had to participate regularly in such training opportunities as were offered, and he had to request reappointment in the ORC at the end of each five-year period. The discouraging lack of training opportunities has already been discussed, and the attrition rate of ORC members, even in the years immediately preceding mobilization in 1940 and 1941, was quite high. During fiscal year 1939, for example, the ORC lost 6,784 active, assignable officers, while 8,956 inactive ORC members had their appointments terminated. By comparison, the ORC gained only 10,682 officers during the year.[34]

This yearly drain of trained Reserve officers meant that when mobilization began in 1940 there were not enough ORC members to fill the Army's needs. By the spring of 1941 the War Department had decided to allow the reappointment of former Reserve officers commissioned after 1933 who had been in an eligible status at the time they had terminated their ORC membership.[35]

The Army, however, rejected the idea of having the ROTC increase its production of lieutenants. With a singular

33. Memorandum from Secretary of War Henry L. Stimson, October 14, 1940, Subject: "Memorandum in Re Appointment of Officers' Reserve Corps from Civil Life," RG 319, Entry 343, Box 103.

34. "Report of the Secretary of War to the President, 1939," *Annual Reports, War Department, Fiscal Year Ended June 30, 1939* (Washington: GPO, 1939), pp. 66–67.

35. Memorandum, Brig. Gen. Wade H. Haislip, ACS/G–1 to Chief of Staff, April 21, 1941, Subject: "Policy with Respect to Reappointment in the Officers' Reserve Corps of Former Reserve Officers, Who are Within the Selective Service Ages (21–36)," RG 319, Entry 343, Box 104.

lack of foresight, Brig. Gen. Harry L. Twaddle, ACS/G–3, scorned the idea of increasing the quota for advanced course ROTC cadets, because he said, the number of lieutenants produced by the ROTC each year "more than meets the contemplated needs of the Army."[36] General Twaddle's thoughts on this subject after December 7, 1941, are not recorded, but a stop-and-go pattern of officer procurement was characteristic of the Army during the war.

On January 12, 1942, Secretary of War Stimson admitted that "there will be a need for the commissioning of a substantial number of men from civil life for administrative and other positions in order to relieve officers qualified for combatant service."[37] A week later minimum age for appointment as an officer was reduced from 21 years old to 18 years old, and a month later the War Department announced the suspension of ROTC summer camps. Cadets would henceforth be sent to basic training courses before commissioning, and the requirement of a college degree could be waived "in special cases."[38]

On February 19, 1942, the Secretary of War announced a more flexible standard for reappointing former ORC members. This policy was more lenient than the previous one in that it applied to officers commissioned after 1931 (as opposed to 1933), and it did not require an officer to have been in an "eligible" status when his appointment in the ORC terminated.[39] This relaxation of policy meant that thousands of officers who had simply let their ORC appointments lapse could now be ordered to active duty in a commissioned status.

---

36. Memorandum, Brig. Gen. Harry L. Twaddle to Chief of Staff, October 23, 1941, Subject: "Increase in Advanced Course Quota, ROTC," RG 319, Entry 343, Box 104.

37. Memorandum, Henry L. Stimson, January 12, 1942, Subject: "In re Appointment of Officers From Civil Life," RG 319, Entry 343, Box 105. Before the war was over, some 100,000 civilians received direct commissions without any military training. Robert R. Palmer, Bell I. Wiley, and William R. Keast, *United States Army in World WAr II, The Army Ground Forces, The Procurement and Training of Ground Combat Troops* (Washington: Historical Division, Department of the Army, 1948), pp. 91–92.

38. War Department Radiogram, January 20, 1942, RG 315, Entry 343, Box 105; War Department Press Release, "Army Suspends R.O.T.C. Camps until Six Months after War Ends," February 12, 1942, RG 319, Entry 343, Box 107.

39. Memorandum, TAG (by order of the Secretary of War), February 19, 1942, Subject: "Appointment of Former Officers in the Army of the United States," RG 319, Entry 343, Box 105.

Even these measures could not meet the Army's needs for commissioned officers during its rapid expansion in 1942, so standards for officer procurement were lowered. By the next year, when mobilization of the ground forces had slowed, the Army had a surplus of junior officers; by 1944 demand exceeded supply again.[40]

WAR-TIME POLICIES

Despite Chief of Staff Marshall's praise of the ORC for providing 100,000 trained officers during the pre-war mobilization,[41] the best interests of Reservists were regarded only lightly—if at all—when personnel policies were implemented during the war.

For example, before May 1942 a Reserve officer who was physically disqualified from active duty was placed in the Inactive Reserve, where he was not subjected to the draft. Beginning in May 1942 the War Department began discharging all physically disqualified Reserve officers who had less than fifteen years of service. These individuals were then subject to being drafted into the Army as enlisted men, because the physical standards for draftees were lower than those for commissioned officers.[42]

Several Reserve officers sent letters of protest to the Executive for Reserve and ROTC Affairs, and on December 4, 1942, he took up the issue with the ACS/G–1. He did not think the policy was fair, stated Col. Edward J. Smith, and he believed that these officers should be reappointed in the ORC or other component if they were physically qualified for even limited service. The next day he discussed the matter in detail with Col. Jenkins of the G–1 staff, and they reached an agreement along the lines that Col. Smith suggested. The physical standards continued to differ for officers and enlisted personnel, however, with the result that men like James P. Chapman continued to be discharged, then drafted. The agreement with Col. Jenkins had not been carried through as War Department policy.[43]

---

40. See Palmer, Wiley and Keast, *Procurement and Training of Ground Combat Troops*, p. 159.

41. "Report of the Secretary of War to the President, 1941," *Annual Reports, War Department, Fiscal Year Ended June 30, 1941* (Washington: GPO, 1941), p. 53.

42. Memorandum, Brig. Gen. Edward W. Smith to Chief of Staff, September 28, 1945, Subject: "Report of Activities of this Office During My Tenure of Office," RG 319, Entry 343, Box 116.

43. Memorandum, Col. Edward W. Smith to ACS/G–1, December

Additional Reserve officers were trapped in this "Catch-22" situation during 1943, and their continuing protests finally led to the announcement of an official change of policy. On October 20, 1943, Maj. Gen. W. G. White, the ACS/G–1, informed the Secretary of War's Personnel Board of the new two-part policy. If a commissioned officer who was discharged for physical reasons after satisfactory active service was subsequently inducted as an enlisted man, he would be reappointed in the grade formerly held. If a commissioned officer who was not serving on active duty was discharged for physical reasons and was later inducted, he would be reappointed to his former grade, *if* a vacancy existed and he was otherwise qualified.[44] This policy still left the possibility that an ORC member could be drafted as an enlisted man, and it was not until May 24, 1944, that War Department Circular 206 eliminated this possibility.[45] The Executive for Reserve and ROTC Affairs had been instrumental in effecting this new policy, but the Army's antipathy toward ORC members was indicated in the time that elapsed after it was brought to the attention of the ACS/G–1 in early December 1942. In disability retirement, too, the Army did not treat the Organized Reserve equitably.

From June 30, 1940, to August 31, 1944, stated the Executive for Reserve and ROTC Affairs, 3864 non-Regular Army officers were relieved from active duty because of physical disability. Of these, only 68 were retired with pay under the Retirement Act, a minuscule percentage that Brig. Gen. Smith thought was evidence of unfair treatment of Organized Reservists. Smith called this discrepancy to the attention of the ACS/G–1, and War Department Circular 205, "Determination of Line of Duty," was changed to make it easier to find "in line of duty" when judging disability.[46]

4, 1942, Subject: "Induction of Former Reserve, National Guard and Other Officers Discharged for Physical Disability" and attached Memorandum for Record, December 5, 1942, RG 319, Entry 343. Box 105; letter, Brig. Gen. Edward Smith to Col. Joseph K. Nicholls, January 1, 1943, RG 319, Entry 343, Box 105.

44. Memorandum, Maj. Gen. W. G. White, ACS/G–1, to Secretary of War's Personnel Board, October 20, 1943, Subject: "Reappointment of Officers Discharged for Physical Disability," RG 319, Entry 343, Box 107.

45. Brig. Gen. Edward W. Smith to Chief of Staff, September 28, 1945, Subject: "Report of Activities of this Office During My Tenure of Office," RG 319, Entry 343, Box 116.

46. "Report on Activities of the Office of the Executive for Reserve

EXECUTIVE OPERATIONS

It is evident that members of the ORC needed someone to represent them—to serve as a sort of ombudsman for them—at the Army Staff level during the war. The Executive for Reserve and ROTC Affairs (ERRA) had long performed this function, and the entrance of the United States into World War II caused no immediate change in the status, activities, or personnel of the office. In March 1942, however, the ERRA was placed under The Adjutant General, and in June it was given independent status under the Chief of Administrative Services, TAG. During that same month the ERRA was designated a member of the "Post-War Planning Board of the War Department."[47]

Brig. Gen. Frank E. Lowe was the first Organized Reserve general officer to serve as ERRA. He had been on the job for a little over one year, and the United States had been at war for some eight months, when he recommended that the office·functions "which pertain to the Organized Reserves be suspended for the duration of the present emergency . . . ." He further suggested that the office be transferred to the Legislation and Liaison Branch of the War Department General Staff, a suggestion that was adopted in September, 1942.[48]

The OERRA functioned during the war with a strength of one brigadier general, one colonel, one lieutenant colonel, one major, and four clerical civilians. In addition to aiding individual ORC members with their problems, the ERRA worked with Brig. Gen. John McAuley Palmer, who was putting together a suggested structure for the post-war Reserve components.[49]

By the spring of 1945 the Organized Reserve had become more important, and the OERRA was placed on the War Department Special Staff. The Executive for Reserve

---

and ROTC Affairs for period 1 October 1942 to 31 August 1944," RG 319, Entry 343, Box 111.

47. "Historical Summary," November 9, 1942, RG 319, Entry 343, Box 106.

48. Memorandum, Brig. Gen. Frank E. Lowe to Secretary of the General Staff, August 13, 1942, Subject: "Office of the Executive for Reserve and ROTC Affairs," RG 319, Entry 343, Box 106; Memorandum, Col. Edward W. Smith to Army HQ Commandant, November 5, 1942, Subject: "Transfer of Office of Executive for Reserve and ROTC Affairs to the Pentagon Building," RG 319, Entry 343, Box 107.

49. Memorandum, Brig. Gen. Frank E. Lowe to Secretary of the General Staff, August 13, 1942, Subject: "Office of the Executive for Reserve and ROTC Affairs," RG 319, Entry 343, Box 106.

and ROTC Affairs gave up his additional duties with the Legislation and Liaison Branch and began to devote full-time to the transition to a peace-time reserve force.[50]

CONCLUSION

The officers of the ORC had served well during World War II, furnishing almost one-fourth of the Army's total officer strength during the conflict. Because of pre-war neglect, the units of the Organized Reserve were not prepared to mobilize in 1940 or even 1941, and by the time the units were called to duty after that time, they were ORC in name only.[51]

The future of the Organized Reserve Corps was problematical, for no one knew for sure how many officers had gotten their fill of military duty during the war and whether demobilization would mark the end of their military affiliation. The War Department had been planning the post-war Army for years, but Congress might not accept these plans. The public outcry for a rapid demobilization could not be resisted, but Soviet ambitions loomed large in the minds of the War Department's planners. It was obvious to most military leaders that Reserve forces were going to be needed in years to come and that the neglect of the post-World War I years simply could not be allowed. The question was whether Army plans, Congressional desires, and public will would fit together in a coherent fashion, sufficient for the National defense.

50. War Department General Orders No. 39, May 17, 1945.
51. From July 1, 1940, to June 30, 1946, some 902,000 men served on active duty as commissioned officers. Of this total, 204,000 were members of the ORC; memorandum, TAG to ERRA, November 26, 1946, Subject: "Data on Commissioned Officers, Regular and Non-Regulars for Reserve Officers Association of the United States," RG 319, Entry 343, Box 126 (320.2).

5

Peace—And War Again, 1946–1953

Even before Pearl Harbor, the Army had begun planning for the post-war, and the services of Brig. Gen. John McAuley Palmer were a valuable part of that effort. General Palmer's service as a member of the War Plans Division of the General Staff immediately after World War I made him a logical and valuable resource, as did his friendship with George Marshall. "I have some personal knowledge of our government's past experience with this problem," wrote Palmer in November 1942. "Some serious mistakes were made at that time [post-WWI]. If we can avoid them after World War II, in my opinion, the whole problem will be greatly simplified."[1]

Palmer and his committee, formed by Chief of Staff Marshall to develop plans for the post-war, worked diligently, and on August 25, 1944, the War Department issued Circular No. 347, a philosophical blueprint for the post-war military establishment that was developed out of Palmer's life-long study of the Army. The military organization envisioned in this document was based upon two stated assumptions: (1) that the United States would maintain "such temporary military forces . . . as may as necessary . . . to lay the foundations for a peaceful world order" and

---

1. Letter, Brig. Gen. John McAuley Palmer to Frederic A. Delano, Chairman, National Resources Planning Board, November 9, 1942, RG 319, Entry 343, Box 107. For a good account of Palmer's work see Michael S. Sherry, *Preparing for the Next War: American Plans for Postwar Defense, 1941–45* (New Haven and London: Yale University Press, 1977).

(2) that Congress would provide for universal male military training. The Circular also emphasized—perhaps more than had any official pronouncement in the past—the role of the reserve forces in this nation's military establishment.[2] The "professional peace establishment," stated Circular No. 347, should be "no larger than necessary to meet *normal* [emphasis added] peacetime requirements." The regular army would be reinforced in wartime by a "properly organized citizen army reserve," a proposal described in the circular as a way of "perfecting a traditional national institution to meet modern requirements which no longer permit extemporization after the outbreak of war."[3]

The tradition of the United States had never been that of maintaining a large standing army, or even a large reserve force, in peacetime; mobilization of the untrained civilian community had long been the US response to the need for a large military force. During the two World Wars the United States was given by its allies the luxury of time—time to induct and train men and time to produce the weapons necessary to arm them. At the close of World War II, however, it was evident that the burden of Western defense would fall increasingly on the United States. It was similarly evident—and the authors of Circular No. 347 were quite aware of it—that if a major war were to occur in Europe there would no longer be the luxury of time, for the Soviet Union could overrun Europe long before the first US draftees reached the front lines.

Though the Soviet Union was very much one of the Allies at the time Circular No. 347 was issued, assumptions about Soviet post-war ambitions may well have been on the minds of the War Department's planners. Understood in this light, Circular No. 347 was an ambitious, yet realistic, approach to US military organization. That it did not prove to be an accurate prediction of the future was not so much the fault of the War Department's planners as it was a reflection of the political realities of the time.

The War Department sought a "cautious demobilization" after the defeat of Japan, largely out of respect for the ambitions and military strength of the Soviet Union, as well as in anticipation of worldwide occupation duties. Such a course, however, was politically impossible. The United States Army stood at over 8 million personnel in 1945, and

---

2. War Department Circular No. 347, August 25, 1944.
3. *Ibid.*

most of these individuals demanded nothing less than a prompt and complete release from active service.[4]

Plans for an Army strong enough to deter possible Soviet aggression ran squarely up against powerful opposition: the normal post-war economy moves in the federal Government and an idea that "the bomb"—the atomic weapons monopoly enjoyed by the US—would prove the ultimate deterrent to an aggressor. The United States had not questioned the financial cost of winning World War II, but the immediate post-war political reaction was that of cutting back drastically on the military part of the federal budget.

President Truman himself set the pattern for military spending during the years from 1946–1950 by using a "remainder method" of calculating the military budget. The federal budget would be balanced, he said, by taking total revenues, subtracting from that total all domestic spending, and giving the rest to the military.

This frugality was complemented nicely by the idea that the US monopoly of the atomic bomb was a cheap, effective, and absolutely fail-safe deterrent. The idea that the next major conflict might not be a nuclear one was given some thought by the War Department, but Congress and the President preferred the economy route.

The years between World War II and Korea were characterized by a not-unprecedented desire to achieve national security at the least possible cost, and one cost-effective way of reaching this goal was to build-up a strong reserve force. In theory this idea worked quite well, but in reality the President and the Congress created a military shell and a false sense of security that was nearly as hollow as were the divisions of the Organized Reserve in the years after World War I.

TERMINAL LEAVE PROMOTIONS

Rebuilding the Organized Reserve was an important assumption of War Department Circular No. 347 and of post-war military strength planning. The Army had very little to offer as an inducement, however, to veterans who were invited to join the Corps. One of the few things the Army did in fact offer its veterans was not even tied to their continued membership in the ORC, and this was the "terminal leave

---

4. Russell F. Weigley, *History of the United States Army* (New York and London: Macmillan Publishing Co., Inc. and Collier Macmillan Publishers, 1967), pp. 486, 569.

promotion" that became such a bone of contention with the Regulars. Reserve promotions had been frozen during the war, while Regular Army promotions had not. The only way an ORC member could receive a promotion during WWII was by being on active duty and in line for a vacancy of the next higher grade. He .was then eligible to be considered for an Army of the United States (AUS) promotion. Without the vacancy, there could be no promotion. As Colonel Charles M. Boyer, Executive Director of the Reserve Officers Association, explained it, " . . . Promotions became the luck of assignment, and if a man was lucky in assignment, he went up rapidly, and if he was assigned to a position where there were no vacancies, he stood still."[5] Figures compiled by ROA indicated that by June 1944—over 2 1/2 years after Pearl Harbor—some 21 percent of the ORC members on active duty had not received even one promotion.[6] A plan was therefore devised to correct some of the inequities of the system, and there was some hope that this would encourage continued participation in one of the Reserve components of the Army.

The rules for receiving a terminal promotion were simple and mechanical and applied to all non-Regular Army officers. Any non-Regular Army officer would be given a one-grade promotion effective the day he went on terminal leave, providing he met the following requirements:

1. Below the grade of 0–6 (Colonel);
2. At least two years active duty after September 16, 1940;
3. An efficiency index of at least 35;
4. No promotion while on active duty;
5. Requisite time-in-grade; i.e., 18 months to First Lieutenant or Captain, 24 months to Major or Lieutenant Colonel, and 30 months to Colonel. In computing time-in-grade, overseas service prior to May 1, 1946, counted an additional 50 percent.[7]

There was, of course, no requirement that the officer be promoted into a vacant position, and this was the key to the

5. "Reserve Officer Personnel Act," *Hearings before the Committee on Armed Services, House of Representatives, Eighty-third Congress, First Session,* p. 1676. Hereinafter cited as "ROPA."

6. "Your Association Wins Promotions for Officers Reverting to Inactive Status," *The Reserve Officer* (November 1945), p. 4.

7. Major W. K., Whichard, "Administering the Reserve," *The Reserve Officer* (December 1946), pp. 10–11.

terminal leave promotion. The system was completely inflexible, and an officer who was only a few days short of the required time-in-grade or a few hundredths under the efficiency index level was not promoted.[8] The elimination of the vacancy requirement was the only relaxation of the wartime promotion system, and as a result only about 40,000 officers—not all of whom were ORC members—received a terminal leave promotion.[9] This was only about 5 percent of the 800,000 Army officers on active duty in 1945, but this small percentage was multiplied again and again in the public mind until it was commonly believed that *all* reserve officers had received a promotion upon their release from active duty.[10]

These terminal leave promotions were important, however, to the officers who received them. It is likely that many of these men did join the Officers' Reserve Corps or continue their affiliation with it after their discharge from active service, in part because the terminal leave promotion removed a source of great and continuing frustration for them. It should be clearly understood, however, that the terminal leave promotions were not *per se* connected with either past or future membership in the ORC. These promotions, in all probability, were of value in ORC recruiting, but only in an indirect way.

REBUILDING THE ORGANIZED RESERVE CORPS

The only appeal the Army could actually make, given the paucity of membership benefits in the ORC, was an appeal to patriotism, and when General George C. Marshall addressed a letter to "All members of the Army" in August 1945, that was the heart of his appeal. "We owe it to our country," he wrote, "and to the comrades who have made the great sacrifice, to insure that never again will Americans be drawn into a war unprepared."[11] These were brave and ambitious words from the Army's Chief of Staff, but the next five years did not demonstrate a national commitment to achieving the goal of military preparedness through the

---

8. ROPA, p. 1676.

9. *Ibid.*

10. See, for example, the statements of Rep. Leroy Johnson (R–CA) and Maj. Gen. Boniface Campbell, DCS/G–1, during hearings on the Reserve Officer Personnel Act. ROPA, pp. 1676, 2038.

11. Letter, Chief of Staff George C. Marshall, August 23, 1945, copy in "Office History, 1916 to Present," Center of Military History.

creation of a strong, effective Organized Reserve and National Guard. One example of this was the national response to proposals for universal military training.

Universal military training was an integral part of the planning for the post-war Organized Reserve Corps. "Without it," wrote the Executive for Reserve and ROTC Affairs (ERRA), "it is our considered opinion that the development and maintenance of any material strength within the ORC is improbable."[12] Universal military training was not, however, enacted by the post-war Congress, and recruitment for the Organized Reserve depended entirely upon voluntary enlistments and commissionings.

Given the pre-war participation of men in the Officers' Reserve Corps, it was probably not unexpected that many officers would continue their Army affiliation by joining the post-war ORC. By January 1946 some 52.5 percent of all demobilized officers had accepted commissions in the ORC.[13]

Medical officer recruitment was a problem, however, and even men who had been in the pre-war ORC were refusing any further military affiliation. The war-time experience of Capt. E. H. Phillips is a good illustration of the way the Army alienated ORC doctors. Capt. Phillips had been a member of the Officers' Reserve Corps and had volunteered for active duty in 1942. He was a board certified otolaryngologist—an ear, nose, and throat specialist—but he was never promoted, because there were no higher level vacancies in the command. There were no vacancies, stated Capt. Phillips, because his civilian contemporaries, men who had no military background and no better medical credentials than he had, were commissioned directly from civilian life as majors and lieutenant colonels. Capt. Phillips was angry about the way he had been treated, and Brig. Gen. Edward W. Smith, the Executive for Reserve and ROTC Affairs, sympathized with him. "Civilians could be offered high commissions," stated Smith, "and Reserve Officers

12. Memorandum, ERRA to Director of Operations and Training, December 6, 1946, Subject: "Clarification of War Department Policies Pertaining to the National Guard and the Organized Reserve Corps," RG 319, Entry 342, Box 14 (370.01).

13. Memorandum, Lt. Col. J. L. Ballard, Jr., Chief, Strength Accounting and Statistics Office, to Executive for Reserve and ROTC Affairs, February 4, 1946, Subject: "Respective Ratios to Latest Date of (a) New Commissions in Officers Reserve Corps to Total Eligible for Commission, and (b) New Appointments in Enlisted Reserve Corps to Total Eligible for Appointment," RG 319, Entry 343, Box 124 (210.8).

could only be promoted under the slow process of regular promotion."[14]

Despite the problem of medical officer recruitment, the Officers' Reserve Corps reached a strength of 274,839 by June 1947, less than two years after the end of the war. Enlisted recruitment, however, did not go as well. The War Department had anticipated that 10–12 percent of the enlisted personnel would join the Enlisted Reserve Corps (ERC), but only 1.3 percent of those discharged (35,578 of 2,700,000) had joined by November 1945. The percentage of enlisted veterans who joined the ERC had increased to 3.2 percent by January 31, 1946, and the number of enlisted members of the ERC reached 467,608 by June 30, 1948.[15]

MISTER BREGER   —By Dave Breger

(Reprinted by special permission of King Features Syndicate.)
"We just can't simply persuade him that just because he's in the Enlisted Reserve Corps is no reason to be constantly on the alert."

The Organized Reserve was generally a recognizable organization following World War II, as is indicated by this 1946 cartoon by Dave Breger.

---

14. Letter, Brig. Gen. Edward W. Smith to Capt. E. H. Phillips, September 20, 1945, RG 319, Entry 343, Box 118 (330.14). See confirmation of this policy in memorandum, ACS/G–1 to Chief of Staff, May 14, 1946, Subject: "Officers Separation Point," RG 319, Entry 343, Box 124 (210.8).

15. "Subsection II f—Civilian Components (2)—Organized Reserve Corps," RG 319, Entry 343, Box 127 (326.2).

This latter figure, impressive as it is when compared with the 1941 ERC strength of 2149, was not nearly up to the levels desired by the War Department. One problem was that there were few units of the Organized Reserve to which the men of the ERC could be assigned.

The War Department's initial plans called for a total of twenty-five Organized Reserve Corps divisions and almost 2400 non-divisional units. For the post-war period, there were four classifications of Reserve units: A–1, A–2, B, and C. A–1 units were service units organized with their full complement of officers and enlisted men. Combat units with their full strength of officers and enlisted personnel were designated A–2. Class B consisted of combat and service units that had their full officer strength plus a cadre of enlisted men, and Class C units had only an officer cadre. The War Department's official position was that "All Organized Reserve Corps units will initially be organized as C units, with officers only."[16] This meant that post-World War II Organized Reserve units would, at least initially, resemble the ORC units of the years after World War I. Enlisted men, stated the War Department, would be assigned to an Active Reserve reservoir.[17]

This policy stemmed largely from the fact that in the years of parsimony between World War II and Korea, the Organized Reserve Corps and the National Guard were in competition—conscious or unconscious—for an inadequate pool of dollars. The fact was that the Organized Reserve fared quite badly in this competition. Though the individual members of the Officers' Reserve Corps had achieved an enviable record of service during the war, the Organized Reserve Corps as an organization suffered by comparison with the National Guard. The small number of ORC units that were designated for Class "A" status was a reflection of the Organized Reserve-National Guard competition. This situation did not go unnoticed at the White House, however.

"It has come to the President's attention," wrote President Harry S. Truman's military aide, ORC member Harry Vaughan, to Chief of Staff Dwight D. Eisenhower, "that there is some controversy largely sponsored, I understand, by the National Guard Association against the creation of

16. Memorandum, Lt. Gen. C. P. Hall, Director of Org. and Tng. to Army Chief of Staff, July 10, 1946, Subject: "Inactive Duty Pay for Organized Reserve Corps Units," RG 319, Entry 342, Box 10.

17. "Approved War Department Policies Relating to Postwar National Guard and Organized Reserve Corps," October 13, 1945, RG 319, Entry 343, Box 117 (326.2).

any A–2 Reserve units for the Organized Reserve. The President directed me to advise you that he thinks these units should be created; in fact, he is of the opinion that there is no use in having a Reserve without them."[18] This part of the question of Organized Reserve versus National Guard was quickly resolved, when less than a month later the Secretary of the General Staff informed Vaughan that Chief of Staff Eisenhower "has asked me to advise you now that a decision has been reached, and organization of units of this type is being directed."[19]

The Organized Reserve divisions were not, however, the Reserve units that the War Department had in mind for A–2 status. Priority for divisional organization at the A–2 level of readiness was clearly given to the National Guard. War Department policy, for example, even after the exchange between Vaughan and Eisenhower, was that "until such time as it is clearly demonstrated that requirements cannot be met by the National Guard, Reserve divisions will not be organized beyond class 'B' status."[20] Reserve divisions were to be organized initially as Class "C" units (60 percent of authorized commissioned officer strength) and would advance to "B" status only when they achieved 80 percent of their authorized commissioned and non-commissioned officer strength. To reach Class "A", a unit needed its complete authorized cadre, plus 40 percent of its authorized enlisted strength.[21]

Activation of the first post-war units of the Organized Reserve began on July 1, 1946, and by the end of January 1947 a total of 1141 Organized Reserve units had reached Class C status. The number of such units rose steadily throughout 1947, reaching 3,973 by May 23, 4,479 by June 19, and 6,343 by December 5.[22] By the end of December, the strength of the Organized Reserve Corps was as given in Table 5–1.

18. Memorandum, Brig. Gen. Harry H. Vaughan to Gen. Dwight D. Eisenhower, March 29, 1946, RG 319, Entry 342, Box 10.

19. Memorandum, Col. J. W. Bowen to Harry H. Vaughan, April 18, 1946, RG 319, Entry 343, Box 125 (240).

20. Letter, Gen. Jacob L. Devers, CG, Army Ground Forces, to CG's, Armies, May 13, 1947, Subject: "Clarification of War Department Policies Pertaining to the National Guard and the Organized Reserve Corps," RG 319, Entry 343, Box 147 (370.01).

21. "AGF Initiates Reserve Training Mobilization in Six Army Areas," *The Reserve Officer* (August 1946), pp. 7–8.

22. *Ibid.*, p. 7; War Department Press Releases, January 24, May 23, June 6, June 19, and December 5, 1947, RG 319, Entry 343, Box 141 (322).

Table 5–1   Organized Reserve Strength, December 31, 1947.[23]

	Unassigned	Composite Groups	A	B	C	Total
Units			59	887	5,897	6,843
Officers	62,250	167,059	158	6,233	43,133	278,833
Enlisted	325,008	90,717	422	2,382	21,927	450,456

What these figures mean is that fewer than 600 members of the Organized Reserve Corps were in units that would be ready for active duty on M-Day. The implication of these figures had not escaped Brig. Gen. Wendell Westover, the Executive for Reserve and ROTC Affairs. He had earlier informed the Army's Deputy Chief of Staff that "current and mobilization plans are NOT realistic, since they have produced, from 8 May 1945, to date no Reserve force in being. Today, we have in this country less than eighty (80) Class (A) Reserve units, none of which are adequately manned, equipped, and trained; further, most of them are small and of relatively little importance, such as affiliated laundry units, battalion medical sections, and bomb-disposal squads."[24]

The Organized Reserve Corps, wrote Brig. Gen. Westover several months later, only had 355,000 men actually available for use, compared with an authorized strength of 949,000. The "primary difficulties encountered to date," he wrote, "[are a] deficiency of facilities, equipment, and funds . . . traceable to a large degree to the low priorities afforded the ORC and reluctance to accord it requisite support."[25]

The reason for these deficiencies was simple: a lack of determination on the part of the President and the Congress to give the Organized Reserve the financial support it needed. "Economy" was the watch word of the time, and it often seemed as if the legislative and executive branches were trying to outdo each other in cheeseparing. Indeed, the economy measures were so severe that an officer in The Adjutant Gen-

---

23. Staff Study, Brig. Gen. Wendell Westover, ERRA, to Army Chief of Staff, April 6, 1948, RG 319, Entry 343 (CAR), Box 26 (326.2).

24. Memorandum, Brig. Gen. Wendell Westover, ERRA, to Deputy Chief of Staff, March 17, 1948, Subject: "Immediate Program," RG 319, Entry 342 (CAR), Box 26 (326.2).

25. Memorandum, Brig. Gen. Wendell Westover to Chief of Staff, October 13, 1948, Subject: "Draft of Secretary of Defense Letter Relating to Proposed Presidential Directive," RG 319, Entry 342 (CAR), Box 2 (031.1).

eral's Office indicated that because of a lack of funds, "an ad-m[inistrative] restriction has been placed on the enlistments auth[orized] in certain Class A units . . . . "[26]

This failure to support the Organized Reserve Corps was nowhere more evident than in the paucity of training opportunities afforded its members during the immediate post-war years. Without proper and continuing training, the members of the Organized Reserve Corps would in the long run be little better than conscripts, though the fact that most of the Corps members from 1945–1950 were World War II veterans was a decided advantage. Proper training, however, was non-existent in the first three years after World War II, and lack of funds was the primary limiting factor. There would be no Organized Reserve Corps unit training until Fiscal Year 1949, wrote Army Under Secretary William H. Draper in late November 1947, because " . . . the unit training of all Battalions would cost more than the entire appropriation in FY 1949 for all Reserve activi-ties . . . . "[27]

Even the training that was provided was often reminis-cent of the years between the World Wars, particularly for Class C units of the Organized Reserve. The 98th Infantry Division (ORC) conducted its first post-World War II train-ing during the summer of 1948 at Pine Camp (now Fort Drum), New York. The Division had a summer camp strength of 300 men, of whom 75 percent were officers. In the words of an attached public information officer, "Reg-iments were of platoon size; battalions and companies were represented by squads, sometimes attenuated . . . . The MOS distribution bore only a faint resemblance to any T/O."

The total divisional artillery consisted of two 105mm howitzers, which were provided to the unit without sights. Not until the Cornell University ROTC—150 miles away—agreed to loan sights for the weapons were the howitzers anything more than decorative. The division had no organic vehicles, so "the Division walked to work." Lt. Col. George F. Havell, the PIO who wrote about the 98th Division's training, concluded his account with the following observa-tion: "To point out that the 98th Division has a long way to go before it can be welded into an effective fighting unit is

---

26. Memorandum for the Record, Maj. Frey, July 23, 1948, RG 407, Box 1613 (353-Org Res Corps 4/1/48–12/31/48). See Appendix B for a tabulation of ORC funding during this time.

27. Letter, William H. Draper, Jr., to Lt. Col. Robert B. Fentress, November 21, 1947, RG 319, Entry 343, Box 127 (326.2).

to state the obvious. That will take more manpower, equipment, long training, and—above all—time."[28]

CHANGES IN THE DEFENSE ESTABLISHMENT

The Organized Reserve Corps, of course, operated in neither a political nor an organizational vacuum, and in fact the future of the Corps was intimately related to the post-war organization of the military establishment of this country. War-time proposals for unification of the military services resulted in the National Security Act of 1947, which created the National Military Establishment headed by a Secretary of Defense. There were also created three military Departments: Army, Navy and Air Force.[29]

Following the passage of this act, Secretary of Defense James Forrestal appointed on November 20, 1947, a Committee on Civilian Components, headed by Army Assistant Secretary Gordon Gray, to make a "comprehensive, objective and impartial study" of the Organized Reserve and the National Guard.[30] President Harry S. Truman supported the unification of the Organized Reserve and the National Guard, and his military aide, Maj. Gen. Harry H. Vaughan, had previously published an article arguing that military efficiency would be enhanced by unification of the Guard and Reserve and suggesting that there was no longer any real need for a federally-supported state militia.[31]

The "objective and impartial study" required of the Committee was submitted to the Secretary of Defense on June 30, 1948, and its recommendations stirred immediate controversy. The "Gray Board Report," as the study came to be known, proposed that the Organized Reserve and the National Guard be transformed into a federal "National Guard of the United States." The National Guard should remain in existence, suggested the Gray Board, but it "must be directly under Federal control." The Committee members were "convinced that the same forces can no longer be expected to perform both local and national functions and that a

---

28. Lt. Col. George F. Havell, "A Fighting 98th Division Will Be Built," *The Reserve Officer* (November 1948), pp. 14–15, 22.

29. Weigley, *History of the United States Army*, p. 493.

30. Eilene Galloway, *History of United States Military Policy on Reserve Forces, 1775–1957.* Prepared for the use of the Committees on Armed Services, (Washington: GPO, 1957), p. 465.

31. Harry H. Vaughan, "National Guard and Reserve Must Be Unified," *The Reserve Officer* (October 1947), pp. 4–5.

modern Federal striking force cannot be prepared adequately under State control."[32]

The lengthy report drew immediate opposition from the National Guard Association, which labeled the unification proposal as "just another effort over a long period of time by the War Department and the Regular establishment to supplant the National Guard system with a Federal Reserve or Militia."[33] Despite the support of President Truman, the idea of merging or unifying the Guard and Reserve was dropped for the time, and it did not surface again as a serious proposal until the 1960's. In another area, however, the Organized Reserve finally caught up with the Guard, and that was in the matter of compensation for inactive duty training (IADT).

The War Department had long been opposed to inactive duty pay for members of the Organized Reserve, for reasons that were explained in Chapter Four. The post-war need to encourage Organized Reserve membership, however, finally caused a change in the attitude of the War Department. It is quite likely, too, that the Executive for Reserve and ROTC Affairs was instrumental in effecting this change. Col. John V. Rathbone, for example, wrote to the ACS/G–1 on behalf of the ERRA in mid-April 1946. Without pay for IADT, he stated, "It will be impossible to provide the units and personnel in the desired quantity and quality." A month later, Lt. Col. Jay W. Doverspike, Acting Executive Officer of the OERRA, advised that it was "not considered possible to develop the required units within the Organized Reserve Corps unless some provision is made for pay to members of these units, for training other than active duty."[34]

With Defense Department support, the provision of inactive duty pay for members of the Organized Reserve Corps became law on March 25, 1948, though the first payments under this statute were not made until October 1, 1948.[35] Because of limitations on funds, the Department of the Army established four priorities for payment of IADT:

---

32. *Report of the Committee on Civilian Components,* pp. 10–11.

33. Maj. Gen. Ellard A. Walsh, "One Federal Force? No," *The Reserve Officer* (June 1949), p. 6.

34. Memorandum, Col. John V. Rathbone to ACS/G–1, April 17, 1946, Subject: "Legislation for the Organized Reserve Corps," RG 319, Entry 343, Box 117 (326.2); memorandum, Lt. Col. Jay W. Doverspike to Chief, L & LD, May 14, 1946, no subject, RG 319, Entry 343, Box 125 (240).

35. Public Law 80–460; Department of the Army Press Release, October 23, 1948, "Drill Pay Regulations Issued for Army Reserve," RG 319, Entry 343 (CAR), Box 37 (240).

1. Organized Reserve Corps personnel in units that were in direct support of the 18-division Army;
2. Individuals with mobilization assignments as "filler personnel" for Regular Army and National Guard divisions;
3. Members of the Class B Organized Reserve Corps divisions; and
4. Remaining Organized Reserve Corps personnel.[36]

Another legislative battle that was fought and won by the Organized Reserve during the years immediately following World War II was that of retired pay. Pre-World War II proposals for such had run into solid opposition from the War Department, including the Office of the Executive for Reserve and ROTC Affairs. Even late in the war, Brig. Gen. Edward W. Smith, the ERRA, wrote that "The military is an avocation of the Reserve officer, prompted by patriotic motives while employed in a gainful civilian pursuit which, presumably, provides for his own retirement from the active business world."[37]

The difference that a change in Organized Reserve leadership can make is exemplified by the response of Brig. Gen. Edward S. Bres, successor to Brig. Gen. Smith as ERRA. When asked to comment on a similar piece of retirement legislation, the response was quite positive—but for officers only. "This office is firmly of the opinion," wrote Bres, "that provision for retirement pay in some form should be made for Reserve officers. Retirement pay should include credit for both active Federal service as well as inactive duty service. It is believed retirement pay will insure the continued interest of future officers."[38]

The proposal for non-disability retirement pay for reservists—both officers and enlisted personnel—was finally enacted by the provisions of Public Law 80–810 (June 29, 1948). The law provided for payment beginning at the age of 60 to reservists who had served at least twenty years in the reserve and active components. Retired reservists were not yet, however, permitted to use the commissaries or post

---

36. Department of the Army Press Release, "Drill Pay Regulations Issued for Army Reserve," RG 319, Entry 343 (CAR), Box 37 (240).

37. Memorandum, Brig. Gen. Edward W. Smith to ACS/G–1, January 18, 1944, Subject: "Comments on H. R. 3946, providing for 'retirement pay for certain members of the armed forces,'" RG 319, Entry 343, Box 115.

38. Memorandum, Brig. Gen. Edward S. Bres, ERRA, to Chief, Legislation and Liaison Division, March 4, 1946, Subject: "H. R. 5204, 79th Congress," RG 319, Entry 343, Box 124 (210.85).

exchanges, despite a concerted campaign by the Reserve Officers Association.[39]

WOMEN IN THE RESERVES

The question of how to increase the strength of the Organized Reserve Corps had plagued War Department planners since the end of World War II. The same questions, of course, had confronted the active Army during the war, and one source of high quality personnel had been the women of this country. Women had served in American armies, sometimes clandestinely, at least as early as the Revolutionary War. There had been no women in the Organized Reserves, however, before World War II, and there was no legal authority for them to join the Organized Reserves after the war.

This situation changed in 1947 when Congress authorized members of the Army Nurse Corps and Women's Medical Specialist Corps to serve in the Regular Army and the Officers' Reserve Corps.[40] The following year it authorized Women's Army Corps (WAC) members to serve in the Regular Army and the Organized Reserves under the provisions of the "Women's Armed Services Integration Act of 1948."[41]

A restriction, however, was that only prior service personnel were eligible to join the Organized Reserve Corps. This proviso meant that only members of the World War II Women's Army Corps, the Army Nurse Corps, or the female component of one of the other services, could join the Organized Reserves. Despite this restriction, within two years after passage of PL 80–625 the number of women in the Organized Reserve Corps had reached 4000. By May 1950 membership in the Organized Reserve Corps was opened to non-prior service women between the ages of 18 and 34, and a waiver to age 45 was allowed.[42] Women, of

---

39. Letter, Maj. Gen. Edward F. Witsell, The Adjutant General, to Brig. Gen. E. A. Evans, Reserve Officers Association, December 3, 1947, RG 319, Entry 343, Box 137 (210.85).

40. Public Law, 36–80, April 1947.

41. Public Law 80–625, June 12, 1948.

42. Department of Defense Press Release, May 25, 1950, Subject: "Women Without Prior Military Service now Eligible for WAC Reserve," RG 319, Entry 343, Box 2 (000.7); for a good account of the Women's Army Corps during World War II, see Mattie E. Treadwell, *The Women's Army Corps* (Washington: Department of the Army, 1954). The restriction that only veterans could join the Organized Reserves was partially lifted in 1947, when enlistment of a non-veteran was permitted if

course, formed only a small percentage of the active Army during World War II, and by law they could not be used in combat. This combat restriction on women also applied to the Organized Reserve Corps, so what the Army and the Organized Reserves really needed was a large and steady source of men.

SELECTIVE SERVICE AND RESERVE ORGANIZATION

Universal military training would provide a source of manpower, but UMT had been rejected immediately after the war. It was revived, however, in the Gray Board Report in 1948. Congress was still unwilling to embrace the idea completely, but the 80th Congress did pass a new selective service act, which became law on June 24, 1948. This statute provided that men from 19 to 26 years old could be inducted for up to 21 months of active service. They would thereafter serve in a Reserve component for five years, an obligation that could be reduced to three years by service in a unit of the Organized Reserve Corps or the National Guard.[43]

Individuals who were members of Organized Reserve Corps or National Guard units as of the date of the act were exempt from the draft for as long as they continued to participate satisfactorily, as were World War II veterans with more than 90 days of active service. This legislation was of little immediate value in Organized Reserve Corps recruiting, but it did hold forth the promise of funneling men into the Reserves and Guard once they had performed their active duty.[44] As a practical matter, however, the Selective Service Act of 1948 was not immediately effective even at providing soldiers for the active Army, for only 300,000 men were drafted in the first two years after its passage.[45]

President Truman was dissatisfied with the progress— or lack of progress—being made in putting together an effective Army reserve organization, and he undoubtedly realized that the Selective Service Act of 1948 would have only a minimal immediate effect on the Organized Reserve Corps and the National Guard. In October 1948, not quite four months after the Gray Board had submitted its report, he

---

the individual agreed to assignment to and training with a troop program unit. AR 150–5, Ch.3, December 11, 1947.

43. Public Law 80–759, June 24, 1948.
44. *Ibid.*
45. Weigley, *History of the United States Army*, p. 501.

issued an Executive Order calling upon the Secretaries of the Army, Navy, and Air Force to "proceed without delay, utilizing every practicable resource of the regular components of the armed forces, to organize all reserve component units, and to train such additional individuals . . . as may be required for the national security; and to establish vigorous and progressive programs of appropriate instruction and training for all elements of the reserve components . . . ."[46]

Under the provisions of the Executive Order, Army Secretary Kenneth C. Royall asked the Committee on Civilian Components, headed by former Secretary of State James F. Byrnes, for a report of recommendations for the Organized Reserve and the National Guard.

The Byrnes Committee submitted its report to the Secretary on February 21, 1949, and recommended that the strength of the Organized Reserve be set at 579,300. Included in this total would be 96,900 members of 25 Class "B" Organized Reserve divisions (1,876 officers and 2,000 enlisted men per division); 149,400 members of combat support units; 242,000 members of combat service support units; and 91,000 officers and enlisted men who would be used as fillers during the early phases of mobilization. The Committee also recommended that paid administrative assistants be provided for units of the Organized Reserve Corps.[47]

KOREA

The Organized Reserve Corps did not, however, achieve the strength goals outlined by the Byrnes Committee prior to the Korean War. On June 30, 1950, the Corps consisted of 217,435 officers and 291,182 enlisted men, of whom only 68,785 officers and 117,756 enlisted men were participating in paid drills.[48]

The parsimony of the years after World War II was not, of course, restricted to the reserve components of the Army, for the active forces had not fared much better. Some efforts were made in 1948 and 1949 to improve Army readiness and to make the Organized Reserve a force upon which the

---

46. Executive Order 10007, October 15, 1948. It should be noted that fiscal frugality was not thereafter abandoned by the President.

47. Department of the Army Press Release, February 21, 1949.

48. *Study of the Functions, Organization, and Procedures of the Department of the Army; OSD Project 80 (Army), Part VII, Reserve Components* (Washington: Department of the Army, 1961), p. VII–B–7.

United States could depend, but it was a case of too little, too late.

The official history of the Joint Chiefs of Staff puts it this way:

The outbreak of the war was to reveal that these forces were suffering from severe defects, largely stemming from the Administration's efforts to hold military expenditures to a minimum. President Truman had laid down this economy objective in 1948 [there really was not much of a change from earlier], and had held to it in the preparation of the budgets for fiscal years 1950 and 1951. Its effect was to force the services to abandon the plans they had drawn, following the hasty and ill-considered demobilization at the end of World War II, to expand their forces to levels judged necessary for the 'cold war.' Thus the Army, which in 1947 had set a goal of 25 divisions, cut this back to 10 and maintained the lower figure only with some difficulty.[49]

When the North Koreans struck across the 38th parallel on June 15, 1950, the US Army was not in any condition to resist. Five years of neglect had taken its toll, and the weakness of depending for security upon an atomic umbrella was demonstrated by the inability of the Army to respond to anything short of all-out mobilization. General Douglas MacArthur had an immediate need for additional American combat forces for Korea, and it soon became obvious that the active Army was not prepared to offer the required level of support. President Truman quickly received Congressional authorization to order members and units of the Organized Reserve Corps to active service. A call for volunteers had yielded few positive results, so in July 1950 the Army turned to what Army Secretary Frank Pace described as "our sole immediate source of manpower"—that is, to the members of the Organized Reserve Corps and the National Guard.[50]

The first members of the Organized Reserve Corps to be called to active duty were 7,862 captains and lieutenants who were not assigned to units of the ORC. By the end of August 1950 a total of 404 units of the Organized Reserve, plus 10,584 individual Organized Reserve officers, had been

---

49. James F. Schnabel and Robert J. Watson, *The History of the Joint Chiefs of Staff; The Joint Chiefs of Staff and National Policy, Volume III—The Korean War, Part I* (unpublished, 1978), p. 45.

50. Frank Pace, Jr., "The Reserve Forces of the Army," *The Reserve Officer* (March 1952), p. 7.

called to active duty.[51] Unlike World War II, the Army's policy for Korea was that officers and enlisted personnel would not be stripped out of organized units and sent to Korea as replacements.[52] The justification for this policy was that coherent units of the Organized Reserve would be needed in the event that a more general war broke out elsewhere in the world.

A tremendous problem of equity ensued from this decision, however, for two reasons. First, non-unit members of the Organized Reserve Corps had not been receiving inactive duty pay, and might well have received no active duty training, either, since their demobilization after World War II. Since they had received few benefits from their Organized Reserve Corps membership, they felt they should not receive the first call to duty. Second, there were by 1950 many millions of young men who had never served in the military at all. Since most Organized Reserve Corps members were also World War II veterans, the ORC men did not think this double jeopardy call-up was fair.[53]

In September 1951 the ACS/G–1 suggested six priorities for ordering reservists to active duty:

1. Qualified volunteers from the Organized Reserve Corps and the National Guard;
2. Members of Organized Reserve Corps units;
3. Members of the active reserve with less than 12 months of WW II service;
4. Members of the inactive reserve with less than 12 months WW II service;
5. Other members of the active reserve;
6. Other members of the inactive reserve.

The Executive for Reserve and ROTC Affairs non-concurred in the proposed list and suggested that the number 2

51. Msg, G–1, WCL 37558, August 10, 1950, RG 319, Entry 343 (CAR), Box 35 (210.4); letter, Hubert E. Howard, Chairman, Munitions Board, to Secretary of Defense, August 28, 1950, Subject: "Recall Requirements of Reservists," RG 319, Entry 342, Box 15 (CAR) (210.4); Office, Chief of Military History, Department of the Army, *Problems Encountered in Bringing Units Up to Strength and Condition of Readiness for Korea*, p. 2.

52. Presentation by Col. George E. Butler before the Section 5 Committee, September 25, 1950, RG 319, Entry 342 (CAR), Box 38 (334).

53. *Study of the Functions, Organization, and Procedures of the Department of the Army; OSD Project 80 (Army), Part VII, Reserve Components*, p. VII–B–5.

priority—members of units—be moved to the bottom of the list. "To order into the active military service members of Organized Reserve Corps units," wrote Brig. Gen. Hugh M. Milton, echoing a familiar line, "would seriously affect the capabilities of these units to perform their training mission and to assume their planned role in the event of full mobilization."[54]

By the next month—barely a year after the United States had gotten into the fighting in Korea—the ACS/G–1, Lt. Gen. Anthony C. McAuliffe, announced the officer recall program for Fiscal Years 1952 and 1953. Because the active Army had a shortage of some 11,000 officers, wrote McAuliffe, it would be necessary to call additional men to active duty. These men, he stated, would be those who had been in a pay status in the reserve. He recognized the danger this posed to overall US readiness, but he said, "This calculated risk is necessary since it is not politically, nor militarily, practical to order additional members of the Inactive and Volunteer Reserve into active service."[55]

Secretary of the Army Frank Pace soon expanded upon McAuliffe's statements in a memorandum to the Army Chief of Staff. "The Department is limited in its ability," wrote Pace, "to utilize the Volunteer and Inactive Reserve in that it is the desire of Congress that paid reservists be utilized in lieu of those who have not received pay for reserve activity. However, in implementing this Congressional intent, reservists who at any time since the beginning of the Korean conflict have been paid for reserve activity will be considered as available for recall and will be utilized to the maximum extent practicable. This will be without regard to the length of time in pay status," concluded Pace, "whether currently in a pay status, or whether currently in the Organized, Volunteer, or Inactive Reserve."[56]

Although the priority and liability for service varied somewhat among the different groups of the organized Reserve Corps, the fact remains that large numbers of ORC

54. Memorandum, ACS/G–1 to RROTC, September 26, 1951, Subject: "Involuntary Ordering into Active Service of Reservists," RG 319, Entry 342 (CAR), Box 15 (210.4); and memorandum, RROTC to ACS/G–1, October 1, 1951, same subject, *ibid.*

55. Memorandum, Lt. Gen. A. C. McAuliffe to addressees, October 26, 1951, Subject: "Recall Program, FY 52 and FY 53," RG 319, Entry 342 (CAR), Box 15 (210.4).

56. Memorandum, Frank Pace, Jr., to Chief of Staff, January 14, 1952, Subject: "Ordering into the Active Military Service Officers of the Organized Reserve Corps," RG 319, Entry 342 (CAR), Box 15 (210.4).

members were called to active Army service. By the end of the first full year of fighting in Korea, more than 200,000 members of the Organized Reserve and 95,000 National Guardsmen had been called to duty. During this same period, the Army received 550,000 draftees and 175,000 volunteers.[57]

The number of Organized Reserve Corps members who served in Korea has not been determined, though 240,500 ORC members were called to active duty. Fourteen separate ORC battalions and 40 separate ORC companies, plus an unknown number of individuals, actually went to Korea. Many ORC members were in combat units, and with the general lack of combat preparedness on the part of the United States Army, opportunities for heroism were far too numerous. Members of the Organized Reserve received a fair share of recognition for their actions against the enemy. Seven Medals of Honor—five posthumously—were awarded to ORC members, as were approximately 10 percent of the other top combat decorations.[58]

Even reservists who were not called to active duty were subjected to the inequities of the Korean mobilization. Unlike World War II, when the entire country, broadly speaking, was involved in and united behind the war effort, Korea was never even dignified by being a declared war. It was a "police action," and the conduct of the war was not of intimate concern to a large percentage of the American population. Only a fraction of the 2,500,000 members of the reserve components was ever called to active duty, but all Reservists lived, and worked under the daily threat of mobilization.

Although membership in the Reserves carried with it the ultimate responsibility and hardship of responding to a mobilization order, Reservists discovered in 1950 that hardship could occur without their being mobilized. Indeed, within two months of the initial outbreak of war in Korea,

---

57. Dr. Robert W. Coakley, "Highlights of Mobilization, Korean War, Prepared in Office of the Chief of Military History, Department of the Army, 10 March 1959," p. 2 (copy in CMH files).

58. *Semiannual Report of the Secretary of Defense, January 1 to June 30, 1953* (Washington: GPO, 1953), pp. 67–68. The 40 ORC units contained 8651 enlisted personnel. The number of Organized Reserve officers in Korea was undoubtedly substantial, because only 15% of the officers in the Eighth Army were Regulars. For a good discussion see Office, Chief of Military History, *Problems Encountered*, pp. 1–4. Statistics on combat decorations were compiled from Department of the Army General Orders. The percentage is based on a sample.

reports were reaching the Department of the Army that Organized Reserve and National Guard members, because of the uncertainty surrounding their possible mobilization, were having trouble finding permanent employment. This situation did not improve, and in October 1950, Rear Adm. I. M. McQuiston, a member of the Secretary of Defense's Civilian Components Policy Board, addressed the matter in a memorandum to the Secretaries of the Army, Navy, and Air Force:

There is evidence of serious deterioration in the morale of reservists—a deterioration that is progressive and is expanding at an alarming rate. Indications are prevalent that a growing attitude in a large proportion of the members of the Civilian Components is their intent to resign their commissions or terminate their enlisted status at the first opportunity. This is not because of any unwillingness to serve their country in time of war, but because the reservist finds himself unduly penalized in time of limited mobilization.[59]

ARMED FORCES RESERVE ACT OF 1952

The lessons learned from the Korean War mobilization led to renewed Congressional interest in the reserve components, the result being the Armed Forces Reserve Act of 1952.[60] This statute brought together in one place many of the existing laws that related to the reserve components, and it established in much greater detail than ever before the composition, responsibilities, and regulation of the reserves. The reserve components were redefined by this law, which provided that each of the seven reserve components would have a Ready Reserve, a Standby Reserve, and a Retired Reserve. The Officers' Reserve Corps and the Enlisted Reserve Corps were legally eliminated, and the Organized Reserve Corps was renamed the Army Reserve.[61]

---

59. Memorandum, Rear Adm. I. M. McQuiston to the Secretaries of the Army, Navy, and Air Force, October 1950, Subject: "Employer-Employee Relationship under Current Expansion Program," RG 319, Entry 342 (CAR), Box 15 (210.4). Some twenty years after Korea the Department of Defense established the National Committee for Employer Support of the Guard and Reserve in an effort to prevent problems similar to those of the Korean War era. This committee has been of immense help to reservists, but there are continuing instances of employer discrimination. For a recent discussion of this question see Capt. Art House, "Defense Honors Four-Decade Backer of Reserve and Guard," *Army Reserve Magazine* (Spring 1983), pp. 33–34.

60. Public Law 82–476.

61. *Ibid.*, Secs, 202 and 302.

A ceiling of 1,500,000 was set for the Ready Reserve, the members of which would be liable for active duty during wartime or any national emergency declared by Congress or the President. Members of the Standby and Ready Reserves were only liable for active duty under a Congressional declaration.[62] One useful change effected by the act was that reserve commissions would henceforth be given for an indefinite term, rather than for five years.[63] By the end of fiscal year 1953 a total of 247,500 Army Reserve officers had accepted the indefinite-term commissions, while 68,000 had declined them.[64]

Another provision of the Armed Forces Reserve Act of 1952 established within the Office of the Secretary of Defense a Reserve Forces Policy Board of eighteen members. This board provided advice at the Department of Defense level similar to the way the "Section 5" committees did for the Department of the Army.[65]

The Korean War mobilization experience was not ignored by the Armed Forces Reserve Act of 1952. In a strongly-worded section of the act, Congress required that consideration be given to the "duration and nature of previous service, with the objective of assuring such sharing of hazardous exposure as the national security and the military requirement will reasonably permit . . . ."[66] The law further required that "Insofar as practicable, in any expansion of the active Armed Forces of the United States which requires that units and members of the reserve components be ordered into the active military service of the United States, members of units organized and trained for the purpose of serving with a unit shall be ordered involuntarily into active duty only with their units."[67]

As practical matter, neither this law nor any law since 1952 has completely addressed the question of equity. Members of the USAR serve with the idea that they may be called to fight if this country goes to war, and only a political decision—to be discussed in Chapter Nine—kept the Army Reserve from having a large presence in Vietnam.

---

62. *Ibid.*, Secs. 205–207.

63. *Ibid.*, Sec. 224.

64. *Semiannual Report of the Secretary of Defense, January 1 to June 30, 1953*, p. 71.

65. PL 82–476, Sec. 257.

66. *Ibid.*, Sec. 233 (b)(2).

67. *Ibid.*, Sec. 233 (g).

CONCLUSION

The Korean War Armistice was signed in July 1953, just six months after Dwight D. Eisenhower had assumed the Presidency. Korea was over, though the country remained divided. Its legacy, however, would be an important one. The most comprehensive Congressional history of the reserve forces of the United States concluded that the Korean War had caught the Department of Defense largely unprepared.[68] Indeed, the belated efforts to strengthen the Army's reserve components that began in 1948 had barely begun to show results two years later. The extreme frugality of the post-World War II period—a historically typical US reaction—had created what to any reasonable observer was not even an illusion of military strength. The idea that any future war would be an unlimited one, with an exchange of nuclear firepower, had led inexorably to the belief that conventional armed forces were not as important as they once had been. Korea had revealed the flaws in this line of reasoning, and the first American fighting men in that conflict had suffered too certainly the deadly results of this error. Research and development had been neglected; equipment modernization had been delayed; active military strength had been drawn down below safe levels; and the Army's neglect of its own Organized Reserve Corps had created not only inequities and injustices, but also deadly inefficiency. The United States finally achieved a sort of peace in Korea, but the fighting men there paid a terrible price for the parsimony and neglect of the post-war years. Talleyrand was not speaking of military matters when he said it, but he could well have been describing this period in American history: "It [was] . . . worse than a crime; it [was] . . . a blunder."

---

68. Galloway, *History of the United States Military Policy on Reserve Forces, 1775–1957.*

Brig. Gen. Theodore Roosevelt, Jr., was the only general officer who stormed ashore with the first wave on D-Day, June 6, 1944. Shown here with his ever-present cane, Brig. Gen. Roosevelt was awarded the Medal of Honor for his actions that day. The citation read as follows: "After two verbal requests to accompany the leading assault elements in the Normandy invasion had been denied, General ROOSEVELT'S written request for this mission was approved and he landed with the first wave of the forces assaulting the enemy-held beaches. He repeatedly led groups from the beach over the sea wall and established them inland. His valor, courage, and presence in the very front of the attack and his complete unconcern at being under heavy fire inspired the troops to the heights of enthusiasm and self-sacrifice. Although the enemy had the beach under constant direct fire, General ROOSEVELT moved from one locality to another and rallying men around him, directed and personally led them against the enemy. Under his seasoned, precise, calm, and unfaltering leadership, assault troops reduced beach strong points and rapidly moved inland with minimum casualties. He thus contributed substantially to the successful establishment of the beach-head in France." Brig. Gen. Roosevelt, who was serving as Assistant Commander of the Fourth Infantry Division, died of a heart attack the day this photograph was taken, July 12, 1944. (Signal Corps photo #ETO–HQ–44–7576–A)

Army infantrymen hit an unidentified beach in Italy in 1944. The Officers' Reserve Corps furnished almost one-fourth of the Army's officers during WW II, mostly in the middle grades (captain, major, and lieutenant colonel). (Signal Corps photo, #229080)

Tank crew members of the 2nd Armored Division await the signal to move out in pursuit of retreating Germans near Champ Du Bouet, France, August 10, 1944. Some 37 percent of the officers in this division were ORC members at this time. (Signal Corps photo)

Pictured here is Maj. Gen. William J. "Wild Bill" Donovan, member of the ORC and head of the Office of Strategic Services (forerunner of the Central Intelligence Agency) during WW II. Donovan had received the Medal of Honor for his heroism during World War I. (Photo courtesy of Veterans of the OSS)

Sergeant Hiroshi H. Miyamura is shown here receiving a Medal of Honor from President Eisenhower in 1953. Miyamura, who entered the active Army from the Enlisted Reserve Corps early in the Korean War, was serving as squad leader of a machine gun platoon in Korea when the Chinese attacked his position in April 1951. According to the citation for his award, Miyamura "killed more than 50 of the enemy before his ammunition was depleted and he was severely wounded. He maintained his magnificent stand despite his painful wounds, continuing to repel the attack until his position was overrun. When last seen he was fighting ferociously against an overwhelming number of enemy soldiers." Miyamura spent over two years in a Chinese POW camp and was released in August 1953. At least six other Army Reservists received Medals of Honor for their heroism in Korea. (Signal Corps photo #427741–S)

Members of the Eighth Army move across a Chinese-made bridge in the Chugyong-san area of Korea, March 1951. Members of the Organized Reserve were very much in the thick of fighting in Korea, especially during the first year of the war. (Signal Corps photo)

Summer training continued for members of the Organized Reserves, even as the first ORC members were on their way to Korea. Shown here firing the .50 caliber machine gun at Fort Sill, Oklahoma, are members of the 18th FA Battalion in August 1950. (Signal Corps photo)

Members of the 240th Port Co. (ORC), from Miami, Florida, review the proper handling of the carbine. They are undergoing their summer training at Camp Leroy Johnson, New Orleans, Louisiana, in July 1950. (Signal Corps photo)

Crouched beside a tank at Fort Ord, California, members of the 418th Military Police Escort Guard Company plan their attack in June 1951. (Signal Corps photo)

Enlisted reservists undergo the same basic training as members of the active Army. These men of the ERC are completing the final part of the confidence course at Fort Hood, Texas, in November 1950. (Signal Corps photo)

Learning to climb poles is a necessary part of learning to be a lineman. These ORC members from the 494th Signal Construction Company of Birmingham, Alabama, are at their training site at Fort Gordon, Georgia, in August 1951. (Signal Corps photo)

On their second day of summer training at Camp Leroy Johnson, Louisiana, members of the 817th Transportation Truck Battalion of Albuquerque, New Mexico, learn about the assembly of a vehicle engine. (Signal Corps photo, July 12, 1950)

Officers of the 3027th ASU, Organized Reserve Corps, are shown the latest model flame thrower by instructors from the Army's Chemical Corps Training Center, Fort McClellan, Alabama, June 1951. (Signal Corps photo)

"A smart, well-groomed appearance and esprit de corps influence each other. . . . Today's uniform, sold in war surplus stores as work clothes and worn by a legion of displaced persons and ex-prisoners of war, hardly achieves this purpose."—Sec. of the Army Robert T. Stevens, introducing the new Army uniforms in 1954. These members of the 808th Engr. Petr. Distr. Co. (ORC), shown here with a Bailey bridge panel during their 1951 annual training at Camp Polk, La., bear eloquent testimony to the truth of the Secretary's remarks. The ORC received hand-me-downs in virtually every category. (Signal Corps photo, #381379)

The crew of a 90 mm anti-aircraft gun prepares to fire during summer training at Yakima, Washington, Training Center in June 1954. These men are members of the 405th AAA Bn, USAR. (Signal Corps photo)

The Army Reserve today has about one-tenth of the Army's field artillery strength. Shown here twenty-five years ago is a crew of the 446th Field Artillery Battalion, an Army Reserve unit from Lakeland, Fla., firing their 8-inch howitzer during a field problem. (Signal Corps photo, #529549)

Armies have to be fed, and the USAR has a lot to do with feeding of the US Army. Members of the 394th QM Recovery and Disposition Co. are preparing food during two weeks of training at Fort Knox, Ky., during the summer of 1959. (Signal Corps photo, #566606)

Learning the proper techniques for deactivating a land mine are members of the 308th QM Salvage Co. of Chattanooga, Tenn., during their summer training at Fort Campbell, Ky., 1959. (Signal Corps photo, #566601)

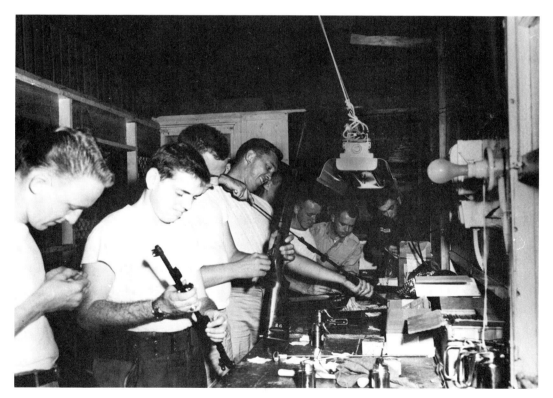

Learning to keep one's weapon clean is an important part of soldiering. These men from an Army Reserve unit seem to be having fun as they clean .30 caliber carbines at Fort McClellan, Ala. (Signal Corps photo, #589772)

Waiting for the green light. Members of the Army Reserve's 12th Special Forces Group prepare to jump during an exercise near Chicago on November 11, 1961. (Signal Corps photo, #588714)

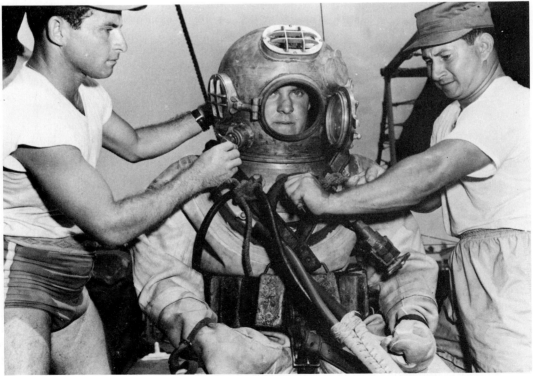

Army Reservists also plunge beneath the surface of the sea. Here getting ready for a dive at the San Juan, P.R., Naval Station is SP5 Jesus Peres Felix, a member of the 428th Engr. Diving Det., USAR, on June 17, 1960. (Signal Corps photo, #591126)

6

The Eisenhower
Years: 1953–1961

The Organized Reserve Corps emerged from the Korean War with a new name—the Army Reserve—and a significantly enhanced reputation. Thousands of individual members of the Organized Reserve (or Army Reserve) served with distinction in non-Reserve units, and the 14 separate USAR battalions and 40 separate USAR companies that fought with the Eighth Army were described by the Secretary of Defense as "uniformly excellent."[1]

There were, however, significant problems that were highlighted by the war. Certain problems such as the creation of a statutory system of promotion consideration for reserve officers were dealt with through the legislative process. Others, such as the number of organized units, drill participation, quantity of equipment on hand in the units, physical facilities, and the number of full-time personnel were affected both by new statutes and by the new administration's policies toward the Army Reserve. The verbal support was tremendous.

"Confronted with the possibility of direct attack," wrote Eisenhower's Secretary of Defense Charles E. Wilson, "our Nation faces the alternative of either maintaining over the years ahead substantially larger active forces than at present or supplementing existing forces with a well-trained, readily available reserve of adequate size. It is the latter course which has been approved by both the President and

---

1. *Semiannual Report of the Secretary of Defense, January 1 to June 30, 1953* (Washington: GPO, 1953), p. 68.

the Congress."[2] Despite this rhetoric, however, the Eisenhower administration's main reliance was on a strategic policy of "massive retaliation," which was simply an updated version of Truman's reliance on "the bomb."[3]

This policy combined quite well with the President's fiscal conservatism, and as a result the Army Reserve was never given support sufficient to correct the neglect of earlier years. Largely because of Congressional support, however, the USAR proportion of the Army budget rose from 0.93 percent in 1953 and again in 1954 to 1.7 percent in 1955. It then rose to 2.9 percent ($211 million) in 1956 and jumped to 4.5 percent ($344 million) in 1957. The percentage and the dollars declined slightly in 1958, dropped significantly in 1959, and rose again in 1960. Compared with the 1960's, the Eisenhower years saw a larger percentage of the Army budget going to the USAR than was the case during the tenure of either John F. Kennedy or Lyndon B. Johnson. It was not until 1965, for example, that the 1960 USAR budget total was surpassed, even though dollars were certainly cheaper by the latter year.[4]

Congress, too, showed an increased interest in the Army Reserve and the other reserve components in the years after Korea. One direct result of this interest was the Reserve Officer Personnel Act of 1954 (ROPA), which is the basic law on the subject today.[5]

ROPA

The existing statutory provisions pertaining to reserve officers prior to ROPA were largely contained in the Armed Forces Reserve Act of 1952. This law required the various service Secretaries to establish "an adequate and equitable system for the promotion of members of the reserve components in an active status."[6] The Army, in fact, had issued

---

2. *Semiannual Report of the Secretary of Defense, January 1 to June 30, 1955* (Washington: GPO, 1956), pp. 18–19.

3. James E. Hewes, Jr., *From Root to McNamara: Army Organization and Administration, 1900–1963* (Washington: Center of Military History, 1975), p. 216; Russell F. Weigley, *History of the United States Army* (New York and London: Macmillan Publishing Co., Inc. and Collier Macmillan Publishers, 1967), pp. 525–26.

4. See Appendix B for budget data.

5. Public Law 83–773; "Address by Senator Margaret Chase Smith to the 29th National Convention, Reserve Officers Association," *The Reserve Officer* (August, 1955), p. 13.

6. Public Law 82–476, Sec. 216.

the required regulations within six months of the passage of this act, but Army Reserve officers were not satisfied.[7]

The Reserve Officers Association lobbied hard for new legislation, and ROA representatives spent a great deal of time testifying before the House Armed Services Committee. The principal witness for ROA was Maj. Gen. Melvin Maas a Marine Corps Reserve officer, former Congressman, and Chairman of the association's Legislative Committee. Maas pointed out the primary difference between the desires of reserve officers and the official position of the Department of the Army. Reserve officers, stated Maas, would "no longer . . . be satisfied with merely saying it is in the regulations. They know regulations can get changed. We know that for years now, every time they come up with a new plan this is going to be fine. This is going to give you a fair break. But they have not found it so. They no longer believe in the regulations. They want to see it in the law now."[8]

This was the very issue on which the Department of the army opposed the bill. "The Army view," stated Lt. Col. A. H. Parker, Office of the Assistant Chief of Staff, G–1, "is that regulations, which have only recently gone into effect and have not yet been thoroughly tested by operating experience, should provide the basis for drafting appropriate legislation on this subject when all the 'bugs' have been worked out of the new system."[9] Reserve officers, however, were not willing to be left to the tender mercies of the regulatory process of the Department of the Army, and their lobbying groups pushed the legislation through the Congress over the objections of the Pentagon.

ROPA was of tremendous importance to officers in the Army Reserve, because it gave to them and other Reservists a statutory basis for promotion and service comparable to that given Regulars by the Officers Personnel Act of 1947. Under ROPA, for example, Reserve officers were not subject to mandatory removal until they had reached a certain number of years of service. For officers in the grades of 0–2 through 0–5, the cut-off was twenty-eight years; for 0–6 and 0–7 it was thirty years; and for Reserve 0–8's it was thirty-five years.[10] The top three grades could, however, re-

---

7. See Army Regulations 135–155, 135–156, and 135–157.

8. *Hearings before the Committee on Armed Services, House of Representatives, Eighty-third Congress, First Session, Pursuant to H. R. 122. Reserve Officers Personnel Act* (Washington: GPO, 1953), p. 1616. Hereinafter cited as "ROPA Hearings."

9. *Ibid.*, p. 1559.

10. Public Law 83–773, Section 327.

main active until they had five years time-in-grade. The
maximum age for active Reservists was set at sixty-two years
for major generals and sixty years for all those of lower
rank.[11]

Mandatory consideration for promotion was also statutorily guaranteed by ROPA. First lieutenants had to go
before a promotion board their fourth year in grade, while
captains and majors had to be considered for promotion by
their seventh year. All of these officers also had to meet
time-in-service criteria. Unit members of the reserve components were given an additional promotion possibility
through "unit vacancy" promotions.[12]

Female Army Reserve officers were subject to the same
promotion procedures as were male officers, with one important exception: promotion opportunities for women were
considerably more limited than were those for men.
Women's Medical Specialist Corps officers could not be promoted above the rank of major, while Women's Army Corps
and Army Nurse Corps officers could only make it to lieutenant colonel.[13]

ROPA authorized 275,000 active Army Reserve officers, a total well above the 145,382 who were actually
members of the Ready Reserve on June 30, 1955.[14] The
number of active Reserve officers, however, could not exceed
the following percentages in each grade:[15]

Colonel. . . . . 2 percent
Lieutenant Colonel. . . . . 6 percent
Major. . . . . 13 percent
Captain . . . . 35 percent

One of the most important provisions of ROPA was its
correction of an anomaly that had plagued the Army Reserve
since 1920. Under the National Defense Act of 1920, the
time-in-grade of a commissioned officer was determined by
taking his date of rank and adding to it his total active duty
service. Inactive duty Reserve participation did not count for
precedence purposes, and discussion of proposals to change
this system for the Army Reserve, Air Force Reserve, and

---

11. *Ibid.,* Sec. 326.
12. *Ibid.,* Secs. 310 and 309.
13. *Ibid.,* Sec. 304.
14. Public Law 83–773, Sec. 304.
15. Public Law 83–773, Sec. 307; *Semiannual Report of the Secretary
of Defense, January 1 to June 30, 1955* (Washington: GPO, 1956), p. 68.

the National Guard occupied a considerable portion of the time devoted to hearings on the proposed legislation.

Col. Charles M. Boyer, the Executive Director of the Reserve Officers Association who worked closely with the members of the House committee as they considered H.R. 1222, delivered the sentiments of ROA on the question. "The Reserve Officers Association," he stated, "strongly recommends that date of rank and date of commission be the same." Former South Carolina Governor (and colonel in the Army Reserve) Strom Thurmond sent a letter to the Committee echoing the same conclusion. "Under the present Army and Air Force policy," wrote Thurmond, "a competent, experienced Reserve officer may, upon mobilization, become junior to a Regular officer who is actually junior in age, experience, and judgement. The sheer inefficiency of a system which requires wholesale revising of dates of rank for thousands of Reserve officers each time they serve a tour of active duty (for as little as two weeks in most cases) is deplorable."[16] Maj. Gen. Melvin Maas, also representing the ROA, called the existing date of rank system "an unworkable monstrosity." "There is not an IBM machine conceived," stated Maas with no small amount of hyperbole, "that could tell you the relative seniority of a Reserve officer at any time, let alone when he is mobilized."[17]

The Navy and the Marine Corps had long since adopted for their reserve components a system like the one proposed by the ROA; the Army and Air Force Reserves and the National Guard, however, used only active duty in determining seniority. Although the Navy and Marine Corps experience had been a positive one, both the Army and the Air Force resisted any change in their own procedures, and the National Guard was ambivalent.[18]

The ranking Army witness was Maj. Gen. Boniface Campbell, Assistant Chief of Staff, G–1, who testified that "The Department of the Army favors continuation of its present concept that seniority on active duty be based on active military experience. It is of the firm opinion," continued Campbell, "that the Reserve Officers Association proposal that seniority on active duty be based on date of appointment is not in the best interest of the Reserve Officers themselves, and certainly not of the service as a whole."[19]

---

16. Public Law 83–773, Sec. 307.
16. ROPA Hearings, pp. 1600–1602.
17. *Ibid.*, pp. 1613–14.
18. *Ibid., passim.*
19. *Ibid.*, p. 2037.

Campbell then raised the spectre of thousands of inexperienced Army Reserve officers being mobilized and assuming their places on active duty. "The impact," stated Campbell, would be " . . . overwhelming under the most favorable conditions. If thousands of the least experienced officers must assume command of and responsibility for the training of our new forces," he warned, "inefficiency would almost certainly result. And the results might be extremely serious, if not disastrous."[20]

Maj. Gen. Campbell was, of course, using the most extreme scare tactics with the committee and was completely ignoring the fine combat record established by reserve officers during World War II and Korea. He was "not familiar with the detailed working" of the Navy and Marine Corps system, stated Campbell, but he speculated that "had the Navy followed the system currently used and advocated by the Army, . . . it is conceivable that they might be as happy with it as they are said to be with their present system."[21]

The original of the bill under consideration—H.R. 1222—proposed to give one day of precedence for each retirement point earned through inactive duty training and each point earned through correspondence course completion. The Department of the Army favored this proposal, as did the Department of the Air Force.[22]

The members of the House Committee adopted in large part, however, the ROA proposal. Under the new formula for computing date of rank, Army Reserve officers received a year's credit for each good retirement year, plus one day for each point earned in a year that was not credited for retirement.[23] ROPA was quite a significant step for the Army Reserve, but it did not purport to address every problem confronting the USAR.

THE RESERVE FORCES ACT OF 1955

On January 12, 1954, President Eisenhower asked Arthur Flemming, Director of Defense Mobilization, to prepare a plan for the development of an improved reserve system. Even before Flemming made his recommendation,

---

20. *Ibid.,* p. 2039.
21. *Ibid.,* p. 2040; see Chapter Four for an account of the Army's reserve officers during WW II.
22. *Ibid.,* pp. 2047–52.
23. Public Law 83–773, Sec. 702.

Eisenhower pledged that the "establishment of an adequate reserve . . . will be a number one item submitted to the Congress next year."[24]

Eisenhower, like many American Presidents before him, had long expressed support for a strong Army Reserve. Writing as Army Chief of Staff, he had stated: "There is no component of more importance to the security establishment than the Organized Reserve Corps . . . . The new Reserve Corps can and must become the well-trained citizen Army Reserve required to supplement immediately, in an emergency, our small Regular Army and our National Guard."[25] Eisenhower as President realized that the creation of a strong Army Reserve was both politically and fiscally desirable, and he quickly adopted the recommendations of the Flemming study, which became known as the National Reserve Plan. Eisenhower submitted his National Reserve Plan to Congress in a special message on January 13, 1955. He pointed out the need for an improved Reserve force and suggested five areas for legislative attention.

First, he recommended that a Reserve group of unspecified size be maintained at a high state of readiness to meet immediate mobilization requirements.

Second, he proposed that young men from 17 to 19 years old be permitted to volunteer for 6 months of basic training, to be followed by 9 1/2 years of service with the Reserves. He also proposed a Reserve forces draft, if there were not enough volunteers.

Third, Eisenhower proposed that enlistees in the National Guard be required to undergo six months of training before joining their units. Additionally, he requested the authority to assign prior-service personnel to National Guard units, if these units were unable to recruit enough personnel.

Fourth, he asked Congress to accept the concept that honorable military service included both active duty and statutory Reserve participation, the idea being that men

24. *Study of the Functions, Organization and Procedures of the Department of the Army, OSD Project 80 (Army), Part VII, Reserve Components* (Washington: Department of the Army, 1961), p. VII–B–6; "Strong Reserve to Be Number One Item for Next Congress-Eisenhower," *The Army Reservist* (November 1954), p. 15.

25. General Dwight D. Eisenhower, "The Reserve Component and Our Future Security," *The Reserve Officer* (July 1946), pp. 9–10; *Semiannual Report of the Secretary of Defense, January 1 to June 30, 1955* (Washington: GPO, 1956), pp. 20–21.

who failed to complete their Reserve requirements would be given less than an Honorable discharge.

Fifth, Eisenhower suggested that the States be permitted to organize militia forces in addition to their National Guard units, so that there would be someone to take over local security missions when the National Guard was federalized.[25]

Both the House and the Senate conducted extensive hearings on the Administration's proposal. Secretary of Defense Charles E. Wilson, Joint Chiefs Chairman Adm. Arthur Radford, Army Chief of Staff Gen. Matthew Ridgway and others—a veritable who's who among the DoD hierarchy—all testified in favor of the President's plan.

Witness after witness told the Subcommittee about the need for a stronger reserve system, and Secretary of the Army Robert T. Stevens hit particularly hard on the need for changes in the status quo. "Our Reserve at the present," stated Stevens, "is inadequate to meet our needs. Its inadequacy is due primarily—yes, I can say almost solely—to the failure to procure the participation of enlisted personnel in adequate numbers in organized units. All other problems associated with the Reserve," concluded Stevens, "are subordinate thereto. Therefore the keystone to a truly Ready Reserve is the procurement of the basically trained personnel who can be integrated, further trained, and retained for a reasonable period of time."[26]

During World Wars I and II, stated Stevens, "we were fortunate in having friends who were able to hold the enemy in check until our forces could be mobilized, trained, and deployed . . . ." The Administration's proposal for the Army Reserve, said Stevens, "is designed to fill the gap between the commitment of the Active Army, and the time when the rawest recruit can be trained to confront the aggressor."[27]

Carter Burgess, Assistant Secretary of Defense for Manpower and Personnel, then told the House Subcommittee that "The plain fact is that our Reserve Forces are not in line with current conditions and requirements." There were not adequate provisions under the current law, stated Burgess, to rectify the situation, and he recommended the Pres-

---

26. "National Reserve Plan," Hearings before Subcommittee No. 1 of the Committee on Armed Services, House of Representatives, Eighty-fourth Congress, First Session, p. 1282; hereinafter cited as "National Reserve Plan Hearings."

27. National Reserve Plan Hearings, pp. 1282–83.

ident's plan as a comprehensive system for supplying men to the Ready Reserve.[28]

Despite the vehement opposition of temperance organizations that did not want the young men of America subjected to the temptations of beer drinking in the Army[29] and of religious and quasi-religious groups that feared the universal military training implications of the National Reserve Plan,[30] the Congress finally enacted a modified version of Eisenhower's proposal. As signed on August 9, 1955, it differed somewhat from the Administration's proposal, but it did hold out the promise of substantial improvements in the Army Reserve.

The Reserve Forces Act of 1955 (RFA) took the form of amendments to the Armed Forces Reserve Act of 1952, just as the National Defense Act of 1920 was written as amendments to the National Defense Act of 1916. The RFA first raised the Ready Reserve ceiling from 1,500,000 to 2,900,000, then it set forth provisions by which these additional reservists would be forthcoming.[31]

After enactment of the RFA, a man had four ways in which he could fulfill his military obligation through some form of service in the Army Reserve:

1. Enlist in the active Army for three, four, or five years, then go into the Ready Reserve. There was a total of five years active duty and Ready Reserve obligation, with an additional year in the Standby Reserve.
2. Enlist in the Army Reserve for six years, two years of which would be spent on active duty. The obligation after that two years was three years in the Ready Reserve and one year in the Standby Reserve. This option was only available before receiving induction orders.
3. Wait for induction into the Army. This would entail two years of active duty, three years in the Ready Reserve, and one year in the Standby Reserve.
4. Enlist prior to age 18½ in a unit of the Army Reserve. This would result in an eight-year military obligation, six months of which would be spent on active duty for training (ADT). Payment during the ADT phase was set

28. *Ibid.*, pp. 1407–10.
29. *Ibid.*, pp. 1856–73.
30. *Ibid.*, pp. 1876–86, 1941–46, 1949–62, and *passim*.
31. Public Law 84–305, Sec. 2(a).

at $50 per month, which was $28 per month less than a draftee received.[32]

Option four was the immediate hope for increasing the strength of the Army Reserve, though in the long run the USAR stood to gain considerable numbers of men who had completed their active duty obligation under one of the other options. The Army Reserve was once again at a disadvantage when competing with the National Guard, however, because enlistees in the Guard had to perform *no* active duty or active duty for training, though the Guardsman was required to participate satisfactorily in unit training to age 28.[33]

President Eisenhower did not approve of this feature of the RFA, because it impaired the readiness of the National Guard. The President was also disturbed that members of the National Guard who volunteered for six months ADT would receive $78 per month for their efforts, compared with the $50 that Army Reservists were paid during the same training. He approved, however, of the provision of the RFA that gave him the authority to order to active duty up to 1,000,000 Ready Reservists—not just Army Reservists—in any Presidentially-proclaimed emergency.[34] The RFA also provided that Army Reserve units would have forty-eight drill periods (inactive duty training) per year and up to seventeen days of active duty for training.[35]

USAR MEMBERSHIP PROBLEMS

One of the long-term problems of the Army Reserve, however, was that it always looked much stronger on paper than it was in reality. As the Reserve Forces Policy Board had put it, "The Ready Reserve as a whole is not ready in fact or by statutory definition."[36] There were entirely too many mem-

---

32. "Choices Available to Fulfill Enlisted Service Obligation," *Army Information Digest* (February 1956), pp. 36–37.

33. *Ibid.* New National Guard enlistees after April 1, 1957, had to take the six months of ADT.

34. "President Eisenhower's Reserve Statement, August 9, 1955," *The Reserve Officer* (August 1955), p. 2; In April 1956 Congress amended the Reserve Forces Act to provide the same pay and disability and death benefits for both Army Reservists and National Guardsmen taking the six months of training. *Semiannual Report of the Secretary of Defense, January 1 to June 30, 1956* (Washington: GPO, 1957), p. 19.

35. Public Law 84–305, Sec. 2(b).

36. *Semiannual Report of the Secretary of Defense, July 1 to December 31, 1954* (Washington: GPO, 1955), p. 13.

bers of the USAR who did not take part in inactive duty training, particularly enlisted men with prior service. There was not much incentive for them to devote their weekends to Army Reserve duty, because military pay at the time was hardly enough to serve as a motivator. The non-participation problem was truly substantial. As of June 30, 1953, only 117,323 of 798,026 members of the Army Reserve (14.7 percent) were in a drill-pay status, and a year later the percentage had fallen even further (136,918 of 1,108,967 or 12.3 percent). By June 30, 1955, shortly before passage of the RFA, membership in the Army Reserve had grown to 1,648,626, and drill participation had risen to 163,137. These figures meant, however, that participation in inactive duty training had fallen to less than 10 percent of the total Army Reserve strength.[37]

There was not in the mid-1950's—and, in fact, there is not today—any particularly effective way to compel Army Reserve participation among men who have completed their military obligation. For men who chose one of the RFA options involving a specified term in the Ready Reserve, however, Public Law 84–305 provided a tool for enforcing the Reserve obligation. Participation in forty-eight inactive duty training drill periods and up to seventeen days annual training was required of all obligated members of the Ready Reserve. Failure to participate satisfactorily could result in an obligated Reservist's being ordered to active duty for training for up to forty-five days. If he attempted to slack off in his last year in the Ready Reserve, his time could be extended for up to six months.[38]

Although the Reserve Forces Act of 1955 did eventually prove beneficial to Army Reserve recruitment, there was initial disappointment with its lack of effect. From August 10, 1955, to June 30, 1956, only 13,012 men chose the two year active duty—three year Ready Reserve—one year Standby Reserve option, and only twice that number—27,272—chose the six months ADT—7 ½ year Ready Reserve program. According to Defense Department estimates, the latter program was expected to produce some 90,000 enlistments per year, so it was evident that the

---

37. *Semiannual Report of the Secretary of Defense, January 1 to June 30, 1954* (Washington: GPO, 1955), pp. 64, 333; *Semiannual Report of the Secretary of Defense, January 1 to June 30, 1955* (Washington: GPO, 1956), p. 296.

38. Public Law 84–305, Sec. 2(b).

young men of America were not exactly falling over each other trying to join the Army Reserve.[39]

For the next six months recruits under the 2–3–1 and 6-month ADT options numbered only 12,850 and 17,934, respectively. The Reserve Forces Policy Board offered its analysis of the problem: "Experience has shown that voluntary enlistments in reserve components have been high when the draft rate is high and conversely low when the draft rate is low."[40] This reasoning has become almost a truism in Army Reserve recruiting, for during the Vietnam War, the young men of America *were* falling over each other trying to join the USAR. The Defense Department, however, rejected the solution recommended by the Board, which was to draft men directly into the Reserve components. It decided to conduct instead "an unprecedented peacetime recruiting campaign . . . to secure voluntary enlistments under Section 262 [the six-month ADT option] of the [Reserve Forces] Act . . . ." Despite the recruiting campaign, the number of men who chose the six-month ADT option grew very slowly. Not until the recession of 1957–58, in fact, did enlistments begin to pick up at all. By the end of fiscal year 1960 only 177,712 men had enlisted under Section 262, and paid drill strength in the Army Reserve had only reached 276,992.[41]

The disappointing lack of enlistments in the Army Reserve was reflected, naturally enough, in the organizational status of USAR units. Of some 7200 company-size units authorized for the Army Reserve on June 30, 1956, only 5284 were in an active status; of the 618,000 personnel required for these units, only 180,000 (29 percent of requirements) were actually assigned. Six months later the Army Reserve had activated 5439 units, to which 210,679 Reservists belonged (32 percent of requirements).[42] The Army Reserve, as discussed later in this chapter, soon re-

---

39. *Semiannual Report of the Secretary of Defense, January 1 to June 30, 1956* (Washington: GPO, 1957), p. 66.

40. *Semiannual Report of the Secretary of Defense, July 1 to December 31, 1956* (Washington: GPO, 1957), p. 11.

41. *Semiannual Report of the Secretary of Defense, January 1 to June 30, 1957* (Washington: GPO, 1958), p. 69; *Annual Report of the Secretary of Defense, July 1, 1959, to June 30, 1960* (Washington: GPO, 1961), p. 101. Recessions always seem beneficial to Army recruiting generally.

42. *Semiannual Report of the Secretary of Defense, January 1 to June 30, 1956* (Washington: GPO, 1957), pp. 66–67; *Semiannual Report of the Secretary of Defense, July 1 to December 31, 1956* (Washington: GPO, 1957), p. 13.

duced the number of units to 4350 under the Pentomic division structure. Accurate comparisons of unit strength and numbers are therefore impossible to make. It can be said, however, that although Army Reserve units in the mid-1950's were more fully-manned than were the ORC units of twenty years earlier, they still did not possess the degree of readiness that would allow them to fulfill their role in the event of a sudden mobilization of the US Army.[43]

MATERIEL READINESS AND TECHNICIAN SUPPORT

Questions about personnel strength, however, were only one of the issues that faced the post-Korea Army Reserve. There were significant problems, for example, in the area of materiel readiness. The Organized Reserve units had never had much equipment, and equipping Army Reserve units was a slow process. Although the Reserve Forces Policy Board was able to say in July 1954 that "The Reserve forces are perhaps the best equipped that they have been in their history," this statement does not really mean much. The Board went on to say, however, that "The chief limitation at present lies not in the unavailability of equipment but rather in the lack of facilities and storage space in which to adequately safeguard the equipment."[44]

The extent of the facilities problems in the USAR was indicated a year later when the Board reported that of the 2570 locations where Army Reserve facilities were needed, only 355 were considered "adequate." Over the preceding four years the Army had spent only $33 million on USAR training centers, and there was a shortfall of some $400 million. As an idea of the priority attached to correcting this deficit, the Army requested for FY 1956 a total of only $31,611,000, to be used for 17 Army Reserve Training Centers, 243 National Guard Armories, and 124 non-armory projects for the National Guard.[45] By the end of fiscal year 1957 the Army Reserve had received facilities appropriations totaling $70 million; the Reserve Forces Policy Board estimated a need for an additional $348 million in the future.[46]

---

43. *Annual Report of the Secretary of Defense, July 1, 1959, to June 30, 1960* (Washington: GPO, 1961), p. 103.

44. *Semiannual Report of the Secretary of Defense, January 1 to June 30, 1954* (Washington: GPO, 1955), p. 66.

45. *Semiannual Report of the Secretary of Defense, January 1 to June 30, 1955* (Washington: GPO, 1956), pp. 74–75.

46. *Semiannual Report of the Secretary of Defense, July 1 to December 31, 1956* (Washington: GPO, 1957), p. 17.

The question of adequate facilities was tied closely with questions relating to equipment issue and full-time USAR maintenance personnel. Until June 1956 equipment pools served all of the Army Reserve units in a given area. This policy changed at the end of FY '56, and USAR units began to receive their own equipment. "This new policy," wrote the Reserve Forces Policy Board, "is being implemented as rapidly as storage and maintenance facilities and the necessary personnel can be provided."[47] The immensity of the problem confronting the Army Reserve is shown in the fact that by June 30, 1957, USAR units had only about 4 percent of their authorized Table of Organization and Equipment (TOE) allowances on hand. "Most of the equipment issued to Army reserves," reported the Secretary of Defense, "is standard, limited standard, or serviceable substitute type items and is adequate, along with equipment available in Army Reserve equipment pools, for training purposes."[48]

By the end of Fiscal Year 1960 the units of the USAR had received 41 percent of their overall TOE equipment allowances. "The majority of the US Army Reserve units," stated the Reserve Forces Policy Board, "can now conduct platoon-level basic unit training with the quantities of equipment on hand." The Board concluded, however, that "Maintenance of all levels continues to be a pressing problem." The primary cause of the maintenance problem in 1960 was the same one as in 1953—too few full-time personnel in the units.

The Army Reserve Technician Program was established in 1950, but it did not experience rapid growth during its first decade. Although President Eisenhower gave lip-service to the need for increasing the readiness of the Army Reserve, his administration was unwilling to give the USAR the number of full-time support personnel required to overcome the maintenance deficit. Eisenhower prided himself on his prudent fiscal management, and part of this management was that of cutting back on the number of civilian employees of the Department of the Army.[49] By fiscal year 1960 the USAR had a requirement for 5,100 technicians,

---

47. *Semiannual Report of the Secretary of Defense, July 1 to December 31, 1956* (Washington: GPO, 1957), p. 18. The Army reinstituted equipment pools for the USAR in the mid-1970's.

48. *Semiannual Report of the Secretary of Defense, January 1 to June 30, 1957* (Washington: GPO, 1958), p. 81.

49. See, for example, the proud statement of how he reduced DA Civilian employment by 13 percent during his first full year in office.

but only 3,046 were authorized by the Department of the Army.[50]

REORGANIZATION

One of the other things that made it difficult for the Army Reserve to attain a high state of readiness was a major structural reorganization, comparable in scope to the pre-World War II change from square to triangular divisions. This time the change was brought about by theories as to the effects of nuclear weapons on the battlefield. In 1957 the Army decided to reorganize and re-equip its combat units into a "Pentomic" divisional structure, an awkward arrangement that combined the latest in nuclear weaponry with the "circle the wagons" mentality of Indian Wars days. The three brigades of the triangular division were replaced under this doctrine by five "highly mobile combat groups organically supported by 5 batteries of light artillery and 1 battery of HONEST JOHN rockets . . . ."[51] The task of reorganizing the active Army's infantry, airborne, and armored divisions into the Pentomic configuration was completed by the end of calendar year 1957, and the number of active divisions was reduced from 18 to 15.[52]

Reorganization of the ten USAR combat divisions to the Pentomic structure was completed by the end of December 1959, one year ahead of schedule.[53] The irony of this accelerated conversion was that the active Army was ready to abandon the configuration because it simply did not work. By fiscal year 1961 the Army, in an attempt "to make our combat divisions more flexible and mobile," embraced the Reorganization Objective Army Division (ROAD). Under the ROAD concept the Army's combat divisions could be tailored to meet a specific battlefield need by adding and subtracting different types of battalions.[54] Conversion of the

Semiannual Report of the Secretary of Defense, January 1 to June 30, 1954 (Washington: GPO, 1955), p. 97.

50. *Annual Report of the Secretary of Defense, July 1, 1959, to June 30, 1960* (Washington: GPO, 1961), p. 104.

51. *Semiannual Report of the Secretary of Defense, January 1 to June 30, 1957* (Washington: GPO, 1958), pp. 3–4.

52. *Semiannual Report of the Secretary of Defense, July 1 to December 31, 1957* (Washington: GPO, 1958), p. 23.

53. *Annual Report of the Secretary of Defense, July 1, 1959, to June 30, 1960* (Washington: GPO, 1961), p. 103.

54. *Annual Report of the Secretary of Defense for Fiscal Year 1961* (Washington: GPO, 1962), p. 60.

Army Reserve to the ROAD division structure would wait, however, until the 1960's.

Other organizational changes during the Eisenhower years were not detrimental to Army Reserve readiness. On December 7, 1954, for example, the Executive for Reserve and ROTC Affairs became the Chief, Army Reserve and ROTC Affairs. This title change, however, had little effect on the operations of the office, though it held out a promise that the CAR would assume more responsibility for the USAR. In July 1956 the Headquarters, Continental Army Command, (CONARC) established the office of Deputy Commanding General for Reserve Forces. This person had the mission of coordinating and supervising the CONARC General Staff in the development of plans and directives for Reserve Component programs in the Zone of Interior Armies. Then on November 1, 1956, the Office of the Assistant Chief of Staff for Reserve components was established at the DA Staff level.[55]

CONGRESSIONAL INTERVENTION

The Eisenhower years were in many ways a time of tremendous growth for the Army Reserve, but in most instances the progress of the USAR was achieved despite the President's policies instead of because of them. In each year from 1958 through 1960 the Eisenhower administration put forth budget proposals calling for a 10 percent reduction in the paid drill strength of both the Army Reserve and the Army National Guard. The first of these proposed reductions was announced on March 31, 1958, by Army Secretary Wilber M. Brucker, who coupled the reductions to the Pentomic structure conversion. Under this proposal the number of Army Reserve combat divisions would be reduced from 10 to 6 by converting 4 infantry divisions to training divisions. The National Guard under this proposal would drop from 27 divisions to 21.[56] Concurrently, the paid drill strength of the Army Reserve was to be reduced from 300,000 to

---

55. James E. Hewes, Jr., *From Root to McNamara: Army Organization and Administration, 1900–1963* (Washington: Center of Military History, United States Army, 1975), p. 400; *Semiannual Report of the Secretary of Defense, July 1 to December 31, 1956,* p. 12.

56. William F. Levantrosser, *Congress and the Citizen-Soldier: Legislative Policy-making for the Federal Armed Forces Reserve* (Columbus: Ohio State University press, 1967), p. 97; Department of Defense News Release, "Fact Sheet on Reorganization of U. S. Army Reserve Components," July 8, 1958, copy in Center of Military History files.

270,000, while the National Guard was to be reduced from 400,000 to 360,000.[57]

Congressional reaction to these plans was immediately unfavorable, and the outraged cries from the Congress caused the Department of Defense to back down quickly. "The Secretary of Defense has modified his previous guidance," said a DoD News Release, "so that the Army has been authorized to develop a plan looking toward the retention of the present 37 divisions in the Reserve Forces Structure . . . provided that this troop structure is maintained with no increase of cost or personnel beyond current programmed levels."[58] Under the "revised guidance," the Army Reserve would consist of 10 Pentomic infantry divisions, 13 training divisions, 2 maneuver area commands, and several hundred supporting companies. Simultaneously, the Army consolidated 46 military districts into 13 US Army Corps (Reserve) Headquarters.[59]

Additional Eisenhower administration attempts to reduce the Army Reserve's budget and paid drill strength in 1959 and 1960 met with similar opposition in the Congress. The primary impetus for cutting the budget of the USAR seems to have come from the Department of Defense level, and not from the Department of the Army. Congressional lobbyists for the Reserve Officers Association attempted in both the House and the Senate to put into the DoD appropriations bill language placing a floor on paid drill strength for the Army Reserve. The move was unsuccessful in the House, but Strom Thurmond was able to accomplish this maneuver on the floor of the Senate. As a result, funds for both the Army Reserve and the National Guard were increased, and a minimum paid drill strength was established.[60]

President Eisenhower was not pleased with this turn of events, which he labeled "an unprecedented departure from past policy." Though he was technically correct, the President was not apparently willing to admit that this latest action on the part of Congress was simply the next logical step in the progression of Congressional oversight of the Reserve Components.[61]

---

57. *Annual Report of the Secretary of Defense, July 1, 1959, to June 30, 1960* (Washington: GPO, 1961), pp. 100, 62.

58. *Ibid.*

59. *Annual Report of the Secretary of Defense, July 1, 1958, to June 30, 1959* (Washington: GPO, 1960), p. 57.

60. Levantrosser, *Congress and the Citizen Soldier,* pp. 110–11.

61. *Ibid.,* pp. 111, 98.

What the President did not realize—or perhaps did not plan for—was that the Army Reserve had developed into a potent political force and that the Reserve Officers Association had honed its political clout with the Congress. The Executive branch had on many occasions surrendered to Congress the initiative on the National Guard's budget, and by the 1950's the same thing was happening with respect to the Army Reserve.[62]

CONCLUSION

The entire Eisenhower era was one of tremendous importance to the Army Reserve. Largely because of the influence and leadership of the Congress, the Army Reserve was strengthened immeasurably by the Reserve Officer Personnel Act of 1954 and the Reserve Forces Act of 1955. Reserve officers finally had a statutory guarantee of promotion consideration paralleling that of the Regulars, and the Army Reserve was provided with a dependable source of manpower for as long as the draft was in operation.

President Eisenhower, though a distinguished soldier and verbal supporter of the reserve components, was overcome by his own fiscal conservatism. The reserves were a convenient concomitant of this conservatism because they were cheaper than active forces, but when he turned to a policy of massive retaliation to the near-exclusion of all other levels of deterrence, the reserves, as well as the active forces, were a logical and convenient place to reduce. That he failed in his efforts to reduce the reserves was not so much a measure of his weakness or lack of resolve as they were an indication of the increasing role of the Congress. The Army Reserve was getting stronger in every way, and the Kennedy and Johnson eras would provide it with the opportunities to demonstrate whether it was a paper tiger or a responsive, effective part of this country's defense.

---

62. For a good discussion of this entire period see *Ibid.*, pp. 97–124, *passim.*

7

The Berlin Mobilization

The 1960's were a decade of major accomplishments for the Army Reserve. More than 60,000 Army Reservists were called to active duty for the 1961 Berlin Crisis in what has generally been termed the most efficient American mobilization up to that time,[1] and nearly 6,000 Army Reservists were mobilized for Vietnam in 1968.

The Berlin Crisis, which lasted roughly from June 1961 to June 1962, occurred at a time when American defense policy was undergoing a fundamental change. The 1950's strategy of massive retaliation had been severely criticized by Gen. Maxwell D. Taylor in his 1960 book *The Uncertain Trumpet*, and Presidential hopeful John F. Kennedy adapted Taylor's thesis of flexible response as a major campaign issue.

Kennedy campaigned hard upon the theme that the Eisenhower Administration had neglected national defense by placing undue reliance upon massive retaliation. Shortly after assuming office, Kennedy set the theme for his administration when he directed Secretary of Defense Robert S. McNamara to reorganize the Defense Department to create a more flexible deterrent.

Early on, McNamara concluded that the Army's Reserve Components were improperly structured and burdened with hundreds of unnecessary units. His conclusions led him to propose a succession of reorganization plans for the Army Reserve, plans that met considerable opposition within and without the Congress.

---

1. *Department of Defense Annual Report, 1962*, p. 66.

Nevertheless, McNamara won a partial victory. The Army Reserve was reorganized along the Army Reserve Command (ARCOM) structure found today, and major changes were made in the force structure. For the first time, Reserve requirements were tied directly to contingency plans,[2] and equipment and manning levels were increased for Army Reserve units. The groundwork was thus laid for the "Total Army" concept of the 1970's.

Army Reserve units were deliberately understrength, based upon the planning assumption that three-quarters of all Reserve Component divisions would have six months or more to build up and train after mobilization.[3] The 10 Army Reserve infantry divisions were manned at 53 to 60 percent of combat strength, and the 4,353 company-sized units of the Army Reserve were manned at 53 percent or less, even though the majority of them would be needed in the early stages of mobilization.[4]

Across the board, Army Reserve units were equipped at less than 50 percent of full combat requirements, and the equipment that was available was generally obsolete material of Korean War or even World War II vintage.[5] Readiness was further hampered by a shortage of full-time employees, and the Army Reserve had only one-third of its required 1,103 reserve centers.[6]

Even so, Maj. Gen. Frederick M. Warren, the Chief, Army Reserve and ROTC Affairs, testified before Congress on May 10, 1960, that the Army Reserve was at its highest state of readiness ever and was basically sound and ready to complement existing ground forces. In less than 18 months, the accuracy of Warren's testimony was tested in the Berlin Crisis call-up.

---

2. On page 114 of his 1968 testimony before the Senate Armed Services Committee regarding the 1969 Defense budget, McNamara stated that for the first time the materiel and personnel requirements of the reserve components necessary to support contingency plans had been included in Defense programs. Also, units for which no military requirement existed in contingency plans had been eliminated and other units which were needed had been added to the force structure.

3. Karl Cocke, *The Reserve Components*, undated manuscript, Center of Military History, p. VIII–4.

4. Maj. Gen. Frederick M. Warren, Posture Statement Presentation before House Armed Services Committee, May 10, 1960. Copy in OCAR Historical File.

5. *Annual Report of the Reserve Forces Policy Board*, June 30, 1961, p. 4.

6. *Annual Historical Supplement*, Office of the Chief U.S. Army Reserve and ROTC Affairs, 1960, pp. 13, 28.

BACKGROUND OF THE CRISIS

The Berlin Crisis was not an isolated incident, but was instead part of a challenge to the position of the United States as a world power.[7] Since World War II, US-Soviet relations had been tense; and the Kennedy Administration came to office during a period of wary maneuvering for advantage.[8] By 1961, recent Soviet space successes had bolstered Soviet confidence, and US failure to support the Cuban Freedom Fighters following their Bay of Pigs landing on April 17, 1961, cast doubt upon the willingness of the United States to employ arms against communist forces.

These circumstances tempted Soviet Premier Nikita S. Khrushchev to pressure the United States to accept a long-standing Soviet proposal for turning Berlin into a "free city." The city had remained under Four Power control following World War II, and the Western sector of Berlin under French, British and US rule had become an island of democracy in East Germany. This island was a haven for refugees fleeing from East Germany and had thereby become an uncomfortable thorn in the sides of the Soviet Union and its allies.

Meeting with Kennedy in Vienna, Austria, on June 3 and 4, Khrushchev told the President that the status of Berlin would be resolved during 1961 with or without the cooperation of the United States. Khrushchev's remarks to Kennedy included a clear implication that the Soviets were prepared to employ military force to achieve their end.[9]

Kennedy was unprepared to give in to such an ultimatum. He had come to office pledging to strengthen American military power to the point where no aggressor would dare challenge US interests. On May 25, he had delivered an address on "Urgent National Needs" to Congress and requested a Defense budget increase of $237 million to expand America's conventional war capability. Kennedy had also directed a realignment of active and reserve forces to improve responsiveness and combat readiness. The Khrushchev ultimatum stimulated an urgent review of American military capabilities in Europe.

---

7. Henry L. Trewhitt, *McNamara* (New York: Harper and Row, 1971), p. 101.

8. Robert W. Coakley, *et al.*, *U.S. Army Expansion, 1961–62*, undated manuscript, Center of Military History, p. I–11.

9. Richard P. Stebbins, *The United States in World Affairs, 1961* (New York: Harper and Brothers, 1962), pp. 22, 35, 37–38.

On June 27, McNamara requested a Joint Chiefs of Staff study to improve the force structure under conditions of a partial mobilization. His guidance was that the active services were to be increased by approximately 500,000 men, with initial emphasis placed upon the use of Ready Reserve personnel and Reserve Component units.

On July 6, the Joint Chiefs of Staff recommended a declaration of national emergency and a mobilization of 559,000 men. The active forces were to be increased by four divisions, and Reserve combat support units were to be mobilized to provide a logistics back-up to the Active Army.[10] Two days later, Khrushchev asserted that the bellicose attitude of the United States over Berlin was forcing the Soviet Union to increase its military expenditures.[11] By July 12, the Joint Chiefs of Staff recommendations had been pared down to a mobilization of 285,500 men, and on July 19 the President decided on a more limited call-up without the declaration of national emergency. The plan was to send six additional divisions to Europe from the stateside strategic reserve by early 1962 while ordering a partial mobilization to reconstitute the depleted strategic reserve.[12]

With his basic plan decided, Kennedy appealed to the nation in a special televised address on the evening of July 25. Citing Khrushchev's grim warnings about the future of the world, Kennedy asserted that "the immediate threat to free men is in West Berlin." He reminded the American people that the fortunes of war and diplomacy had left West Berlin an island of free people 110 miles behind the Iron Curtain and that the United States had a basic right to be in Berlin as a result of victory over NAZI Germany. As 50 million Americans watched, Kennedy called West Berlin the "great testing place of Western courage" and asked for sacrifice on the part of all citizens. He firmly announced his intention to fight over Berlin if necessary.[13]

MOBILIZING THE RESERVES

The next day, Kennedy requested Congressional authority to order to active duty up to 250,000 Ready Reservists—units and individuals. The Congress responded quickly, and Public Law 87–117 was enacted on August 1 by a vote 403 to

10. Coakley, *U.S. Army Expansion 1961–62*, pp. II–1 through II–4.

11. Stebbins, *United States in World Affairs, 1961*, p. 40.

12. Coakley, *U.S. Army Expansion, 1961–62*.

13. *New York Times*, July 26, 1961, p. 10.

2 in the House and 75 to 0 in the Senate. The authority was in effect until July 1, 1962, and allowed the President to call the Reservists to duty for up to 12 months. The President could also extend all terms of active military service.

On August 13, communist forces sealed the borders to West Berlin, halting the flow of refugees which had reached thousands a day. As construction on the Berlin Wall started, there was a renewed sense of urgency in the Pentagon. McNamara pushed for an earlier reinforcement of Europe, and on August 15, he accepted the idea of sending regular units to Europe while replacing them stateside with Reserve units.[14]

The next day, the Army alerted 113 Guard and Reserve units for possible active duty and extended 84,000 active duty enlisted men beyond their normal release date. Secretary of the Army Elvis J. Stahr, Jr. then announced a 12-month extension for Reserve officers presently on active duty for six-month training tours. Ready Reserve obligations were also extended for one year. In all, a dozen measures were taken to allow the United States to reinforce its units in Europe while doubling from three to six the number of combat-ready divisions in the Strategic Reserve of the stateside active forces.[15]

On August 23, the Army staff proposed calling 46,519 Reserve Component soldiers to active duty—the 23,626 in the units previously alerted, 4,396 members of the USAR's 100th Training Division who would open a training center at Fort Polk, La., and 18,497 soldiers to man non-divisional units for the Strategic Reserve Army Forces (STRAF). McNamara obtained Kennedy's approval and on August 25 announced a call-up of 210 units, including the 100th Training Division. All except the 100th were to report for duty on October 1. The 100th was ordered into service on September 25.[16]

Intensified combat readiness training was ordered for 479 units of the Army National Guard and Army Reserve on September 6, with four Guard divisions and 146 smaller units being told to add another weekend drill to their monthly training schedules. These units were alerted for possible call-up. Meanwhile, Stahr told an Association of the

---

14. Coakley, *U.S. Army Expansion, 1961–62*, p. II–27.
15. Press Release 57, Army News Service, August 17, 1961.
16. Coakley, *U.S. Army Expansion, 1961–62*, p. II–37.

US Army convention that the build-up would soon permit reinforcement of Army units in Europe.[17]

In less than two weeks, the warning order had become an active duty call as the Army told two National Guard divisions—the 32nd Infantry Division from Wisconsin and the 49th Armored Division from Texas—and 248 non-divisional·Reserve Component units to report by October 15. The 49th was sent to Fort Polk, which in turn forced the 100th Training Division to mobilize at Fort Chaffee, Ark., and establish a new training center there. The 4009th US Army Garrison was told to help the 100th get ready for its first shipment of 1,000 trainees on October 17. The 100th Training Division's mission was to turn out 60,000 new soldiers over the next year.[18]

Morale appeared to be high among the recalled Reservists. According the the *New York Times,* attitudes ranged from a patriotic sense of duty to eagerness to engage the Russians, the latter feeling personified by Sgt. Nikolai Klinkowski. Klinkowski, a member of New York's Company B, 101st Signal Battalion, was a 25-year-old refugee from communist-controlled Poland, and he wanted very much to "go right now, fight right now and even die right now" to free his country.[19]

A week later, the *Times* reported that a Yankee Stadium souvenir vendor, PFC Marvin Belsky would be losing a small fortune—$35 to $50 a day—by missing the World Series. In Belsky's words, he was now earning peanuts— $99.10 a month—instead of selling them. Other members of the Bronx, N.Y., 920th Transportation Company gave the call-up mixed reviews.[20]

PROBLEMS OF THE CALL-UP

Most reserve units reported to active duty without all of the equipment authorized by their Tables of Organization and Equipment (TOE). This was due in part to the reduced allowances authorized for training purposes. More importantly,

---

17. *New York Times,* Sept. 7, 1961, p. 1.
18. *Army Information Digest,* July 1962, pp. 2–14. The 100th Training Division was warmly praised by the Army leadership for doing an outstanding job. Special mention is made of the 100th in 1961 and 1962 annual historical supplements, and Chief of Staff Gen. George H. Decker made special mention of the 100th as well as the 301st Logistical Command in a March 1962 article in *Officer* magazine.
19. *New York Times,* Sept. 24, 1961, p. VI–32.
20. *New York Times,* Oct. 2, 1961, p. 16.

many items were in short supply nationally, highlighting the common complaint that the Army had been neglected during the later Eisenhower years.

For years, austere funding had not kept pace with the consumption of Army equipment through wearout and obsolescence. For four of the six years prior to 1961, the appropriation for Army materiel did not cover day-to-day losses and likewise failed to provide for modernization. Consequently, by June 30, 1961, the materiel readiness of the Army was substantially below that required for a modern, combat-ready force.[21]

In addition, much of the equipment on hand was approaching the end of its useful military life and was of little value except in training new soldiers. The unsatisfactory situation was made worse by the fact that Operation and Maintenance (OMA) appropriations had been constrained in the 1950's, leading to an impressive maintenance and rebuild backlog. The result was that the Army entered the Berlin build-up handicapped by past neglect and forced to take expedient measures.

Among the measures quickly adopted by the Army was to withdraw equipment from those Army Reserve units not mobilized. Mobilized units did receive additional equipment to aid in training, but the bulk of the equipment efforts were directed toward Europe in support of the planned build-up there.[22]

Equipment was not the only problem. Guard and Reserve units were deliberately undermanned and required the recall of some 38,827 individual Reservists to bring them to full strength. Of these, 15,734 were sent to the 444 mobilized Army Reserve units, and 23,053 filled out Army National Guard units.[23]

The selection and call-up of individual Reservists was not fully satisfactory either. According to McNamara, "The lack of adequate information on the status of individual Reservists recalled as 'fillers' and the urgent requirement for men with special skills requiring long training combined to produce some inequities and some misassignments."[24] The Army was in the midst of a changeover from manual to

---

21. Coakley, *U.S. Army Expansion, 1961–62*, pp. VII–1 and VII–2.

22. *Ibid.*, pp. VII–2 through VII–4.

23. *Summary of Major Events and Problems*, Office of the Chief, Army Reserve and ROTC Affairs, 1 July 1961 to 30 June 1962, p. I–2.

24. *Department of Defense Annual Report, 1962*, p. 22.

machine-processed Reserve personnel records, and the recently reorganized command structure for the Army Reserve magnified the problems associated with a rapid call-up of individuals.[25] The objective of the call-up was to produce additional operational units as quickly as possible. Although the lack of equipment and the infusion of filler personnel delayed the start of training in some cases, Reserve units began an intensified, five-phased training program.

Phase One, lasting three weeks, was devoted to a general shakedown, receipt of filler personnel, and cadre training. During the next two-week phase, units concentrated on squad, section and crew training. Weeks six and seven, comprising Phase Three, were for small unit and team training. The fourth phase, weeks eight through ten, covered platoon and company training, essentially basic unit training. The final phase lasted another three weeks. This was for battalion, battle group and division field exercises. Units also participated in command post and logistical exercises.[26]

The last of the 68,883 Army Reservists mobilized for the crisis had hardly been on duty two weeks when McNamara gave indications that additional recalls would not be necessary. In a November 17 press conference, McNamara expressed confidence in the build-up and said that 300,000 men had been added to the armed forces in recent months while 45,000 had been sent to Europe to reinforce combat units there. He said that the build-up was ahead of schedule and that there was no need to call additional Reservists.[27]

DISCONTENT AMONG RESERVISTS

This announcement cheered those Reservists alerted for additional recalls, but it did little for the rapidly growing mood of discontent among some mobilized Reservists. The honeymoon of the first few weeks was coming to a close, and by the end of November the press was questioning Kennedy about the rumors of discontent and low morale among Reservists.

Kennedy responded that the stories were "wholly wrong" and that it should be clearly explained to all Reservists that they were performing valuable service. Kennedy

25. Irving Heymont, *Review and Analysis of Recent Mobilization, U.S. Reserve Components* (General Research Corporation, 1972), pp. 4–5.
26. *Summary of Major Events and Problems*, p. I–3.
27. *New York Times*, Nov. 18, 1961, p. 1.

added that he intended to release the Reservists from active duty as soon as possible.[28]

Four days later, the front page of the *New York Times* proclaimed "Why Us?". It appears that Kennedy's effort to explain to Reservists why they were in uniform again had about the same effect as a peashooter on a tank.

Aside from classic gripes about food and housekeeping details, Reservists were questioning the call-up procedures. Some, called as individual fillers, wanted to know why they were recalled when men who had never served were not being drafted. Others complained about a lack of work; and one young man, SP5 Willard M. Miller, wrote a letter of complaint to the Boston *Herald,* receiving an Article 15 (non-judicial punishment) for being so bold as to complain about being recalled from his college classes. He had violated a standing order about writing for publication without prior approval, and he also stirred up quite a bit of controversy.[29]

Army Secretary Stahr immediately cancelled Miller's punishment of two weeks' restriction and extra duty, but the Secretary had to answer to the Pentagon press corps. Stahr called a December 4 news conference to explain the Miller situation and to counter the impression fostered by newspaper articles that the Army had received a landslide of complaints from Reservists and National Guardsmen. Stahr explained that the regulation was misapplied to Miller and was meant to cover speeches and articles, not letters to editors. He also said that letters of complaint represented less than one percent of the Reserve Component soldiers recalled, which was about the normal complaint rate for the Active Army.[30]

In his prepared statement, Stahr said that "It is recognized that many individual reservists were not happy to leave families and civilian pursuits and opportunities for military service. However, the individual obligor and volunteer, with rare exception, had accepted the call of his country and has displayed admirable spirit, willingness and 'can do' attitude."

While admitting to equipment shortages and problems in identifying individual replacements, Stahr said that the call-up had proven that the Reserve system would work and work very well. He referred to a special investigation made

---

28. Transcript of Nov. 29, 1961, news conference as reported in the *New York Times*, Nov. 30, 1961, p. 14.
    29. *New York Times*, Dec. 4, 1961, pp. 1 and 19.
    30. *New York Times*, Dec. 5, 1961, pp. 1 and 29.

by Gen. James A. Van Fleet on behalf of the Chief of Staff. Van Fleet reported that the spirit of the citizen-soldier was truly magnificent and reflected the readiness of America to answer the call of the President. In short, Stahr concluded that the 1961 call-up was "far superior to any previous mobilization in this country."[31]

Stahr's opinion was seconded by seasoned journalist Hanson W. Baldwin, who called many of the complaints "cry-baby" and recalled the far more serious problems of the Korean War when many who fought in Korea had undergone the "double jeopardy" of serving in two hot wars. The inconveniences of a cold war were minor by comparison.[32]

Nevertheless, in a move to reduce complaints from the field, the Army issued on December 15 a pamphlet entitled "Why Me." More than two months after recalling Reservists to active duty, the Army finally explained to the troops that a call-up was the only way to immediately increase strength and that larger draft calls would not provide the needed strength in time. In general, the pamphlet answered the most serious questions on Reservists' minds, but it did not end the controversy surrounding some aspects of the call-up.[33]

MCNAMARA AND THE ROA

The issues of mobilization and recall had become entangled in a debate over the future of the Army's Reserve Components. Early in his administration, Kennedy had directed McNamara to reorganize the Defense Department to maximize capabilities while increasing flexibility. This reorganization naturally affected the Reserve Components when McNamara concluded that "not only did the reserve structure make very little sense in terms of size, [but that] its mission was obscure to say the least."

McNamara wanted the reserve components to be ready to replenish the strategic reserve in a timely manner, and he set about to reorganize the Reserves with this thought in mind.[34] The serious discussion of alternative Army National

31. Secretary Stahr's remarks are reported in *Army News Service* Release, No. 100, dated Dec. 5, 1961.

32. *New York Times*, Dec. 5, 1961, p. 8.

33. The text of the pamphlet is contained in *Army News Service* Release, No. 107, dated Dec. 15, 1961, as well as several major newspapers.

34. William W. Kaufman, *The McNamara Strategy* (New York: Harper and Row, 1964), p. 65.

Guard and Army Reserve force structures was underway when the Berlin Crisis overwhelmed all other planning. The crisis and subsequent mobilization put reorganization plans on hold, but in some quarters any discussion of the 1961 mobilization was inextricably linked with the threat of Reserve reorganization.[35]

The matter was made worse by the perception within the Reserve Officers Association (ROA) that McNamara had deliberately failed to defend Reserve Component honor against criticism in the press. The organization's membership also concluded that the Pentagon hierarchy didn't know very much about its Reserve Components.[36] On December 21, these smoldering feelings broke into the open when the ROA accused McNamara of "a national libel" against the Reserves. The Association charged that McNamara had failed to heed Congressional advice on how to carry out a mobilization.[37]

The ROA claimed that "there is no secret about the desire on the part of some authorities in the Defense Department to undermine and eliminate from the National Defense complex the Reserve programs . . . . [This has been] reflected in the continuing efforts during the post-Korea period to substantially reduce—and actually to phase out over a period of several years—the Reserve Forces."[38]

It would be difficult to fully substantiate the ROA charges, but the Association's outburst stimulated Congressional interest in the 1961 mobilization. Subsequently, Rep. Carl Vinson (D–Ga.), Chairman of the House Armed Services Committee, directed Rep. F. Edward Hebert (D–La.), to head a comprehensive inquiry into the defense posture of the Reserve Components. Vinson wrote Hebert that the "desirability of such an inquiry was significantly heightened by the recent partial mobilization of Reserve Components under PL 97–117."[39]

The newspaper reports of poor use of Reservists and the accusations by the ROA coincided with demobilization plan-

35. The McNamara reorganization plans will be discussed in detail in the next chapter.

36. John T. Carlton and John F. Slinkman, *The ROA Story: A Chronicle of the First 60 Years of the Reserve Officers Association of the United States* (Washington: ROA, 1982), pp. 455–62.

37. *New York Times,* Dec. 22, 1961, p. 1. Additional details are also found in the *Army-Navy-Air Force Register,* Jan. 13, 1962, pp. 14–15, and the *Officer,* Feb. 1962, Vol. 38, pp. 12–13.

38. *Army-Navy-Air Force Register, op. cit.*

39. Letter, Vinson to Hebert, reprinted in *Military Reserve Posture,* House Committee on Armed Services, Aug. 17, 1962.

ning and served to make the national leadership sensitive to the public relations impact of demobilization.[40]

DEMOBILIZATION

Once the Reservists had been called to active duty, the balance of staff planning actions for the call-up shifted from the problem of getting Reservists into uniform to that of returning them to civilian status. As early as the first week of December, the Army Deputy Chief of Staff for Operations (DCSOPS) proposed releasing some individual fillers by January 6, 1962, with a proposed release schedule for mobilized Army Reserve units later in the month. The two Army National Guard divisions would be released in March and May.

On December 28 and 29, the Army proposed releasing 32 units with 7,426 personnel because they could not be used effectively, mainly because of equipment shortages. Emphasis was placed upon having enough time to develop an effective public relations plan to explain the demobilization.

The President was reluctant to release units until two new active Army divisions could be organized and trained, and McNamara was unwilling to accept shortages of equipment, lack of useful mission or long lead-time training requirements as reasons to release Reserve units. It would be difficult to explain why the units had been mobilized if they had no mission or could not be trained.[41]

Later, potentially adverse public reaction and the unpredictable reaction of Reservists themselves influenced a decision not to deploy Reserve units overseas. When the rumblings of discontent by some Reservists continued, Army Chief of Staff Gen. George H. Decker recommended on March 2 that overseas deployment of the Reserve Components should not be considered unless there were overriding changes in the situation.[42]

---

40. This particular aspect of demobilization planning is covered in historical context in DA Pamphlet 20–210, *History of Personnel Demobilization in the United States Army* and is cited in Marvin A. Kreidberg and Merton G. Henry, *History of Military Mobilization in the United States Army, 1775–1945* (Washington: Dept. of the Army, 1955), p. 377.

41. Coakley, *U.S. Army Expansion, 1961–62*, pp. VIII–67 through VIII–81.

42. Memorandum, Decker to Under Secretary of the Army, March 2, 1962, Subject: "Overseas Utilization of RC Units/Personnel."

Decker took the discontent seriously. Artillerymen at Fort Bragg, NC, had boycotted their mess hall March 1–4 demanding an early release. Approximately 30 wives had demonstrated in front of the main gate of Fort Devens, Mass., calling for their husbands' release; and members of the 49th Armored Division at Fort Polk, La., had held a two-hour demonstration on March 5.

On March 13, Decker sent a message to the field emphasizing that commanders down to the company and battery level must fully explain the problems facing the United States and emphasize the need to retain Guardsmen and Reservists on active duty. In part, Decker stated that the United States was in a very real sense at war and that the threat against Berlin had not disappeared.[43]

The memo was made public on March 21, and on March 22, Kennedy told a news conference that he would release Reserve Component soldiers "at the first possible date consistent with national security." He noted that the two new Regular Army divisions intended to replace the Army National Guard divisions would be ready in August or September.[44]

By early April, McNamara was ready to release Reserve units as the US military posture improved. On April 6, he proposed to the President that the Reserve Components should be released about August 1 and that a minor degree of risk could be accepted while the two new divisions achieved full combat capability.

Kennedy agreed. His decision was made public on April 12.[45] The next step was to plan the release.

Detailed demobilization instructions were issued by Department of the Army and supplemented by a Continental Army Command (CONARC) letter of instruction. Units could be released from readiness mission as early as July 15, but none could depart for home until August 1. All units had to leave their mobilization station by August 11, and all mobilized Reservists had to return to civilian status by August 31.

The demobilization was not accomplished very smoothly. For example, Army Reserve garrison commands had to outprocess other Reserve Component units while try-

---

43. Coakley, *U.S. Army Expansion, 1961–62,* pp. VIII–81 through VIII–83.
44. *Army News Service*, Release No. 25, March 22, 1962.
45. *Army News Service*, Release No. 30, April 12, 1962.

ing to clear post themselves.[46] Also, as the Reserve units were released, critical items of equipment such as generators, trucks and communications equipment had to be turned in before departure for home station.[47]

ANALYSES OF THE MOBILIZATION

The last Reservist had barely left for home when the first official post-mortem of the 1961 mobilization was published. For months, the Hebert subcommittee had been delving into the problems and accomplishments of the call-up. On August 17, the subcommittee made its findings public, and these findings were not very complimentary.

The subcommittee zeroed in on the chronic problems of the Reserve Components—not enough equipment, not enough men and not enough training. The Army was scored for allowing Reserve policy matters to "rock and stumble along without any imaginative or aggressive effort to resolve them."[48]

However, the subcommittee saved its greatest concern for the Army's lack of information about the Reserve Components. Specifically, "for reasons the subcommittee was unable to ascertain, the Department of the Army did not have available to it records and reports which should have reflected the essential facts relating to the readiness of Reserve units".[49] Additionally, the Congressmen pointed out that the "military departments had not prepared contingency plans which contemplated a partial mobilization and hence were unable to properly select units for recall."[50] This was a major lesson that the Army should have learned from the confused Korean War mobilization.

The lack of knowledge and inability to partially mobilize was highlighted by the problems faced by the individual Ready Reserve members who had to fill out the understrength Guard and Reserve units. The overwhelming majority of these Reservists were veterans who the Army said had "hard skills" not found in the Reserve units. Nevertheless, the subcommittee estimated that less than half of these for-

---

46. Fifth US Army, after-action report: Subject: "Release of Reserve Component Units."
47. Coakley, *U.S. Army Expansion, 1961–62,* p. VIII–92.
48. *Report of Subcommittee No. 3 on Military Posture,* p. 6640.
49. *Ibid.,* p. 6657.
50. *Ibid.*

mer Active Army soldiers served in their primary Military Occupation Specialty (MOS) during the call-up. Clearly, in the subcommittee's opinion, the Army didn't know whom to recall and where to send them once they were recalled.

The Defense Department seconded the subcommittee's findings when McNamara wrote in his 1962 Annual Report that "equipment shortages existed in many units and had to be met by redistribution from other Army assets. The assigned personnel strengths of the recalled units averaged 70 percent of full active duty strength, making it necessary to fill existing vacancies with individual reservists".[51]

McNamara promised to prevent future inequities and misassignment of individual Reservists and asked for increased procurement in his 1962 and 1963 budgets to improve Army Reserve readiness. He also promised to raise the authorized manning level of Reserve units and stated his intent to match units with current contingency plans.

In summary, he said that the recall of Reservists during the summer of 1961 made it possible to meet urgent readiness requirements. Despite their problems, "Army Reserve units and individuals were in a higher state of readiness than ever before."[52] McNamara's conclusion begs the question: Did the mobilization of 1961 achieve its purpose?

CONCLUSION

The 1961 mobilization was a demonstration of national will (or more likely, a demonstration of Presidential will) and was intended to prevent a war rather than fight one. Because the Berlin Crisis did not deteriorate into a hot war and because Berlin was saved as a democratic symbol in the heart of East Germany, the mobilization has to be rated as a qualified success.

On the other hand, the active forces were not much strengthened by the call-up. In his contemporary *SECRET* report, Robert W. Coakley concluded that the mobilization bought time for the Army to add two divisions to its strategic reserve while increasing the number of combat ready divisions in the United States.[53]

---

51. *Department of Defense Annual Report, 1962*, pp. 22–23.
52. *Ibid.*
53. Coakley, *U.S. Army Expansion, 1961–62*, pp. VIII–199 through VIII–200.

In 1972, a Research Analysis Corporation study concluded that the mobilization had achieved its purpose but that the greatest failings were severe weakness in the management of the individual Reservists and the lack of planning for partial mobilization. The study argued that the Reserve system in effect in 1961 was inadequate.[54]

McNamara had made the same argument in 1961 when he first proposed a revamping of the Army's Reserve Components. The Berlin mobilization experience strengthened his resolve and placed him in direct conflict with the Congress and the professional associations of the Reserve Components. The battle over Reserve reorganization was ready to begin in earnest—a battle which did not end until 1967.

---

54. Heymont, *Review and Analysis*, pp. 4–10 and 4–11. Heymont's criticism of the Berlin mobilization is essentially the same as for the Korean War call-up. This opinion is also evident in the Hebert report as well as Coakley's analysis. A review of previous chapters in his work will show that the Berlin and Korean mobilizations suffered from nearly identical problems—haphazard recall of individuals, undermanned and underequipped units, lack of partial mobilization plans and the misuse of mobilized units. Essentially, if the Army had learned anything at all from the Korean effort, those lessons had yet to be effectively applied by the time of the Berlin mobilization nearly a decade later.

8

Reorganizations Lay the Groundwork for the Total Army Policy

For a full decade, from the announcement of the One Army concept in 1958 to the establishment of the two-star US Army Reserve Commands (ARCOMs) in 1968, the Army Reserve was in a constant state of turmoil and reorganization. As previously discussed, the USAR changed from the triangular division structure to the Pentomic structure to the ROAD structure.[1]

Likewise, it was a time for new strategic choices, with the massive retaliation policy of the Eisenhower era giving way to the Kennedy emphasis on counterinsurgency and limited, "brush fire" wars. More importantly, the national leadership recognized that the Reserve Components must be linked to specific contingency plans in order to be a cost-effective military asset.

To increase flexibility and reduce costs, the Army's Reserve Components were weaned from an outdated, inflexible, full-mobilization mission and given discrete responsibilities in support of specific war plans. However, this was not accomplished easily. Although the Kennedy administration was determined to streamline the Army Reserve, their efforts were initially blocked by a Congress jealously protecting its Defense prerogatives.

The reorganization tactics of Secretary of Defense Robert S. McNamara were heavy-handed and angered the Congress as well as the politically powerful Reserve Officers Association. The result was seven years of vicious in-fighting, during which the Army Reserve was left to muddle

---

1. See Chapter Six for a discussion of these changes.

along without firm guidance or clear prospects for the future.

A reasonable compromise was reached in 1967, and the Army's Reserve Components achieved a mix of units that has remained substantially unchanged into the 1980's. The reorganizations of the 1960's eliminated low-priority units from the Army Reserve and gave the Army Reserve a clearer role in national defense. The stage was thus set for the Total Force policy of the 1970's and 1980's.

As stated previously in Chapter Seven, Kennedy had campaigned upon the theme that the Eisenhower Administration had neglected national defense by placing undue reliance upon the nuclear strategy of massive retaliation. Like Truman before him, Eisenhower subordinated military needs to a conservative fiscal policy that placed first priority upon balancing the federal budget.

Because it was impossible to be ready for a wide range of conflicts and still balance the budget, the nuclear deterrent was given first priority as a cost-effective way of achieving more bang for the buck. Even so, the United States did retain a conventional, non-nuclear capability and was able to project its power when inclined to do so—such as during the 1958 intervention in Lebanon.

THE KENNEDY STRATEGY

What Kennedy did was to remove the fiscal strait jacket of the Truman and Eisenhower administrations. By placing defense needs ahead of a balanced budget, Kennedy allowed Defense planners to seek flexible solutions to potential threats.

In keeping with his desire to be able to respond to a wide range of threats, Kennedy directed McNamara to reappraise America's entire defense strategy. McNamara was told to develop the force structure necessary to meet foreign policy objectives without regard to budget ceilings. Once the force structure was decided upon, McNamara was told to produce it at the lowest practical cost.[2]

McNamara in turn emphasized America's ability to respond in the "gray areas" of the world—the Far East, Southeast Asia and Latin America. This emphasis led to the increased importance of conventional forces, with the Reserve Components being responsible for significantly augmenting

---

2. William W. Kaufmann, *The McNamara Strategy* (New York: Harper and Row, 1964), p. 47.

the Active Army. The Reserves were also to provide a base for large-scale mobilization in the event of general war.[3]

Consistent with its desire to strengthen conventional forces, the Kennedy administration moved swiftly to improve readiness by reorganizing the Reserve Components. The groundwork for the 1962 Army Reserve reorganization was laid in mid-May 1961 when the Assistant Secretary of Defense for Manpower, Personnel and Reserves, Carlisle P. Runge, directed the Secretary of the Army to submit a plan to streamline the Army's Reserve Components.

The Army was given ten days to propose a reorganization that would significantly improve the Reserves' responsiveness and combat readiness for conventional, limited-war contingencies. Runge imposed no restrictions on the composition or size of the Reserve force structure. However, an earlier review in March 1961 indicated a need for a total Army force of 42 divisions, with 14 or 15 divisions in the active Army.[4]

Based upon the March review, the Army proposed a reduction in the Reserve Component combat force from the existing 37 divisions to 29 divisions. While the number of divisions was being reduced, the manning levels for the remaining divisions and their support units were to be increased. The remaining divisions were to be reorganized along ROAD lines, and the amount of equipment procured for training would be increased. There would also be an increase in the number of technicians, and provisions were made for up to 100,000 men of the Ready Reserve Reinforcement Pool (today's Individual Ready Reserve) to receive two weeks of Annual Training a year.

Overall, the proposal would increase the Army's Reserve Component budget by 43 percent, to $1.1 billion in 1962. The intent was to have two high-priority Reserve divisions available for emergency combat operations on three-week's notice, with two more Reserve Component divisions available with five-weeks' notice. Six additional divisions and their support forces were to be ready to fight on eight-weeks' notice or less.

On May 22 and 23, this ten-division plan was presented to the General Staff Committees on Army National Guard and Army Reserve Policy (otherwise known as the Section 5 Committees, from their authorization by Section 5

3. *Ibid.*, pp. 97–98.
4. Karl Cocke, *The Reserve Components* (undated manuscript, Center of Military History), pp. VIII–3 through VIII–4.

of the 1920 amendments to the National Defense Act of 1916).[5] The Committees agreed with the plan in principle, and McNamara concurred on May 25.[6] That evening, Kennedy made a special address to Congress in which the ten-division plan was made public. Kennedy announced a complete reorganization of the Army's division structure to increase its non-nuclear firepower while improving flexibility and tactical mobility.

With regard to the Reserve Components, Kennedy said, "The Army is developing plans to make possible a much more rapid deployment of a major portion of its highly-trained reserve forces. When these plans are completed, and the reserve is strengthened, two combat-equipped divisions, plus their supporting forces, a total of 89,000 men, could be ready in an emergency for operations with but three weeks' notice." He explained that "these new plans will allow us to almost double the combat power of the Army in less than two months, compared to the nine months hithertofore required."[7]

Kennedy's statement was expanded upon on June 13 when the Army issued a fact sheet saying that a realignment of the Reserve Component structure was necessary to make the Reserve Components more responsive to strategic plans. Although the Army National Guard and the Army Reserve had achieved the best readiness posture in the peacetime history of the nation, the fact sheet said that it was necessary to close the gap between the readiness posture of active Army units and top-priority reserve units.[8]

On June 21, Secretary of the Army Elvis J. Stahr, Jr. explained the reorganization in an address to the 35th Annual Conference of the Reserve Officers Association (ROA) in San Antonio, Tex. Stahr, who was a former Reserve Officer and an ROA member, said that the Kennedy defense policy was geared to the belief that American forces were more likely to have to fight limited wars than a "no-holds-barred" global war.

Stahr emphasized that the Reserve Components would assume an increasingly important role in the 1960's. He illustrated his point by noting that the "forward strategy" of the United States placed seven Army divisions overseas—

5. 10 U.S.C. 3033.

6. Cocke, *Reserve Components*, pp. VIII–5 through VIII–8.

7. *New York Times*, May 26, 1961, p. 12.

8. Army News Service Fact Sheet, "Army Plan for Realignment of Reserve Component Structure," Release No. 40, June 13, 1961.

five in Europe and two in Korea. This left six active divisions in the United States, three—including the two airborne divisions—in the Strategic Army Corps, and three devoted to training new soldiers. The fourteenth Army division on active duty was split between Hawaii and Okinawa. According to Stahr, the three training divisions could not be deployed without the extensive use of Reserve Component combat and combat support units.

Beyond this augmentation role, the Reserve Components maintained seven divisions for strategic Army forces, and the Army Reserve itself had 10 divisions to meet the deployment requirements of a truly major war. In addition, the Army Reserve had 13 training divisions, for a total USAR force structure of 4,338 company-sized units and an average paid drill strength of approximately 300,000. In all, the reinforcement echelon of the Ready Reserve was 748,000 strong, with 330,000 of these men dedicated to bringing the active duty divisions to full strength.[9]

Stahr said that the Reserves were organized, trained and equipped on the assumption that units would have up to six months to be prepared for combat. However, this assumption was no longer valid as the United States and the Soviet Union moved toward conflict over Berlin. In Stahr's words, "in view of the critical world situation, it is imperative that measures be taken promptly to improve the deployment readiness posture of our Reserve Components and make them more responsive to strategic plans. The pace and nature of modern warfare require that reaction time be measured in weeks rather than months."[10]

Summarizing the argument for Reserve Component reorganization, Stahr said that "the proposed realignment of the Reserve Component structure was developed to meet a changed world situation. Unless such a realignment is accomplished, it is difficult to justify reliance on Reserve Forces, most of which could not be used until several months after an emergency arose."

The implication was that the Reserve Components had to reorganize in order to justify their existence. As Stahr put it, the Army staff was enthusiastic about the reorganization,

---

9. Strength figures cited in Stahr's text can be confirmed in *Summary of Major Events and Problems,* Office of the Chief, U.S. Army Reserve and ROTC Affairs, 1 July 1960, to 30 June 1961, pp. 12–16.

10. To place Stahr's remarks into perspective, the Vienna summit between Kennedy and Khrushchev was June 3 and 4. See the previous chapter for the details of increasing international tensions.

and it was up to the individual Reservists to assume an overriding personal responsibility to make it work.[11]

The groundwork had been laid for the first McNamara reorganization of the Reserve Components, but the reorganization did not occur because the Berlin Crisis, as described in the previous chapter, diverted attention from reorganization to partial mobilization. The crisis and mobilization also changed the Administration's attitude toward the Reserve Components.

The Berlin call-up had raised questions in the minds of President Kennedy and Secretary McNamara over the value of Reserve Components. Defense officials decided on September 22 to hold Reserve Component drill strength at 700,000, while reducing previously planned Reserve budget increases.[12] The reorganization plan had been through 19 revisions by November 1961,[13] and the Army staff had to make further revisions as DoD reduced the combined Guard and Reserve paid drill strength by 30,000, to 670,000. Finally, by mid-November, the action was shifted to the Office of the Assistant Secretary of Defense, Comptroller, where Dr. Merton J. Peck took the lead.

THE PECK PLAN

The resulting "Peck Plan" called for 670,000 Ready Reservists (Guard and Army Reserve) in a paid drill status—a 27 division force. Ten excess divisions would be reduced to operational headquarters. Six new ROAD combat brigades would be formed, and 100,000 members of the Ready Reserve Reinforcement Pool would receive two weeks' training annually. The plan also called for a 4,000-man increase in the number of Army Reserve technicians, a cost which was to be offset by converting 160,000 paid drill slots to 24 paid drills a year status, a decrease from the customary 48 paid drills.[14]

Before the Peck Plan could win final Administration approval, the *New York Times* reported on the plan to cut the Army's Reserve Components. Citing unhappy experiences with the Berlin call-up, the *Times* said that "the Pentagon

11. The Stahr address is quoted extensively in *The Army Reservist,* Sept.–Oct. 1961, pp. 3–6.
12. Cocke, *Reserve Components,* p. VIII–8.
13. *Ibid.,* p. VIII–9.
14. *Ibid.,* p. VIII–10.

has all but abandoned plans to place increased reliance upon the Reserve forces for emergency use."[15]

The *Times* article recalled the Eisenhower attempts to cut 70,000 slots from the combined Army Guard and Army Reserve strength, thus reducing the total to 630,000, and predicted that the latest idea to reduce the Army's Reserve Components would mean political trouble for the Administration. A key stumbling block was predicted to be a law which required the consent of a state's Governor before a National Guard unit could be transferred.

On December 14, Hanson W. Baldwin reported in the *New York Times* that Defense officials thought that expenditures for Reserve Forces were too high and that the existing troop basis was too large. Baldwin pointed out that Defense thinking had reversed itself since the Berlin Crisis. Prior to the Crisis, the idea was to increase Reserve Component strength while keeping the active Army strength steady.[16] Now, wrote Baldwin, the Army was going to increase its active force to 16 divisions, a gain of two divisions.[17]

On December 17, the *New York Times* quoted Deputy Defense Secretary Roswell L. Gilpatric as saying that the President had profound second thoughts about the call-up of Reservists. According to the *Times,* the move to reduce the strength of the Army's Reserves was caused by a reluctance to support sizeable reserve forces in an era of possible nuclear war. The argument was that hostilities might well be over before Reserve units could be brought into combat service.[18] On the other hand, the hostilities over the Army's Reserve Component reorganization were just beginning.

As was discussed in Chapter Seven, the Reserve Officers Association objected strenuously to McNamara's reorganization attempts.[19] It was evident that the issues of the Berlin call-up and the reorganization of the Army's Reserve Compo-

---

15. "Pentagon Maps Cut In Army's Reserves," *New York Times,* Dec. 3, 1961, pp. 1 and 11.

16. "Reserves Facing Ten-Division Cut," *New York Times,* Dec. 14, 1961, p. 1.

17. This is, of course, exactly what happened. The active Army was increased by two divisions during 1962, and the two mobilized Army National Guard divisions—the 32nd Infantry Division and the 49th Armored Division—were released from active duty along with all of the other mobilized Army Reserve Component units by Aug. 31, 1962.

18. "Fight Is Brewing On Reserve Role," *New York Times,* Dec. 17, 1961, p. 17.

19. "Reserve Officers Accuse Pentagon of Call-Up Libel," *New York Times,* Dec. 22, 1961, pp. 1 and 11.

nents were intertwined,[20] and on January 13, 1962, *The Army-Navy-Air Force Register* called for a "dispassionate survey of what has been gained or lost by the recent emergency call-up."[21]

The result of this call was the Hebert committee, also discussed in the preceding chapter. This subcommittee's August 17, 1962, report devoted most of its attention to the Peck reorganization plan which had eclipsed the readiness posture issue by the summer of 1962.

The General Staff Committees on Army National Guard and Army Reserve Policy, the Section 5 committees, were briefed on the Peck Plan on January 26, and they objected to it. The Section 5 committees endorsed a counter-proposal calling for the retention of all 37 Reserve Component divisions and an increase in paid drill strength to 716,000—a net gain of 16,000 instead of the loss of 30,000 under Peck. The Reserve Forces Policy Board concurred with the Section 5 committees on February 1, 1962. Ignoring the proposals of these two statutory bodies charged with advising the Secretary of the Army and the Secretary of Defense, respectively, on reserve matters, the Army moved ahead with its realignment plans.[22]

On April 4, 1962, the Army announced its plans for Reserve Component realignment. These included reducing four National Guard and four Army Reserve divisions to headquarters status, with the simultaneous activation of eight brigades as non-divisional units. The brigades were to be formed under the ROAD concept using the personnel of the "realigned" divisions. At the same time, the top-priority Reserve Component divisions would be maintained at 75 to 80 percent of TOE strength as compared with 52 to 78 percent in the past.[23]

The realignment also cut 58,000 paid drill positions from the Army's Reserve Components, reducing them to a

---

20. Jonn T. Carlton and John F. Slinkman, *The ROA Story, A History of the Reserve Officers Association of the United States,* (Washington: ROA, 1982) pp. 456–63. This work sheds considerable light upon ROA attitudes during this period, but it is unfortunately without footnotes and frequently omits dates from its narrative.

21. "Reserve and Guard Hassle," *Army-Navy-Air Force Register*, Jan. 13, 1962, p. 14.

22. Cocke, *Reserve Components,* VIII–11 to VIII–13. An excellent contemporary explanation of the organization, responsibilities and authority of the Section 5 committees can be found in the Nov. 1963 issue of *Army Reservist,* pp. 8 & 9.

23. "Army Announces Plan for Reorganization of Reserve Components," *Army News Service,* Release No. 29, April 5, 1962.

total drill strength of 642,000—a level 28,000 below the 670,000-man force proposed in the Kennedy fiscal year 1963 budget.[24] The reduction would allow a savings of $53.1 million that year, according to testimony before the Hebert subcommittee on May 11.

In addition to the divisional realignment, the 1962 reorganization plan called for the modernization of non-divisional Reserve Component units. In the words of a May 21, 1962, press release, the reorganization was "the result of a thorough study of the actual needs of the Army." The goal was to make the Reserve Components "more responsive to the needs of the Army in the event of rapid mobilization."

Among the changes proposed were the elimination of 90 mm anti-aircraft gun battalions, air observation detachments, and special services companies, the latter being the units designed to provide entertainment and recreation programs for troops overseas. In turn, the reorganization proposed to add corps and army-level aviation companies, armored cavalry squadrons, and armored medical companies to the Reserve Components. There was also to be an increase in Nike-Hercules air defense battalions at the expense of the older Nike-Ajax units, an increase in self-propelled artillery, and a reduction in towed artillery.[25] In all, approximately 800 units would be eliminated from the Army's force structure.

REACTIONS TO THE PLAN

The reorganization plan was not well received outside of the Pentagon. According to one study, "The Army plan for realigning the Army National Guard and the Army Reserve received a cool reception on Capitol Hill, where it came under the close scrutiny of the Armed Service and Appropriations Committees of both the Senate and House of Repre-

24. "Pentagon Revamps Reserves: 58,000 Pay Spaces, 8 Divisions Go," *Armed Forces Register,* April 7, 1962, pp. 1 and 46.

25. "Fact Sheet on Reserve Realignment," *Army News Service,* Release No. 34, May 21, 1962. It should be noted that while some of these force structure decisions have stood the test of time, such as increasing the ratio of self-propelled artillery to towed artillery, the decision to abandon air defense guns in favor of complex missile systems can be faulted. Lessons learned from Vietnam combat showed that a combination of conventional air defense artillery and missile systems to be more effective against jet aircraft than either system alone. Also, the Army invested heavily in the Nike-Ajax and Nike-Hercules missile systems only to abandon stateside missile defense sites in the early 1970's.

sentatives." Congressional resistance forced a compromise on the number of ready reservists to be maintained in a paid status, and the fiscal year 1963 appropriations act established a paid drill strength of 700,000 for the Army Reserve Components.[26]

The Reserve Officers Association and the National Guard Association opposed the reorganization. Articles in *The National Guardsman* derided the idea that a 58,000 cut in strength could actually result in greater readiness,[27] and the Stackpole Company rushed into print a volume entitled *Reserve Forces and the Kennedy Strategy,* which plainly stated that it was impossible to grow stronger by cutting muscle. This book made the observation that "in any case, money is the key to more readiness. If we want a truly ready reserve, keyed to forseeable requirements of a strategy of freedom of action and adaptable either to general or limited emergencies, we are going to have to pay for it. More drill-pay spaces, more full-time technicians, higher schedules of annual drills, higher levels of equipment, speed-up of weapons procurement, an increased flow of six month trainees—all these things cost money."[28] All of these solutions have been applied with success since the advent of the Total Force policy in 1970, but McNamara was not prepared in 1962 to accept solutions that *increased* the cost of the Army's Reserve Components.[29]

More important than the opposition of the Reserve Component professional associations was the reluctance of state governors to accept any cutback in National Guard strength. In an attempt to win support for his reorganization plan, McNamara spoke before the July 2, 1962, National Governor's Conference at Hershey, Penn. McNamara stated that the revised structure would increase readiness by matching the Reserve Component structure to the "detailed, time-phased, unit requirements established by our military

26. Cocke, *Reserve Components,* pp. VIII–16 and VIII–17.

27. See "The Big Slice," *The National Guardsman,* May 1962, pp. 6–7 among others.

28. George F. Eliot, *Reserve Forces and the Kennedy Strategy,* (Harrisburg, Penn.: Stackpole Co., 1962), pp. 39–52 and 68–69.

29. For FY 1961, the Army Reserve's share of the Army's Total Obligation Authority (TOA) was 3.1 percent. McNamara reduced this share to 2.4 percent in 1964, 2.0 percent in 1966 and 1.6 percent for FY's 1967 and 1968. Under the later Total Force concept, the Army Reserve's share of the Army's TOA rose to 2.6 percent in 1971 and 2.8 percent in 1972 and then stabilized in the 3.2 to 3.5 percent range for the fiscal years 1973 through 1983.

planners." Even though 1,700 obsolete units would be eliminated, more than 1,000 other units would be added to the
force structure. The result, McNamara promised the governors, would leave approximately the same dispersion of units
as before the reorganization. He claimed that only 16 National Guard armories would lose all of their units and that
the Guard would be left with 4041 units, which he contended was sufficient to meet state responsibilities.[30]
McNamara did not succeed, however, in winning the state
chief executives to his side, and their opposition was seconded by the August 17 report of the Hebert subcommittee.

The subcommittee came down four-square against the
McNamara reorganization, finding it "difficult to com-
prehend how a reduction of 58,000 men in Reserve drilling
units would result in an increased mobilization capability."
The subcommittee unanimously opposed the Peck plan because it would lower morale, would not increase readiness,
would hurt retention of trained enlisted personnel, and
would offer no solution to the Reserve Component equipment shortages.[31] Unable to win Congressional or state-
house support, Defense planners went back to the drawing
boards.[32]

By mid-November, a reorganization plan which retained a drill strength of 700,000 was developed, and on
December 3, after a personal briefing, Hebert informed
McNamara that the plan was acceptable. Although Defense
spokesmen had denied as recently as November 30 that any
concessions would be made on reorganization,[33] the Army
announced that it would go ahead with a 700,000-man reorganization on December 4 and dropped any hint of reducing paid drill strength.[34]

Gov. Albert D. Rosellini of Washington, Chairman of
the National Governor's Conference, immediately announced
his opposition to the December 4 plan, while the Reserve
Officers Association quickly withdrew its opposition. Not-

30. "Proposed Army Reserve Component Reorganization," *Speech
File Service,* No. 7–2–62.

31. See report on "Military Reserve Posture," Aug. 17, 1962,
(Washington: GPO), pp. 6644 and 6667–76.

32. The extent of the governors' opposition is chronicled on pages
3–5 of the Aug. 1962 issue of *The National Guardsman.* Additional details are found in the Oct. 1962 issue of *The National Guardsman.*

33. See *New York Times,* Nov. 30, 1962, p. 30.

34. "Army's Revision of Reserve Units and Guard Begins," *New
York Times,* Dec. 5, 1962, pp. 1 and 25.

ing that the December plan contained many concessions to the positions maintained by Congress and the ROA, the association's spokesman, Col. John T. Carlton, summed up the ROA position by saying that "it's hard to be against proposals for modernization."[35]

COMPROMISE

The Pentagon immediately set about to convince Gov. Rosellini and several other governors who were still opposed to the December plan. By early January 1963, a Defense concession to convert Army National Guard divisions to the ROAD organization was apparently sufficient to obtain the necessary state-level support, and the reorganization moved ahead.

Approximately 1,850 company or detachment size units were dropped from the force structure, and approximately 1,000 new units added. This represented a 10 percent drop in the 8,807 unit structure of the Army's Reserve Components. The 700,000 drill strength—400,000 for Army National Guard and 300,000 for Army Reserve—was retained, while McNamara was able to drop four divisions each from the Guard and Reserve and replace them with separate brigades. Meanwhile, higher recruiting standards were set for the Reserve Components to bring them up to active Army levels. The civilian full-time technician force was expanded, and the manning levels for top-priority Reserve units were increased.[36]

McNamara did achieve his basic goal of bringing the Army's Reserve Components into closer alignment with mobilization requirements. The remaining 23 Army National Guard divisions and the six Army Reserve divisions were reorganized at higher levels of authorization, and the entire process was completed by May 1, 1963.[37] The important point is that the Army Reserve ended the 1963 fiscal year better able to support the new Kennedy strategy of flexible response. There was also increased emphasis upon the development of early-deploying Reserve forces in accordance with contingency plans.[38]

35. "Reserve Drop Fight on Revision," *New York Times*, Dec. 6, 1962, p. 25.

36. Cocke, *Reserve Components*, VIII–20; also, see *Army Reservist*, Jan. 1963, pp. 3–4.

37. "Army Reserve Components Complete Reorganization," *DOD News Release*, No. 665–63. May 10, 1963.

38. Cocke, *Reserve Components*, p. VIII–22.

Along with the reorganization, the Reserve Component priority system was changed to reflect a dichotomy within the force structure. Those units which would be needed promptly for reinforcing the active Army, deploying overseas or expanding the mobilization base were designated as Priority I and Priority II and were called the Immediate Reserve. The remaining Reserve units, Priority III, were needed for full mobilization and were identified as the Reinforcing Reserve. The Immediate Reserve met the requirements for rapid response and flexibility. The Reinforcing Reserve met the needs of a broad-based mobilization. In addition to dividing Reserve Component units into an Immediate and Reinforcing Reserve, the reorganization subdivided the Ready Reserve Mobilization Reinforcement Pool (RRMRP) of individual Ready Reservists.

The higher priority individual pool of the RRMRP was preassigned to the units of the Immediate Reserve—both Army National Guard and Army Reserve. The Army National Guard was given the authority to recruit volunteers for an Inactive National Guard, while the Priority III units of the Army Reserve were prohibited from recruiting men who had a Ready Reserve obligation. The idea was to channel obligated Reservists into the Immediate Reserve while staffing Reinforcement Reserve units with non-obligated volunteers. The result was to reduce the need for fillers in high-priority units. This would reduce one of the glaring problems of the Berlin mobilization when large numbers of filler personnel created problems for mobilized units.

REORGANIZATION AND REALIGNMENT

At the same time, the Army staff was being reorganized. The change having the greatest influence upon the Army Reserve was the creation on January 2, 1963, of the Office of Reserve Components. For the first time, the responsibility for policy, direction and the control of the Reserve Components was under a single three-star officer. The Chief, National Guard Bureau and the Chief, Army Reserve were placed under the general supervision of the Chief, Office of Reserve Components (CORC). This ended the situation where the Chief, National Guard Bureau was essentially independent while the Chief, Army Reserve was a relatively minor official on the Army staff.[39]

---

39. Details of the reorganization of the Immediate Reserve and the Reinforcing Reserve may be found in the *Annual Historical Supplement,*

Two other problems identified by the 1961 mobilization were also addressed at this time. Starting in July 1962 the records of the Standby and Retired Reserve were removed from the 14 corps and centralized in St. Louis. On February 20, 1963, the decision was made to centralize non-unit Ready Reserve records in St. Louis to prevent a repeat of the confused call-up of Individual Ready Reservists during the Berlin Crisis.

REP—63

Another problem unearthed during the Berlin call-up was the lack of a uniform obligation among Ready Reservists, with Guardsmen and Reservists having different obligations. The Army sought a single six-year obligation for all Ready Reservists in the summer of 1962, and this was ultimately achieved by means of Public Law 88–110. This law created a new Reserve Enlistment Program, commonly called REP–63, still in effect today.

Specifically, the REP–63 program established a single six-year Ready Reserve obligation, ending the eight-year obligation which had existed under a 1955 amendment to the Armed Forces Reserve Act of 1952. The National Guard lost exclusive recruiting rights to non-prior service personnel ages 17 to 18½, and prior service personnel could now complete their Ready Reserve obligation by joining either the Guard or Reserve. The act required a minimum initial active duty training period of at least four months while permitting as much active duty training as was necessary to become military occupation specialty (MOS) qualified. Reserve Component enlistees were no longer limited to a fixed, six month initial active duty training. The result was that many MOSs were now open to non-prior service Army Reservists.[40] Despite the gains achieved by the 1962–63 reorganization, the improvements provided only a foundation for changes to come.

Office of Reserve Components, July 1, 1962–June 30,1963. Similar information is presented in the May and June 1963 issues of *The Army Reservist* and on pages 62–63 and 120 and 124 of the *Department of Defense Annual Report, 1963.*

40. See the sources cited above as well as "Building the Strength of the Army Reserve," *Army Reservist,* Nov. 1963, pp. 3 and 4. This conclusion is specifically drawn on page 28 of *The Department of Defense Annual Report for Fiscal Year 1964.*

FORCE STRUCTURE PLANNING

A hint of events to come was clearly given in the *Department of Defense Annual Report for Fiscal Year 1964*. The report states that "despite the gains of 1964, further assignment of manpower and materiel to high priority units, particularly to those of the Army reserve components, is required to provide on short notice a properly balanced reserve for the augmentation of our general purpose forces . . . . This progress provides the foundation for further advances being planned."[41]

As a matter of fact, the new 29-division Reserve Component force structure had already become outmoded, because new Army analysis indicated that a total active-Reserve 24-division force was adequate for the limited war situation anticipated over the next decade. With the active force set at 16 divisions, this left a Ready Reserve requirement for only 8 divisions—21 less than what was being carried in the force structure.

A basic problem facing Army force structure planners at this time was the hard, cold reality that equipping a 29-division force in the Reserve Components plus fully supporting a 16-division active Army was a fiscal impossibility. Throughout the two previous administrations, the Army had been unable to obtain sufficient funds to adequately equip the active force. There was a modernization backlog for the entire Army, and the situation was exacerbated by the fact that the Army had never programmed funds to equip fully its Reserve Components.

Army planners estimated that at best they could equip 29 division equivalents—24 divisions plus 16 brigades—without resorting to new procurement. To equip the other 21 divisions—all Reserve Component—would cost an estimated $10 billion at a time when the entire Army budget was running only $11 to $12 billion a year. Furthermore, once the low-priority Reserve divisions were equipped, the equipment would have to be maintained and modernized at regular intervals.[42]

Through the expedient of limiting contingency plans to limited war situations, planners were able to balance the force that could be equipped and sustained at present fund-

---

41. *Ibid.,* p. 24.
42. The logic of this argument is found on pages 3616 through 3626 of the *Hearings on the Merger of the Army Reserve Components*, March 25, 1965, through Sept. 30, 1965.

ing levels with the force required. The 45-division requirement for waging general war could be ignored on the assumption that such a general war would require total
mobilization on the level achieved for World War II. In
such an all-out war, peacetime budget restraints would be
abandoned, and the issue of Defense costs would become
moot. This intellectual drill was nothing more nor less than
balancing the benefits and costs of a limited war capability
versus the risks and costs of an extensive conventional capability short of general war.

Although the risk analysis technique is routine today, it
created considerable anxiety in 1964 when individuals refused to believe that there was ever justification for reducing
the size of forces.[43] Realizing this, it is easier to understand
why the December 12, 1964, proposal to reduce again the
Army's Reserve Components raised so much furor—a situation which created much heat of controversy without shed-
ding much light upon the problem.

The impetus for the 1964 proposals came when Secretary of the Army Stephen Ailes recommended to McNamara
in July that consideration be given to "bringing manpower,
equipment and war plans into consonance," and that a single management system be developed for the Reserve Components. Responding to McNamara's request to expand upon
his recommendation, Ailes appointed a small group under
Brig. Gen. Thomas A. Kenan on October 6, 1964, to find
ways the Reserve Components could achieve better balance,
readiness and management.[44]

MERGER PROPOSED

The Kenan committee studied the deficiencies of the Reserve
Components, the costs of maintaining two separate Reserve
systems, the impact reorganization would have upon the
states, and the related political ramifications. Despite the

43. A consistent argument made by opponents of the reorganization
and merger plans announced on Dec. 12, 1964, was that any reduction
in forces automatically reduced America's defense capability. These individuals failed to see that maintenance of undeployable and ineffective
units was actually a drain upon resources which in turn lowered the
capability of the rest of the force. Maintenance of a large force, which
appears stronger on paper than it actually is in reality, creates a false
sense of security. This is akin to the pre-World War II days when the 27
ORC divisions represented very little real military power.

44. *Hearings, ibid.,* pp. 3601, 3628 and 4158.

political hazards involved, the committee recommended the merger of all Army Reserve units into the National Guard, while the Army Reserve would consist solely of individual Reservists.[45]

Two weeks later the recommendations were tentatively approved by Ailes and sent to the Army Staff for comment. The staff coordination was completed in approximately three weeks, with Maj. Gen. William J. Sutton, the Chief, Army Reserve (CAR) first learning of the plan on November 4. The Section 5 committees had not yet been consulted on Ailes' proposal, and this fact, combined with the late involvement of the CAR, gave Reservists the impression that the plan to abolish Army Reserve units was being concocted in secret.[46]

The failure to include the CAR and the Section 5 committees in the planning process subsequently angered many Congressmen who were more upset over the failure to follow the policies enacted by Congress than by the particulars of the merger plan. The Section 5 committees had been specifically created by Congress to insure that Reserve Component interests were fully considered before the Army took any action affecting the Reserves.

On December 11, McNamara approved the merger plan to transfer all Army Reserve units to the National Guard while reducing the Army's Reserve Component drill strength by 150,000. By this time, reports were appearing in the newspapers of a forthcoming merger, and Defense officials later contended that "leaks" had forced a premature announcement on December 12, 1964. This was one day before the planned December 13 meeting of the Section 5 committees—a date when they were supposed to be informed of the merger.[47]

MCNAMARA AND THE CONGRESS

McNamara's December 12 press conference contained some tactical errors which in all probability contributed to Congress' ultimate rejection of the merger. When asked if the merger could be handled without Congressional approval,

---

45. Cocke, *Reserve Components*, p. VIII–25.
46. *Hearings*, pp. 3678 and 4058.
47. *Hearings*, pp. 3632 and 4234. For an example of articles in the press, see "Plan to shift Reservists Faces a Fight at Capitol," *New York Times*, Dec. 11, 1964.

Table 8–1   Comparison of Present and Proposed Reserve Component Structure.

Unit Category	Present Structure				Realigned Structure	
	Army National Guard	US Army Reserve	Total	Manning Level(%)	Army National Guard	Manning Level(%)
UNITS FOR WHICH THERE IS A MILITARY REQUIREMENT:						
Air Defense	7,400	—	7,400	85	7,400	85
Units to Round Out Active Army & Reserve (units will be added)	76,500	78,600	155,100	80	160,020	80
Bdes (now 11 to be increased to 16 bdes)	25,000	16,300	41,300	75–80	69,614	80
Mobilization Base	2,600	66,600	69,200	75–100	69,200	75–100
6 Div Forces	118,000	64,100	182,100	75–80	189,860	80
2 Special Purpose Div. Forces	25,600	2,600	28,200	70	33,520	80
Support to Other Svc	1,900	9,300	11,200	70	11,200	70
State HQ	4,000	—	4,000	100	8,500	100
Total	261,000	237,500	498,500		549,314	
UNITS FOR WHICH THERE IS NO MILITARY REQUIREMENT:						
Other Div. (21 div—15 Guard & 6 Reserve)	122,800	45,600	168,400	55–60	—	
Non Divisional Units	15,450	16,300	31,750	55	—	
Comd Hq's, Divisional	750	600	1,350		—	
Total	139,000	62,500	201,500		—	
TOTAL	400,000	300,000	700,000		549,314	

* Equipment procurement now authorized for on site Air Defense; Round Out units; support to other SVCS; Part of Mobilization Base; 6 Div Forces; and 11 Bdes. Equipment will be authorized for these forces plus 2 Special Purpose Divs and 5 Bdes.

† Unit composition will change in a number of instances.

Source: *The Army Reserve Magazine*, January 1965, p.12.

McNamara replied "Yes, it can be." He also announced that he was ending the practice of offering Reserve commissions to Congressmen, and he hurt his case when he said that he intended to transfer to the Standby Reserve the 100 or so Congressmen who were Reservists. This was in addition to an earlier McNamara decision to abolish the special Congressional training detachments where Congressmen were able to earn enough retirement points to give them a "good" year toward retirement.[48]

The merger proposal was also prejudiced by being presented as a *fait accompli*. A December 12 memorandum from the Secretary of the Army to Army Reserve commanders told the Reservists that their positions were being abolished because the Army needed a "quick reaction force." Ailes explained that he couldn't abolish the National Guard because it was needed on the state level for natural disaster and civil disturbance missions. Since he was determined to have only one Armed Reserve Component, he was left with no choice but to abolish the Army Reserve units.

The arguments about economy, simplified command, and faster reaction time did little to assuage Reservists who would have to join the National Guard if they wanted to continue in a troop unit. The problem was particularly acute for senior Army Reserve officers who had understandable doubts about their ability to obtain corresponding positions within the National Guard structure.

ROA AND OTHER OBJECTIONS

The reaction by senior Reservists and their professional association, the Reserve Officers Association, was swift and predictable. They had suspected that the merger plan was forthcoming,[49] and McNamara had no sooner made the merger public than the ROA fired off a telegram to President Johnson asking him to hold off any action on the merger until public hearings could be held. Johnson refused the ROA requests, citing the need to take Defense economies wherever possible.

As the organization most actively opposed to the merger, the ROA encouraged its membership and friends to express opposition to the plan. While the ROA drew up a 30-point rebuttal to the merits of the merger, the basic strategy

---

48. In order to count a year toward the 20-year requirement for a Reserve Component retirement at age 60, a Reservist must earn 50 retirement points a year. Retirement points are earned at the rate of one point for every day of active duty and one point for every drill (of at least 2 hours length) attended. Reservists may also earn points by taking correspondence courses and by performing certain specific equivalent duties. By far the easiest way to earn points is by attendance at drills or meetings with a unit, and the abolition of the Congressional detachments made it much harder for Congressmen with their busy schedules to earn points. The "good" year term applies to any year in which 50 points are earned.

49. See the *New York Times*, Nov. 25, 1964, Section C, p. 10.

was to agitate for Congressional hearings. This was a sound strategy, because McNamara had strained relations with several key Congressional committees. Furthermore, his attitude and the unfortunate handling of the merger announcement gave the impression that McNamara was being contemptuous of Congress.[50]

While the political storm clouds gathered, the Army moved ahead on the merger proposal. A steering committee was formed in the Office of Reserve Components, and representatives of the National Guard and Army Reserve were asked to compile troop lists for the merger. At the Department of Defense level, the Reserve Forces Policy Board voted 6 to 6 on the merger; and at the Army level, the General Staff Committee on the National Guard and Reserve Affairs approved of the merger,[51] over the unanimous dissent of its Army Reserve members. The USAR members prepared several alternative plans, which were rejected out-of-hand by the Army staff because they all called for the retention of both Army Reserve and Army National Guard units.[52] The assumption apparently made by the Army staff was that the Army Reserve and the Army National Guard would have to contain identical units to be independent of each other and totally self-sufficient. The concept of mutually supporting and mutually dependent components making up a Total Army as we have it today was totally incomprehensible to the Army in early 1965.

Meanwhile, ROA had been effective in mounting a grass roots movement against the merger. ROA chapters and individual members had been vigorous in contacting their Congressmen to demand public hearings on the merger. Their efforts were also having an impact upon editorial opinion. Although initial reporting had been generally favorable to the merger, the attitude changed in January and February.

Probably one of the more damaging articles to appear was Brig. Gen. S. L. A. Marshall's piece in the January 23, 1965, *New Republic* entitled, "McNamara's Latest Reform: Why His National Guard Merger Scheme Won't Work." Marshall referred to the unsuccessful 1948 attempt by the Gray Board to merge the Reserve Components, a move

50. William F. Levantrosser, "Army Reserve Merger Proposal," *Military Affairs,* Fall, 1966, pp. 137–39.
51. *Ibid.,* p. 139.
52. Details of the alternative plans are found in pages 3714 to 3784 of the *Hearings* cited above.

which floundered when the Guard opposed tighter federal control over its operations. Marshall exhumed every traditional criticism of the National Guard, from incompetent training and political generals to the interference of governors in national defense matters. He argued that only a federal reserve could attract the specialists and uniquely skilled individuals needed on a standby basis. Whether Marshall was right or wrong, his opinions received national circulation and were later quoted in hearings against the merger.[53]

CONGRESSIONAL HEARINGS

A significant factor in the debate over the merger was the attitude of Congress. In general, veteran lawmakers sensed a challenge to Congressional prerogatives in Defense matters. The new chairman of the House Armed Services Committee, Rep. L. Mendel Rivers (D–S.C.), felt a need to assert Congressional authority over Defense policy; and Sen. John Stennis (D–Miss.) led opposition to the merger. Another outspoken critic was Sen. Strom Thurmond (R–S.C.), who was a retired Army Reserve major general and a former president of the Reserve Officers Association.[54]

Hearings were called by subcommittees of both the House and Senate Armed Services Committees, with the hearings before an Hebert House subcommittee being particularly hostile toward McNamara and Army Secretary Ailes. What was developing was a confrontation between the Executive and Legislative Branches over authority to merge the Reserves.

McNamara refused to concede a need for Congressional approval, except that he would require an increased appropriation for a larger National Guard. Hebert directly challenged this contention. Another key point in the hearings was whether the Defense Department had made proper use of the statutory groups created to advise on Reserve Component matters. Considerable time and effort were expended to

---

53. *Hearings*, p. 3642.
54. Thurmond was not the only Reserve general in Congress. Sen. Barry Goldwater, R–Ariz., was an Air Force Reserve major general; and Sen. Howard W. Cannon, D–Nev., was an Air Force one-star. In all, 83 members of Congress were members of the Ready Reserve; and the ROA counted 170 members on the Hill. See page 84 of the Dec. 13, 1964, *New York Times* for a complete listing of Congressional Ready Reservists by grade and service.

establish the fact that these committees had not been consulted until after McNamara had decided to move ahead
with a merger.

Defense officials were hard pressed to deny that they
had circumvented the intent of Congress. One particularly
notable verbal blunder was made by Ailes when pressed by
Hebert on authority of the Section 5 committees. Ailes conceded that legislative language gave the committees the authority to oversee Reserve-related matters. In Ailes' words,
"That is what the language literally says, but I never assumed it means that."[55]

The Army was also embarrassed to admit that on October 22, 1964, Army General Counsel Alfred B. Fitt had
rendered the legal opinion that the Secretary of the Army
was utterly lacking in authority to compel the merger. Fitt
opined that Army policy would be thrown upon the mercies
of the governors.[56]

Hearings on the merger, which continued through
March and April, temporarily ended with a joint press conference May 15, 1965, between Hebert and McNamara. The
conference announced a face-saving compromise in which
McNamara indicated that he would seek legislation to clarify some of the aspects of the merger, and Hebert expressed
satisfaction that the Congress had reached full partnership
with the administration in discussing the merits of the merger.[57]

The merits of the merger from the Department of Defense point of view can be summarized as follows:

1. The merger would create a single chain of command
   through the National Guard Bureau, as opposed to separate Army Reserve and National Guard chains.
2. Approximately 200,000 paid drill spaces in unnecessary
   units would be eliminated with a concurrent cost savings.
3. The manning level of the remaining units would be increased, with these units going from 498,500 troops
   prior to the merger to 549,314 troops afterwards.
4. Because of reduced drill strength, future retirement costs
   would be reduced. McNamara made this point at his
   December 12, 1964, press conference.

---

55. *Hearings,* p. 3697.
56. *Hearings,* pp. 4320–36.
57. Levantrosser, "Army Reserve Merger Proposal," p. 142.

5. Equipment levels in the retained units would be increased as equipment was transferred from abolished units.
6. Concurrently, personnel assets in the full-time support force of the Reserve Components would be redistributed among fewer units, thereby increasing Reserve readiness.[58]

The case against the merger was made by ROA's Carlton in testimony on April 8, 1965, before the Hebert subcommittee. Describing the plan as "not militarily sound," Carlton's lengthy arguments can be summarized thusly:

1. The claim of increased manning levels is false. Most units would not receive increased manning levels, while the strength of state *headquarters* would be doubled.
2. The command structure would not be simplified. Instead of having the units of the Army Reserve under a single commander, the merger would place these assets under 50 different commanders—state governors.
3. Readiness would be decreased while the Reserve Components go through the transition from one chain of command to another and while new senior personnel are assigned under National Guard leadership. Carlton contended that this readiness loss would take several years to reverse.
4. A 29 division-equivalent force would be inadequate to meet the threat. According to the ROA, the fact is that our mobilization base should be structured to counter enemy capabilities, and not what some economy-minded comptrollers may conceive the enemy's intentions to be.[59]
5. It is imprudent to reduce the strength of our Reserve Components at a time of increased troop commitments in Vietnam.[60]

---

58. The entire DoD position is found in the January 1965 issue of *The Army Reservist* which reprints Ailes' letter to commanders of Dec. 12, 1964, the DoD press release on the merger, the press' questions and answers from that date and a detailed chart showing how the force structure would change. The plan for the execution of the merger is found on pages 7 and 8 of the March 1965 issue of *The Army Reservist*.

59. This particular argument is found on page 11, March 1965 issue of *The Officer*.

60. For Carlton's entire testimony, see *Hearings, ibid.,* pp. 4189–4219. The ROA's case for the Army Reserve is explained in detail in the May 1965 issue of *The Officer* and runs nearly 30 pages.

The issue of Vietnam was a serious one. By mid-April 1965, the United States had 33,500 troops in Vietnam, with the combat role of 5,000 Marines there openly acknowledged. In late April, McNamara obtained a strength increase to 75,000 Americans; and the United States forces in Vietnam reached 50,000 by the end of May.[61]

Gen. William C. Westmoreland has since written that he had come to the conclusion that some sort of a national mobilization would be required.[62] In any case, the decision to commit a larger segment of the active forces to Vietnam made clear the need to maintain a continental reserve. Even though the President subsequently chose to bolster manpower levels through the draft rather than by calling up Reserve units, the very fact that a call-up of Reserve forces had been under consideration was instrumental in convincing many Congressmen that the merger and reduction in Reserve Component strength was unwise.

Amidst signs of increasing Congressional opposition to the merger, the Hebert subcommittee resumed House hearings in early August. Deputy Secretary of Defense Cyrus R. Vance, the principal pro-merger witness, restated the same arguments previously made before the committee. He insisted that the merger would strengthen the national defense, but most of the subcommittee remained highly critical of the plan. The subcommittee shelved the merger by a vote of 8 to 1 on August 12 with Rep. Lucien N. Nedzi (D–Mich.), being the sole McNamara supporter.

In announcing the subcommittee decision, Hebert said that the full committee would oppose any effort to destroy the Army Reserve by merging it with the National Guard. Committee Chairman Russell supported Hebert's position; and the ranking minority member of the House Armed Services Committee, Rep. William H. Bates (R–Mass.), seconded the chairman. However, the committee held open the door for compromise by saying that it would not rule out a reorganization of the Reserves as long as an Army Reserve structure was retained.[63]

61. Donald C. Odegard, *Non-Mobilization and Mobilization in the Vietnam War,* (Carlisle Barracks, Penn.: Army War College, 1980), pp. 11–13.

62. William C. Westmoreland, *A Soldier Reports* (Garden City, NY: Doubleday and Co., 1976), pp. 140–141. The subject of Reserve Component mobilization for Vietnam will be covered in detail in the next chapter.

63. Cocke, *Reserve Components,* pp. VIII–39 & VIII–40.

The House Appropriations Committee and its Senate counterpart had already recommended separate funding for the Army Reserve and Army National Guard. The Senate committee had even inserted restrictive language into the 1966 Department of Defense Appropriations bill to prohibit the merger. The language was modified in conference committee, with the subsequent September 29 appropriations act stating that a realignment of reorganization of the Army Reserve Components could take place only with the approval of the Congress.[64] This act also had a proviso that the Army Reserve be programmed for a paid drill strength of 270,000 and that the Army National Guard attain an end strength of 380,000. This was 50,000 less than previous legislation.

MCNAMARA ACTS

On November 13, McNamara ignored the Congressional rebuff of the merger and announced that he would inactivate 751 Army Reserve units containing 55,000 Reservists. He contended that there was no further use for these units. The directive to the Chief, Army Reserve to abolish the units was accompanied by an authority to establish Reinforcement Training Units (RTU) to replace deactivated units.[65] The RTUs allowed Reservists to earn retirement points in a non-paid status through weekly meetings or work on special projects. Within a year, the number of RTUs rose from 364 to 526, and their membership increased from 6,675 to 11,346. Altogether six divisions, 19 battalions and 126 smaller units were chosen for a December 31, 1965, phase-out.

At the same time, McNamara announced the formation of a Selected Reserve Force (SRF). Consisting of 976 Army Reserve and Army National Guard units, the SRF would be a 150,000-man force to quickly back up active forces in case of disturbances outside of Vietnam. The SRF consisted of three divisions and six independent brigades from the National Guard and 232 combat support and combat service support units of 31,519 men from the Army Reserve.

The SRF units were authorized 100 percent of their combat strength instead of their former 70 to 80 percent manning levels, and the number of unit training assemblies was increased by 50 percent, to 72 a year. All of these as-

---

64. Sec. 639, 79 U.S.C. 879. (Public Law 89–213).
65. *Army Reserve Magazine*, Dec. 1965, p. 27; Levantrosser, "Army Reserve Merger Proposal," p. 143.

semblies had to be four hours long, as compared with the two-hour minimum then allowed other Reserve Component units.

In addition, battalion-sized units and larger commands were authorized up to 96 drills a year to update plans and SOPs as well as to conduct exercises. The SRF units received top priority on active duty training quotas for new enlistees, and they were alerted for a special, more rigorous period of active duty during 1966.[66] Although the formation of the SRF was said to be only precautionary, there were ample reasons to be concerned about Reserve Component Readiness at this time.

The proposed merger had thrown the Army Reserve into turmoil. The Army Reserve had just begun to recover from the Berlin Mobilization, which had resulted in a severe post-mobilization personnel loss. When its future was placed in doubt, all Army Reserve construction was terminated and the recruitment of non-prior service personnel virtually stopped in early 1965. The number one concern of the Army Reserve leadership was for its own future.[67]

The uncertain Army Reserve situation was made worse by developments within the active force. The build-up of active forces for Vietnam taxed the training base to the extreme, making it virtually impossible for even SRF units to obtain training. Despite increased priority for equipment, SRF units did not see substantial gains in their equipment posture, and some SRF units even lost equipment to active forces.[68] A drawdown of Army Reserve equipment for Vietnam had begun.

CONGRESS AND THE MERGER

Meanwhile, the main battle between McNamara and the Congress over the future of the Army's Reserve Components continued. Several reasons, which also seem to have currency today, help explain why such a clash of wills occurred between the Executive and Legislative branches.

According to one study, the merger was an attractive arena for Congress to exert its prerogatives in Defense policy-making, because force levels and organization charts are easily understood in layman's terms. Many Congressmen had

---

66. *Army Reserve Magazine,* Dec. 1965, pp. 4–6.

67. Odegard, *Non-Mobilization and Mobilization,* pp. 9 and 10.

68. Based on author's own observations while assigned to the 198th Artillery, Delaware Army National Guard.

first-hand knowledge of the military through active or Reserve service, and quite a few were members of military professional organizations. There was no widespread organized opposition among the general public to Reserve forces, and the citizen-soldier tradition allowed legislators to discard any worry about offending constituents. On the contrary, because the Reservists were only part-time soldiers, their unrestricted political activity was a very positive political benefit to their Congressional supporters.[69]

When McNamara submitted his 1967 budget to Congress in January 1966, he kept the merger issue alive by again proposing no expenditures for Army Reserve units. Once more, Congress opposed McNamara's plans, and the Senate Preparedness Investigating Subcommittee unanimously recommended against the merger. The subcommittee was piqued by the December 31, 1965, deactivation of 751 Army Reserve units, including all six of the Army Reserve's remaining combat divisions.

The full Armed Services Committee declared that any future Army Reserve or Army National Guard deactivations of the 1965 magnitude should be taken only after consultation with the Congress.[70] In response, Defense officials countered that there was no military requirement for the 751 units and that it made no sense to spend money on them. Officials said that 25,400 of the 55,000 men affected did transfer to other units and that nearly all of the remaining men were assigned to the Ready Reserve Mobilization Reinforcement Pool (RRMRP). A Defense statement also said that the Reserve Components were in excellent condition and that the merger proposal of the previous year was still valid.[71]

The protests of Defense officials notwithstanding, Congress once more blocked the merger. The 1967 Defense Appropriations Act required a minimum Army Reserve paid drill strength of 260,000, and the House went so far as to pass a bill requiring a permanent Army Reserve unit strength of at least 260,000.[72]

It was rapidly becoming evident that the merger would never gain Congressional approval, and the latest House ac-

69. Levantrosser, "Army Reserve Merger Proposal" p. 143.
70. "Senate Preparedness Committee Blasts Merger," *The Officer,* June 1966, pp. 5 and 6.
71. DOD News Release, No. 417–66, May 14, 1966.
72. The bill passed the House by a 332 to 6 vote on Sept. 21, 1966.

tion implied that Congress would legislate strict strength and organization guidelines unless McNamara dropped his proposal to abolish all Army Reserve units. Without formally conceding the fight, McNamara announced that alternative approaches were being taken to alleviate the Army's Reserve Component problems.

The moderation of McNamara's stance came in his January 23, 1967, statement on the 1968 budget before a joint session of the Senate Armed Services Committee and the Senate Preparedness Subcommittee. It was the only rational option open to him, because declining Army Reserve readiness demanded an end to the struggle between McNamara and Congress.

While the merger debate had raged, the condition of the Army Reserve deteriorated. Because the future was uncertain, the Army had not converted the Army Reserve units to the more modern Tables of Organization and Equipment (TOE) then in the active Army. The Army also deferred reorganizing Reserve combat service support units to the new COSTAR (Combat Support to the Army) concept, where the old technical service units were functionalized into combat service support units. Active Army and Army Reserve units were no longer compatible. They were not organized and equipped in such a manner as to allow rapid integration into the active Army upon mobilization, and this defeated the "One Army" concept and reduced readiness.[73]

MCNAMARA ACQUIESCES

McNamara accommodated Congressional desires by proposing a 1968 end strength of 400,000 drilling Army National Guardsmen and 260,000 Army Reservists. He contended that there were still unnecessary units in the force structure but that it would be possible to bring the Reserve Components into line with Defense needs.[74]

The decision by Defense leaders to work within Congressional guidelines rather than trying to push a merger past Congress lessened the conflict over policy prerogatives.

---

73. These points were made in a February address to the ROA Midwinter Conference, 1967, by Lt. Gen. C. W. G. Rich, Chief, Office of Reserve Components. The address is reprinted on pages 4–6 of the April 1967 issue of *The Army Reserve Magazine*.

74. McNamara's address is reprinted in the March 1967 issue of *The Army Reserve Magazine*.

Army planners were finally able to draft a proposal to bring the Reserve Components in line with mobilization requirements.

On May 24, 1967, Lt. Gen. C. W. G. Rich, Chief of the Office of Reserve Components, signed a plan to realign the Reserve force structure. The plan had been approved by the Chief of Staff on April 21 and endorsed in an 11–10 vote by the Section 5 committees on May 4. Despite the non-concurrence of the Chief, Army Reserve, the plan was approved by Secretary of the Army Stanley R. Resor on May 31.

NEW RESERVE COMPONENTS PLAN

Basically, the plan called for a Reserve Component of 698,100 men in eight divisions and 16 independent brigades complete with the appropriate support increments. In addition, the Reserve Components would include 6⅓ support increments (Combat Support and Combat Service Support) to round out active Army organizations. The command structure of the Army Reserve would be modified. Although Army Reserve units would still be commanded through the Continental Army Command (CONARC), the 14 corps would be eliminated. The Reserve units would be commanded by new two-star Army Reserve Commands (ARCOMs) that would answer to CONARC through the numbered Continental US Armies (CONUSAs). The goal was to convert Reserve units to the new "G" series TOEs and the COSTAR organization starting Sept. 30, 1967, and to have the entire process, including the creation of the ARCOMs, finished in time for Annual Training in the summer of 1968.[74]

On June 2, 1967, McNamara announced the approval of the above plan with the only major difference being a reduced paid drill strength of 640,000—400,000 in the Army National Guard and 240,000 in the Army Reserve. According to McNamara, 92 percent of the units in the new structure would come from the old structure with little or no change in unit organization.

The Army National Guard would be composed of mostly combat units while the Army Reserve would have only combat support and combat service support units. The Army Reserve would retain its 13 training divisions.

This latest plan met little opposition in Congress, except that the Committee on Armed Services insisted that some combat units be retained in the Army Reserve. The result was a compromise by Army officials and the develop-

Table 8–2   Force Structure and Organization—Three Brigade Plan.

Units	Structure, End FY 1967 ARNG IR/RR[1]	USAR IR	Total	Future Structure[2] ARNG	USAR	Total
Combat Divisions	8/15	0	23	8	0	8
Training Division	0	13	13	0	13	13
Command Hq Divisional	0/5	0	5	0	0	0
Combat Brigades	7/0	4	11	18	3	21
Maneuver Area Cmds	0	2	2	0	2	2
Air Defense Bns	44/0	0	44	31	0	31
Field Army Supt Comd	0	0	0	0	1	1
Support Brigades	0	3	3	1	4	5
Adjutant General Units	36/0	96	132	40	120	160
Civil Affairs Units	0	77	77	0	51	51
COSTAR Units	0	38	38	122	134	256
Finance Units	1/0	18	19	1	26	27
JAG Units	0	196	196	0	226	226
Hospital Units	15/0	107	122	15	106	121
Military Police Bns	6/0	4	10	7	4	11
Public Info Units	34/0	25	59	34	24	58
PSYOPS Units	0	8	8	0	6	6
Garrison Units	0	18	18	0	9	9
Terminal Units	0	19	19	0	19	19
Total Companies and Detachments	2,520/1,480	3,575	7,575	2,900	3,450	6,350
Paid Drill Strength (000)	307.9/110.6	260.0	678.5	400	260	660

[1] IR—Immediate Reserve: Manned at 80% or higher of full wartime strength; necessary equipment being procured. RR—Reinforcing Reserve: Manned at 50% of full wartime strength; no equipment being procured.
[2] Manned at 90% or higher of full wartime strength; to be fully supported with equipment, technicians, spare parts.

ment of the "three brigade" plan whose unit structure is shown in Table 8–2.

The three brigade plan was outlined by Resor in a July 12, 1967, letter to Sen. Richard B. Russell (D–Ga.), Chairman of the Senate Committee on Armed Services. Three separate brigades would be dropped from the National Guard and given to the Army Reserve. The Army Reserve would also have 10 infantry battalions, 15 separate artillery battalions and 16 combat engineer battalions, while increasing in strength from 240,000 to 260,000.

To balance this, units originally planned for the Army Reserve were placed in the National Guard. These included 13 hospitals, 52 composite service companies, 6 construction engineer battalions and 8 ordnance companies. The National Guard paid drill strength would stay at 400,000. There was a net decrease in the number of Reserve Component units, but this loss was offset by increasing the manning levels to an average of 92 percent of full wartime strength—up from the former average of 75 percent.[75]

The acceptance of the three brigade plan allowed the Army to finally reorganize the Army Reserve. The concept for the new ARCOM organization was made public in July 1967, with the target date for the change-over from the corps structure being December 1968.

The locations of the 18 new ARCOMs were announced on December 21, 1967. Their mission was to insure attainment and maintenance of mobilization readiness of attached and assigned units. By commanding units within their geographical area of responsibility, the ARCOMs were to supervise and coordinate training, supervise materiel readiness, coordinate public and troop information programs and supervise the preparation of unit mobilization plans.[76] This is essentially the mission performed by the ARCOMs today.

The reorganization was completed by May, 1968. The elimination of the Corps, which had been staffed by active Army personnel, was a basic revision in the command concept for the Army Reserve. For the first time, all Army Reserve units were under the command of an Army Reserve general officer, and this implied substantially greater responsibility for Reserve commanders.[77]

Army Reservists also gained a formal voice at the Department of the Army level as a result of the reorganization controversy. Although there had been a full-time officer on the Army Staff responsible for Army Reserve matters since 1927, this position, known today as the Chief, Army Reserve, was not statutory until the passage of Public law 90–168.

This law resulted ultimately from the 1965 hearings on McNamara's reorganization proposals. At that time, the

---

75. See CORC, 24 May 1967, "Proposed Plan for Reorganizing the Army's Reserve Components," signed by Lt. Gen. Rich. Copies are in the possession of US Army Center of Military History and the Public Affairs Office, Office of the Chief, Army Reserve.

76. Testimony, Army Secretary Stanley R. Resor, Senate Committee on Appropriations, July 12, 1967.

77. *Annual Report of the Secretary of Defense on Reserve Forces, 1968,* p. 9.

House Committee on Armed Services expressed serious reservations about Reserve readiness. On October 23, 1965, the Committee announced its intention to prepare comprehensive legislation early in the next Congressional session to clarify and resolve the future status of the Reserve Components.

This legislation, H.R. 16435, the "Reserve Forces Bill of Rights and Vitalization Act," was introduced in July 1966. In addition to setting minimum drill strengths for the Reserves, the bill provided for statutory Chiefs of the Army Reserve and Air Force Reserve. The bill passed the House 322 to 6 on September 21, 1966, but the Senate was unable to act on the legislation because it was too late in the session. Meanwhile, one of the objectives of H.R. 16435 was temporarily achieved in the 1967 Department of Defense Appropriation Act, which established a minimum drill strength for the Army National Guard and Army Reserve.

Subsequently, Hebert introduced substantially the same legislation into the 90th Congress on January 10, 1967, with H.R. 2. The bill moved quickly through the House, receiving passage February 20, 1967, by a vote of 324 to 13. The Senate began hearings in June and passed an amended version on November 8, 1967. After a conference committee reconciled differences, the two chambers agreed to the conference committee report on November 16, and the measure became Public Law 90–168 on December 1, 1967.

Also entitled the "Reserve Forces Bill of Rights and Vitalization Act," H.R. 2 and the debates surrounding it reflected the very essence of the struggle between the legislative and executive branches over defense policy prerogatives. The House, according to Hebert, had a fundamental responsibility for raising armies and supporting a Navy, and this responsibility extended to the Reserve Components.

While the Defense Department agreed that the Congress had prerogatives in the defense arena, the executive branch contended that Congressional prerogatives were limited to broad oversight responsibilities. These responsibilities, in the eyes of DoD officials, did not include setting exact requirements for the force structure or dictating the internal organization within an agency of the Army.[78]

---

78. Report No. 13, House of Representatives, 90th Congress, 1st Session, Feb. 13, 1967, p. 2. Levantrosser suggests that the extreme interest in the Reserve Components was a departure from the norm and

The House version of the legislation was far more detailed than the final Senate version and reflected a distrust of the Defense Department. The House bill established a minimum drill strength for each of the seven Reserve Components and established the Chief, Army Reserve as the commander of the Army Reserve. The legislation even went so far as to describe how the Office of the Chief, Army Reserve was to be organized. Similar guidance was given for the Air Force.

The House also wanted to create an Assistant Secretary of Defense for Reserve Affairs, while the Senate preferred to have a Deputy Assistant Secretary of Defense for Reserve Affairs to serve within the Office of the Assistant Secretary of Defense for Manpower and Reserve Affairs. The House acceded to the Senate's desires on this point.

Both bodies were concerned about the role of the Reserve Forces Policy Board. The purview of the board was expanded by allowing any member of the board to bring matters forward for consideration. Previously the board could consider only matters referred to it. The individual service secretaries were given the authority to appoint board members, a right which formerly belonged to the Secretary of Defense. Some modifications were also made in the Army Reserve Forces Policy Committee—the Section 5 Committee—and its Air Force counterpart.

The final legislation also contained benefits for National Guard technicians and an authority for the Air Force Reserve and the Air National Guard to exceed temporarily former limitations on field grade officers.

The final version of the bill resolved House–Senate differences over drill strength policy by providing that authorized personnel strength of the Selected Reserve of each Reserve Component would be set by Congress each year as part of the appropriations process. This satisfied the desire of House members to include some minimum strength provision or other language which would prevent the Secretary of Defense from making drastic cuts in the Reserve Components without Congressional consent. The role of the Chief, Army Reserve was subject to somewhat more debate.

Testifying before the Senate Committee on Armed Services, Secretary of the Army Stanley R. Resor said on September 27, 1967, that the Army had no objection to creating a statutory Chief of an Office of Reserves since it

was more of a reaction to McNamara's perceived arrogance than a desire to dictate detailed policy. See Levantrosser, *ibid.*, p. 144.

paralleled the present law which had established the National Guard Bureau. Resor did object, however, to provisions which set forth that office's organization in great detail. He felt that such matters were properly the responsibility of his office or the Army Chief of Staff.

Resor also objected to language which made the Reserve office an operating agency responsible for preserving the integrity of the Reserve Component. He believed that this would establish two chains of command. The Defense Department objected to the provision which made it mandatory for the Chief, Army Reserve to be a Reserve officer. Defense officials believed that such a requirement would restrict them from appointing the best possible officer to the position.[79]

In the end, the Senate Committee on Armed Services agreed with Resor that the Chief, Army Reserve (CAR) should be an advisor to the Chief of Staff on Army Reserve matters. But, the CAR was to come from the officers of the Army Reserve and had to have at least 10 years commissioned service in the Army Reserve. The CAR was to be appointed by the President to a four-year term, with the advice and consent of the Senate. The Chief was to be a major general and was eligible to succeed himself.

Maj. Gen. William J. Sutton, who was already serving as the Chief, Army Reserve under the Chief, Office of Reserve Components, became the first statutory Chief, Army Reserve. Subsequently, the CAR became the appropriations director for the Reserve Personnel Army (RPA) and Military Construction Army Reserve (MCAR) appropriations[80] with responsibility for testifying annually before Congress. This in effect gave the Army Reserve a national spokesman.

Although the Congress has retained a high degree of interest in the Reserve Components, the passage of Public Law 90–168 put an end to the acrimonious debate over Reserve Component policy. The Army was able to turn its attention to the 1968 reorganization. Assured that their component would continue to exist, Army Reservists were able

---

79. Resor's testimony is found on pp. 124–137 of "Reserve Components of the Armed Forces and National Guard Technicians," Hearings, Committee on Armed Services, United States Senate, June 26 to Oct. 3, 1967.

80. At this time Army Reserve Operations and Maintenance funds were a sub-account of the Operations and Maintenance Army (OMA) appropriation. The Operations and Maintenance Army Reserve (OMAR) appropriation was not created until 1973.

to concentrate on repairing the damage inflicted by years of uncertainty; and the Army Reserve began to make real progress toward readiness goals.

While the 1968 reorganization was taking place, forty-two Army Reserve units were mobilized in April. Most were sent to Vietnam, but a few reinforced the strategic reserve forces on active duty in the United States.

A second Selected Reserve Force (SRF) was organized on May 1, 1968, allowing the first SRF to be relieved of its expanded mobilization responsibilities. Experience with the first SRF showed that Reserve units could achieve full TOE strength with notable increases in readiness. On the negative side, officials learned that drills at the rate of 72 per year over a sustained period would cause drop-outs by non-obligated Reservists.[81]

The SRF continued until August 1, 1969, when it was relieved of its mission. Personnel pressures had forced the number of drills to be reduced to 58, 10 more than required for other Reserve units; and equipment shortages remained until the end. It was easy to assign higher priorities to Reserve Component units, but it was not always so easy to sustain them or to provide adequate training facilities. The active Army came first.[82]

CONCLUSION

In summary, the Army Reserve changed significantly from 1960 to 1969. The Army Reserve began the decade with 4,338 company-sized units with a drill strength of approximately 300,000. By 1970, the Army Reserve had 3,478 company-sized units with a membership of 260,000. The number of Individual Ready Reservists increased from 748,000 in 1960 to 931,000 in 1970.

The manning levels of Army Reserve units increased from the 55–70 percent level in 1960 to 93–100 percent as the decade ended. Despite the equipment drains of Vietnam, the Army Reserve did make modest equipment gains. Unit TOEs were modernized, and Reserve units were able to replace their World War II rifles and trucks.[83]

---

81. *Annual Report of the Secretary of Defense on Reserve Forces, 1968,* p. 13.

82. Cocke, *Reserve Components,* p. VIII–55.

83. When the author enlisted in the early 1960's, his Reserve Component unit was firing M1 rifles, two generations behind the active force. These weapons were collected and M14s were issued in 1965. The older M1s were eventually issued to irregular forces in Vietnam.

More important, the Army Reserve force structure was modified to meet contingency plans. Low-priority units were abolished, and the three components were no longer a mirror image of each other. They had started to take on today's structure of mutually dependent and mutually supporting parts of the Total Army.

Army Reservists gained greater control of their component. Reserve generals took command of all Army Reserve units under the supervision of the Continental US Armies (CONUSAs); and the Army Reserve gained a national focus and spokesman in the person of the Chief, Army Reserve. These events did not occur without considerable debate and anguish along the way, but these birth pains were necessary to set the stage and make possible the Total Army concept of the 1970's and 1980's.

The third and final tier of a 3000 barrel water tank is put into place by the 461st Pipeline Co. of Cody, Wyo. This USAR unit built the water tank during two weeks of training in June 1961. (Signal Corps photo, #591581)

Most of the Army's smoke generator units are in the USAR. Reservists from the 375th Chemical Co., 472nd Chemical Bn (USAR), create a smoke screen during summer training at Camp McCoy, Wisc., in 1961. (Signal Corps photo, # 585646)

The Army Reserve contains all of the Army's railroad assets. This USAR maintenance team is working on the boiler of a steam locomotive at Fort Eustis, Va., in 1962. (Signal Corps photo, #596511)

Army Reservists also learn to destroy things. Shown here is a member of an Army Reserve Special Forces Group as he instructs a class in demolition at Fort McClellan, Ala., in 1966. (Signal Corps photo)

When Hurricane Agnes swept through Pennsylvania in the summer of 1972, over 1000 Army Reservists were called to duty to help with rescue and clean-up operations. Shown here are members of the 469th Engr. Bn, of Caven Point, NJ, who are constructing a Bailey bridge in Schickshinny, Penn. (US Army photo)

Women have helped defend this country since before the American Revolution. It was not until after World War II, however, that women were allowed to join the Army Reserve. In 1982, women comprised approximately 14 per cent of the Ready Reserve of the USAR. Shown here is the change of command ceremony (September 1973) by which Capt. Ruth Glaspey, WAC, became the first woman to take command of an Army Reserve Transportation Unit. (US Army photo)

Thirty-five USAR units were sent to Vietnam in 1968, including the 513th Maintenance Bn, from Boston, Mass. Members of the Direct Support Platoon of the 513th are shown here as they work on a 5-ton truck. (US Army photo)

US soldiers on patrol near Hue, South Vietnam, 1971. Over 100,000 individual members of the USAR served on active duty each year from 1967 through 1971, and many of these men and women did serve in Southeast Asia. (US Army photo)

Long Binh, Republic of Vietnam, was an incredible complex built up by the United States to support its effort in Southeast Asia. Several of the USAR units that went to Vietnam in 1968 operated out of Long Binh. (US Army photo)

Army Reservists of the 737th Transportation Co. present arms during welcome home ceremony on August 13, 1969, in their home town of Yakima, Wash. This USAR unit was one of 35 that was sent to Vietnam in 1968. It served with the 1st Log. Command near Chu Lai and was awarded the Meritorious Unit Commendation for its service. (US Army photo)

A public affairs specialist with the 1209th US Army Garrison, Mattydale, NY, conducts a field interview during her unit's annual training at Fort Drum, NY, May 1982. (US Army photo)

The ROTC cadet shown here is typical of the young men and women who have taken advantage of the Army Reserve's Simultaneous Membership Program, which allows a Senior ROTC cadet to enlist in an Army Reserve unit at the same time he or she is attending college. The cadet receives both Army Reserve drill pay and pay for Annual Training, in addition to cadet allowances. (US Army photo)

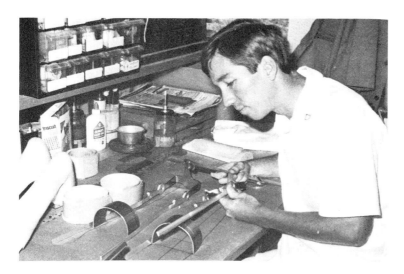

An Army Reserve orthopedic specialist assembles a leg brace during training at Walter Reed Army Medical Center, Washington, DC. Many of the skills taught to Army Reservists are directly transferrable to civilian employment opportunities. (US Army photo)

While other crew members watch, the section chief repairs the firing mechanism of an 8-inch self-propelled howitzer during his unit's annual training at Fort Drum, NY, in 1982. (US Army photo)

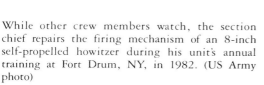

The Army Reserve celebrated its 75th Birthday on April 23, 1983, with a cake-cutting ceremony at the Pentagon. Shown here is Lt. Col. D. Y. Dunn, 92-year old retired Army Reservist, who represented the oldest group of those who have served in the USAR. Behind Dunn is Eric Heginbotham, whose swearing-in at the ceremony made him the newest Army Reservist. (US Army photo)

9

The Army Reserve and Vietnam

The 1968 decision to mobilize units of the Army Reserve came three years after Secretary of Defense Robert McNamara first raised the idea with President Lyndon Johnson. In May and June of 1965 South Vietnamese forces suffered a string of defeats, and in July the Defense Secretary went to Vietnam on a fact-finding mission. McNamara returned with a recommendation that the number of US personnel in Vietnam be raised immediately from 75,000 to 175,000, with an increase to 275,000 early in 1966. A large part of this increased strength in Vietnam would come from the Army's Reserve Components, from which McNamara wanted to call up 125,000 men.[1]

The question of calling up the reserves was only a part of the much broader debate that went on with the Johnson administration. Indeed, the critical decision in July 1965 was whether to pull out of Vietnam entirely, to maintain the current level of involvement, or to "give our commanders in the field the men and supplies they say they need."[2]

In examining the various options, wrote Lyndon Johnson in his autobiographical account of his Presidency, "I realized what a major undertaking it [McNamara's proposal] would be. The call-up of a large number of reserves was part

---

1. Col. Donald C. Odegard, *Non-Mobilization and Mobilization in the Vietnam War (Draft Report of the Study Group) 10 January 1980* (Carlisle Barracks, Penn.: Strategic Studies Institute, US Army War College), pp. 13–15.

2. *Ibid.*, p. 16.

of the package. This would require a great deal of money and a huge sacrifice for the American people."[3] Johnson thereupon summoned a group of what he called his "top advisors" to the White House on July 21, 1965, the day after McNamara's return from Vietnam.[4] After a series of meetings that included General Earl C. Wheeler, Chairman of the Joint Chiefs of Staff, President Johnson had made his decision.

I had concluded that the last course [expanding the number of men and amount of materiel in Vietnam] was the right one. I had listened to and weighed all the arguments and counter-arguments for each of the possible lines of action. I believed that we should do what was necessary to resist aggression but that we would not be provoked into a major war. We would get the required appropriation in the new budget, and we would not boast about what we were doing. We would not make threatening noises to the Chinese or the Russians by calling up reserves in large numbers.[5]

After what amounted to a perfunctory discussion with Congressional leaders, Johnson made part of his decision public in a July 28 press conference at the White House. "I had asked the Commanding General, General [William C.] Westmoreland, what more he needs to meet this mounting aggression. He has told me. We will meet his needs." Johnson went on to say that he was increasing the number of troops in Vietnam from 75,000 to 125,000. "Additional forces will be needed later," he said, "and they will be sent as requested." He was raising the monthly draft calls from 17,000 to 35,000 men, stated the President, but he had concluded that it was "not essential to order Reserve units into service now. If that necessity should later be indicated, I will give the matter most careful consideration and I will give the country—you—an adequate notice before taking such action, but only after full preparations."[6]

Johnson was doing everything he could to minimize the impact of his decision, even to the extent of not revealing the full measure of it. He said he had rejected the idea

---

3. Lyndon B. Johnson, *The Vantage Point: Perspectives of the Presidency, 1963–1969* (New York, Chicago, and San Francisco: Holt, Rinehart, and Winston, 1971), pp. 146–47.

4. *Ibid.*, p. 147.

5. *Ibid.*, p. 149.

6. *Public Papers of the Presidents of the United States. Lyndon B. Johnson, Containing the Public Messages, Speeches, and Statements of the President, 1965, II* (Washington: GPO, 1966), p. 795.

of declaring a national emergency—which was a necessary prerequisite to calling up the Reserves—because he saw no reason for it. In answer to a question from the press, the President indicated that he did not want to choose between guns and butter, but would have the government do all it could to continue the "unparalleled period of prosperity."[7]

There was at the press conference no discussion of why the Reserve components were not being called up for Vietnam, and Johnson did not mention the subject in his autobiography. As mentioned previously, General Earl C. Wheeler, Chairman of the Joint Chiefs of Staff, was present for at least one of the White House meetings in late July. Research conducted by the Historical Division of the Joint Chiefs has not, however, discovered any evidence that the topic of Reserve mobilization was discussed at the July meeting from the standpoint of military efficacy.[8]

The best historical judgment of the decision not to employ Reserve Component units—particularly the Army Reserve and the Army National Guard—in Vietnam is that Johnson had made an almost purely political decision. Lyndon Johnson was gradually involving the United States in a land war in Asia, yet he was disguising his every move. The short-range success with which he accomplished this goal was exemplified by a front page headline in the next day's *New York Times:* "Most in Congress Relieved by the President's Course."[9] There was "general satisfaction" in the Congress, reported E. W. Kenworthy for the *Times,* "that the President had decided to increase the draft and postpone a decision on calling up reserve units." The President had become "increasingly sensitive," reported the *Times,* "to the possible political effects of a reserve call-up." Thirty-three House Democrats confirmed the political repercussions of Reserve forces mobilization, saying that they had been getting "'heavy flak' from families that would be affected by a reserve call-up."[10]

Calling-up the Reserve Components, stated one study of this period, would not have been consistent with John-

7. *Ibid.,* p. 800.

8. *The History of the Joint Chiefs of Staff. The Joint Chiefs of Staff and the War in Vietnam, 1960–1968,* Part II. (Top Secret). (Unpublished work: Historical Division, Joint Secretariat. Joint Chiefs of Staff, 1 July 1970). See especially Chapter 22, "Growth of Forces in RVN to End of 1965."

9. *New York Times,* July 29, 1965, p. 1.

10. *Ibid.,* pp. 1, 11.

son's attempts to portray Vietnam as "a limited war of short
duration which could be fought with little domestic disloca-
tion and without interfering with his administration's war
on poverty."[11] Another author described the process somewhat more cynically:

He was using force but using it discreetly, and he was also handling the military. They were moving toward war, but in such
imperceptible degrees that neither the Congress nor the press
could ever show a quantum jump. All the decisions were being
cleverly hidden; he was cutting it thin to hold off opposition. If
there were no decisions which were crystallized and hard, then
they could not leak, and if they could not leak, then the opposition could not point to them. Which was why he was not about
to call up the reserves, because the use of the reserves would blow
it all. It would be self-evident that we were really going to war,
and that we would in fact have to pay a price. Which went
against all the Administration planning: this would be a war
without a price, a silent, politically invisible war.[12]

Whether a substantial mobilization of the Army Reserve and Army National Guard—McNamara had suggested
125,000 men—in 1965 would have made any difference in
Vietnam is certainly open to debate. McNamara's attempt to
merge the two components had been squelched by the Congress, but the Army Reserve was still in a state of
McNamara-induced turmoil; the Army National Guard was
undoubtedly in better condition for mobilization.[13] From a
purely military point of view, 125,000 men could have been
sent to Vietnam much quicker by mobilizing the Army Reserve and the Army National Guard than was possible
through the long, slow process of the draft. No one knows
whether this would have made any significant difference in
the military outcome in Vietnam, but a Reserve forces call-
up would almost certainly have precipitated a closer public
and Congressional scrutiny of the war itself. As Baskir and
Strauss put it, "Reservists and guardsmen were better connected, better educated, more affluent, and whiter than
their peers in the active forces, and the administration

---

11. Lawrence M. Baskir and William A. Strauss, *Chance and Circumstance: The Draft, the War, and the Vietnam Generation* (New York: Alfred A. Knopf, 1978), p. 50.

12. David Halberstam, *The Best and The Brightest* (New York: Random House, 1969, 1971, 1972), p. 593.

13. Odegard, *Non-Mobilization and Mobilization,* pp. 9–10, 15.

feared that mobilizing them would heighten public opposition to the war."[14]

The US role in Vietnam grew ever-broader in the 2½
years following the July 28, 1965, announcement. The
number of Army troops in Vietnam rose steadily all during
this period, but the increase in active duty strength came
almost exclusively from draftees and draft-motivated volunteers. In 1966 and 1967—as in 1965—the Johnson administration was unwilling to admit publicly that Vietnam was
anything other than a limited war of short duration. That it
had been going on for years before the US ever thought of
getting involved was not considered relevant by Johnson and
his advisors.

In the years from 1965 to 1968 it became even more
politically difficult to consider a Reserve call-up, because the
Reserve components had become havens for those who
wanted to avoid active military duty—and Vietnam. According to Baskir and Strauss, who wrote what is perhaps
the most comprehensive book on the draft and its effects
during this time, "A 1966 Pentagon study found that 71
percent of all reservists were draft-motivated," and anyone
who was associated with any of the Reserve Components
during those years can remember the long lists of men who
wanted to join the unit.[15]

THE RUSSELL AMENDMENT

Even as it became more politically difficult to call-up the
Reserves, however, it became legally easier. Under the
Armed Forces Reserve Act of 1952, a Presidential declara-
tion of emergency was required before Reserve components
could be ordered to active duty. To the Fiscal Year 1967
Department of Defense Appropriation Act, however, Senator
Richard B. Russell (D–Ga) added the "Russell Amendment," which gave the President the authority, until June
30, 1968, to "order to active duty any unit of the Ready
Reserve of an armed force for a period of not to exceed
twenty-four months."[16] A June 1967 amendment to the
Universal Military Training and Service Act gave the President authority to order non-unit members of the Ready Re-

---

14. Baskir and Strauss, *Chance and Circumstance,* p. 50.
15. *Ibid.,* p. 51.
16. Public Law 89–687, October 15, 1966.

serve to active duty until they had completed a total of twenty-four months service.[17]

This expanded legal authority for the President did not make the political decision any more palatable, however, so all through 1965, 1966, and 1967 Reservists sat at home and draftees went to Vietnam. This was almost the exact opposite of the first year in Korea, when Army Reservists and National Guardsmen had borne the burden with the members of the active components. This is not to imply that Army Reservists were not fighting in Vietnam during these three years, because most of the officers on active duty with the Army held Reserve commissions, the product of the Army's ROTC programs. Members of Army Reserve units, however, as well as members of the Individual Ready Reserve, were not sent to Vietnam during these three years.[18]

PUEBLO AND TET

The next year—1968—was to prove different, however, though not as different as it might have been. The year began most inauspiciously for the United States when the North Koreans seized the *U.S.S. Pueblo,* a Navy spy ship, off the coast of North Korea on January 23. Two days later President Johnson used the authority given him by the Russell Amendment (Public Law 89–687) to mobilize twenty-eight units of the Air Force Reserve, Air National Guard, and Naval Reserve. This mobilization had nothing directly to do with Vietnam, though some of these men were eventually sent to Southeast Asia.[19]

Less than a week after the *Pueblo* incident the North Vietnamese launched their Tet Offensive. Tet was a military defeat for the North Vietnamese, but it was a psychological

---

17. Public Law 90–40, June 30, 1967.

18. In a unique exception to the usual pattern, thirteen second lieutenants with USAR commissions were called to active duty in 1966 from the 4th Bn, 198th Artillery (AW) (SP), Delaware National Guard. These individuals had incurred an active duty obligation as a result of their ROTC commissioning, and they were called-up as individual Army Reservists, despite their being in the National Guard. One of these men was 2Lt. Richard B. Crossland, co-author of this study.

19. Odegard, *Non-Mobilization and Mobilization,* pp. 43–44; "Where Are They Now? Activated Reservists Just Waiting Around," *Wall Street Journal,* March 15, 1968, p. 1; Major John D. Williams, "Public Affairs Aspects of the 1968 Reserve Mobilization," *Air University Review/Air Force Review,* November-December 1971, pp. 59, 63.

defeat for the United States, coming as it did when US officials were proclaiming that the Viet Cong and North Vietnamese were on the verge of military collapse.[20]

According to General William C. Westmoreland, the US Commander in Vietnam, the Tet Offensive "had at last presented the right opportunity" for calling-up the Reserves. Westmoreland, who states in his autobiography that he had earlier opposed a Reserve mobilization, now felt that "with additional strength and removal of the old restrictive policy, we could deal telling blows—physically and psychologically—well within the time frame of the reservists' one-year tour. The time had come to prepare and commit the Reserve."[21]

PLANNING FOR MOBILIZATION

US forces in Vietnam at the time numbered about 500,000 of the 525,000 approved to that point by the President. General Westmoreland wanted 10,000 more troops sent to Vietnam immediately. In response to a request from Secretary of Defense McNamara, the Joint Chiefs of Staff began to look at various possibilities for reinforcing Westmoreland, including Army, Navy, Air Force and Marine Corps assets in their deliberations. The Army Staff worked feverishly to develop force structure packages in support of overall JCS goals, but the Army planners were severely handicapped by several factors. First, time pressures were enormous. During the eleven-week planning period the Assistant Chief of Staff for Force Development (ACSFOR) issued some seventy-five different force packages, generally under such short suspenses that there was often no time to coordinate them with anyone outside the DA staff.[22]

Coordination was effected, however, with the Office of Reserve Components (ORC), the Chief, Army Reserve (CAR), and the Chief, National Guard Bureau (CNGB). Because of what was described as "the need to maintain security," however, ORC was not allowed to contact the Continental United States Armies, US Army Reserve Commanders, or State Adjutants General. Data on which to base the various force packages, then, had to be compiled from information on hand in

---

20. Odegard, *Non-Mobilization and Mobilization*, p. 44.

21. General William C. Westmoreland, *A Soldier Reports* (Garden City, NY: Doubleday Co., Inc., 1976), pp. 193, 354.

22. Department of the Army, *After Action Report: Mobilization of Reserve Forces, 1968* (Declassified from Secret), pp. 1–1, 1–2.

the Army Staff offices. A further problem, which aggravated
the situation at the Department of the Army level, was that
the Army's Reserve Components had begun a major reorganization on December 1, 1967, a reorganization that was not completed until May 31, 1968.[23]

All of this frenetic activity at the Army Staff level was
in turn being driven by political and other decisions being
made higher up. The Joint Chiefs of Staff, for example, was
busily considering three different overall plans for the mobilization, with a total strength mix ranging from 90,000 to
126,000 men.[24]

The question of mobilizing the Reserve Components
was top-most in the minds of the JCS, because only through
such a mobilization could the United States maintain any
sort of strategic reserve, if additional active forces were sent
to Vietnam. The JCS had long been urging a Reserve forces
mobilization, and the JCS recommendation, which General
Wheeler offered in a February 12 meeting with the President, was that "Deployment of emergency reinforcements to
Vietnam should not be made without concomitant call up of
Reserves sufficient at least to replace those deployed and provide for the increased sustaining base requirements of all
services."[25]

Defense Secretary McNamara, however, had done a
turnaround from his 1965 advocacy of a Reserve call-up.
McNamara had gotten his knuckles rapped for his earlier
position, and he now opposed mobilization of the Reserves
for Vietnam duty. President Johnson asked McNamara and
Wheeler to "study the problem further and to agree on a
recommendation."[26] The Secretary of Defense was not prepared to wait for JCS agreement with his position. Instead,
he immediately recommended, and President Johnson ordered, the deployment to Vietnam of one brigade of the
82nd Airborne Division and a Marine regimental landing
team—a total of 10,500 men.[27] The Joint Chiefs thereupon
urged on February 13 the call-up of 32,000 Army Reserve

---

    23. *Ibid.,* p. 1–2.
    24. *Ibid.,* p. 1–5.
    25. Quoted in *United States-Vietnam Relations, 1945–1967,* Vol 5,
Printed for the use of the House Committee on Armed Services (Wash-
ington: GPO, 1971), iv.c.6.(c), p.3. The twelve volumes of this set com-
prise the "Pentagon Papers."
    26. Johnson, *Vantage Point,* p. 386.
    27. JCS Msg 9926, 130218Z Feb 68, Subject: "Deployment of
Brigade Task Force of 82nd Airborne Division to SVN (S)," cited in
United States-Vietnam Relations, Vol. 5, iv.c.6.(c), p.6.

Component, 12,000 Marine Corps Reserve, and 2,300 Naval Reserve personnel. The Army personnel were needed, stated the JCS, "to replace the forces deployed from the strategic reserve, to provide support units to meet anticipation requirements in I CTZ and to provide a wider rotation base of requisite ranks and skills."[28]

According to President Johnson's account, McNamara and Wheeler continued to disagree on the question of a Reserve forces call-up.[29] McNamara's tenure ended on February 28, however, and he was replaced by Clark Clifford, who was believed at the time to be more inclined to mobilize the Reserves. At the same time, General Wheeler returned from a trip to Vietnam and presented Westmoreland's request for 206,000 additional troops.[30]

For the next month the President and his advisors considered various levels of reinforcement for Vietnam, and with every change of nuance a new force structure package had to be developed by the Army Staff. On March 31, President Johnson announced in a nation-wide television address that he would not run for re-election.[31] The last real political obstacle to a Reserve-forces call-up for Vietnam had now been removed. The final troop list was submitted to the JCS on April 2 and was based on the mobilization of 54,000 men in three increments, a total far short of the number Westmoreland had said he needed. The total of 54,000 men was modest enough in itself, but even this figure would not stand for long. Just two days later, Secretary of Defense Clifford stated that this option was too expensive, and he pared the call-up to only the first increment. A final revised troop list was prepared by April 8, calling for the mobilization of seventy-six Army Reserve Component units with a total of 20,034 personnel, not all of whom would go to Vietnam. It was this list that the Secretary of Defense announced in an April 11 press conference.[32]

---

28. JCSM 96–68, 13 Feb 68, Subject: "Emergency Reinforcement of COMUSMACV (C)." quoted in *United States-Vietnam Relations*. Vol.5, iv.c.6.(c), pp. 7–8.

29. Johnson, *Vantage Point*, p. 387.

30. Odegard, *Non-Mobilization and Mobilization*. pp. 44–45.

31. *Public Papers of the Presidents of the United States. Lyndon B. Johnson. Containing the Public Messages. Speeches. and Statements of the President. 1968–69. Book I* (Washington: GPO, 1970), p. 476.

32. *After Action Report: Mobilization of Reserve Forces. 1978*. p. 1–5; OSD Memorandum for Secretaries of the Military Departments and Chairman of the Joint Chiefs of Staff, April 4, 1968, Subject: "Reserve Recall," cited in Odegard, *Non-Mobilization and Mobilization*. p. 46.

202   TWICE THE CITIZEN: A HISTORY OF THE USAR, 1908–1983

The final selection of types of Reserve units was based
on specific requirements set forth by the US commander in
Vietnam, plus units needed to reconstitute the Strategic
Army Forces. The threat of civil disturbances was a major
factor in the elimination of particular National Guard units
from consideration, though it had no bearing at all on the
units of the Army Reserve. The DA goal was to select Army
Reserve and National Guard units based upon the propor-
tional strengths of the two components, and the final mix-
ture of 31.9 percent USAR to 68.1 percent ARNG compared with actual force percentages of 40 percent to 60
percent. Units were spread geographically as much as possible, the final troop list representing thirty-four states. Every
attempt was made at Department of the Army level to select
the most operationally ready units of each type required, but
a lack of up-to-date information hindered this effort. Of the
seventy-six Army Reserve Component units in the final
troop list, fifty-nine were current or former members of the
Selected Reserve Force (SRF); two units had no SRF counterpart. The other fifteen units were selected after considering
such factors as readiness status, location (for geographic balance), civil disturbance role, command and control requirements, and length of time the unit had been organized.[33]

The irony was that after all the planning and changing
and revising and considering of the proper mix of units
needed for support of the war in Vietnam, the total of seventy units mobilized was decided in the end by financial
considerations. "The major factor governing the final decision on the size of the force in the 1968 Partial Mobilization," concluded the Army's official after action report, "was
. . . the financial support required for such a force and not
operational requirements for additional forces to cope with a
worsening world military situation."[34] Lyndon Johnson had
apparently concluded that the American people could not
continue to have both guns and butter, and he was therefore
cutting back on the rate of procuring the guns.

THE USAR MOBILIZATION

Regardless of the reasons that went into their selection,
forty-two units of the Army Reserve were mobilized in this
relatively-small call-up. The types of units are shown in
Table 9–1.

33. *After Action Report: Mobilization of Reserve Forces, 1968,* pp. 1–6
to 1–8.
34. *Ibid.,* p. 1–5.

Table 9–1   USAR Units Mobilized.[35]

Type Unit	Number	Total Auth Strength
Inf Bn	1	782
MI Det	2	64
AG Units	4	190
Composite Svc Units	8	1,552
Med Units	11	667
Fin Units	1	40
Ord Units	2	313
QM Units	3	457
Trans Units	10	1,814
Total	42	5,869

Most of the members of these units first learned of their call to duty through the media, rather than through official Army notification channels. According to the Army's after action report, the Department of Defense had prohibited DA from following the procedures developed and prescribed after the 1961 mobilization. "This action," concluded the report, "caused confusion, embarrassed field commanders and contributed to a general feeling of consternation among many reservists."[36]

Nevertheless, over 5000 Army Reservists reported to their home stations (see Appendix C) on May 13, 1968, and within a week they were on their way to active Army mobilization stations. There was considerable local publicity given the mobilized units, and in at least one instance there were special ceremonies to mark the mobilization. When the 737th Transportation Co (Med Truck Petr) left Yakima, Washington, for Fort Lewis on the morning of May 14, the town of Yakima was ready. From 8:30 a.m. to 9:00 a.m. the men of the 737th were treated to a special "send-off" party by the Greater Yakima Chamber of Commerce, attended by "mothers, wives, children, relatives, girl friends, and citizens." Music was provided by the Davis High School Band.[37] Other Army Reserve units may not have received

35. *Annual Historical Summary, RCS–CSHIS–6 (RZ), Office of the Chief, Army Reserve, 1 July 1967 to 30 June 1968,* Part I, p. 3. A complete listing of these units, with their home stations, is at Appendix C. The figure of forty-five USAR units mobilized is sometimes seen. This figure refers to "company/detachment" size units and as such counts the 100th Bn, 442nd Inf as four units (HHC and three line companies).

36. *After Action Report: Mobilization of Reserve Forces, 1968,* p. 2–1.

37. "737th Mobilizes at Center" and "737th Earns Proud Sendoff from Yakima," both in *Yakima Herald-Republic,* May 14 and 15, 1968.

such fanfare, but they convoyed to their mobilization stations nevertheless, and for the next three to seven months underwent the training needed to make them of maximum value in Vietnam.

Few of these Army Reserve units had 100 percent of their authorized strength, so the Department of the Army had to find filler personnel for them. There had been no national emergency declared in conjunction with the call-up, so there were in reality few options within the Army Reserve system. One primary source of fillers for the mobilized units was to be found among certain Reserve Enlistment Program— 1963 (REP–63) personnel in the Individual Ready Reserve (IRR). Some 4,132 of these men had enlisted for a six-year hitch in the Army Reserve, and after their initial active duty for training, they were obligated for 5½ years of satisfactory unit membership. For one reason or another, however, they had been transferred to the IRR, and they were fair game for a call-up.[38]

Of the 4,132 REP–63 personnel who were screened for active duty orders, 1,380 were exempted from call-up for reasons ranging from hardship and dependency (371) to inability to locate them (325). Eventually, 1,692 IRR personnel were assigned to the mobilized USAR units, and 1,060 were given assignments with the active Army. Over 1,800 enlisted vacancies in the Army Reserve units were filled with active Army personnel, as were any officer vacancies.[39]

Army Reserve units––even those in the SRF––had never received all of the equipment required by their TOE, and the forty-two mobilized units were no exception. By July 12, however, all mobilized units had received equipment necessary to bring them to a C–1 Readiness Condition. According to the after action report, "No significant [equipment] problems occurred after that date."[40]

The standard training week for the mobilized units was forty-four hours long. General training guidance was provided by DA for all units, while the thirty-five Vietnam-bound units were given additional training, including a minimum of sixteen hours with the M16 rifle.[41] There were few complaints from Army Reservists who claimed they were not being given meaningful training or things to do,

38. *After Action Report: Mobilization of Reserve Forces, 1968*, p. 3–10.
39. *Ibid.*, pp. 3–11, 3–3, 4–7.
40. *Ibid.*, p. 3–4.
41. *Ibid.*, p. 3–6.

in marked contrast to many such complaints from the Air
Force and Navy Reservists who had been mobilized earlier in
the year.

CHALLENGES TO MOBILIZATION

This is not to say, however, that there were *no* complaints
from the Army Reservists. When Rep. Charles A. Vanik visited the Fort Meade, Maryland, training site of the 1002d
Supply and Service Company from Cleveland, Ohio, members of the unit complained to him about "the lack of combat training, pass policies, laxity in the conduct of physical
training tests, and low morale."[42]

Other major Congressional interest in the mobilization
came from the Senate delegation from Massachusetts, composed of Edward Kennedy and Edward Brooke. As early as
May 27, barely two weeks after reporting for duty, eighty-
eight enlisted members of the HHC, 513th Maintenance
Battalion, signed a letter of complaint to Sen. Brooke.
These men charged that the 513th was not prepared for active duty, much less for deployment to Vietnam, and should
not have been mobilized. The Army response was that "At
the time of selection the 513th was the best qualified unit
of the six available in the US Army Reserve."[43]

Controversy surrounding the 513th continued later,
however, when sixteen members of the unit filed suit in US
District Court in Baltimore charging that they had not received all of their mandatory training.[44] Senator Kennedy
asked the Army to postpone the 513th's deployment after
sixty-seven additional units members corroborated the complaints of the sixteen men who had filed the suit. Kennedy
asked Secretary of the Army Stanley R. Resor to "conduct a
full and prompt investigation" of the claims and to "keep
this unit available until an appropriate inquiry is satisfactorily completed." Resor declined Kennedy's request, and a
spokesman stated that the Army had investigated "as far as

42. *Ibid.*, p. 3–16.
43. DF, CAR to CORC, June 12, 1968, Subject: "Mobilization of
the 513 CS Bn," with enclosures, found in Records of the Chief, Army
Reserve, Washington National Records Center, Suitland, Maryland, Ac-
cession No. 71A–3109, 402–05, "Congressional Correspondence, 68,
A–G."
44. "Boston Reservists Fight Viet Duty," *Boston Herald-Traveler,*
October 4, 1968, p. 1.

they're going to and as far as they are concerned, it's a closed case."[45]

Both political and legal challenges failed, however, as the US Supreme Court, in an 8–1 decision from which Justice William O. Douglas dissented, turned down the plea from members of the 513th and five other Army Reserve units. A total of 256 plaintiffs had joined in the suit, which had two major claims: (1) that in being called-up for twenty-four months they were not given credit for active duty time already served and (2) that they could only be called up after a declaration of national emergency. The plaintiffs were thus challenging the constitutionality of the Russell Amendment.[46]

THE VIETNAM EXPERIENCE

The 513th—all 251 members of it—did go to Vietnam, as did the members of thirty-four other units of the Army Reserve. In December 1982 Lewis C. Brodsky, Chief of Public Affairs for the Office of the Chief, Army Reserve, sent letters to each of these units, asking for their help in compiling the story of the Army Reserve in Vietnam.[47] Many units responded to this request with newspaper clippings, letters of commendation, general orders, unit lineages, after action reports and other documents generated during or immediately after their tour of duty in 1968–69. Together with information gleaned from other sources, this material has allowed at least a paragraph or two to be written about many of the Army Reserve units that went to Vietnam, and these narratives are contained in Appendix C. There are many common threads of experience that run throughout the record of these units, and the author does not believe that focusing on the particularly units about which information could be obtained will lead to an erroneous impression

45. "Ted Pleads for Boston Reservists," *Boston Herald-Traveler*, October 8, 1968, p. 1.

46. "Dissidents in Uniform: Supreme Court Rejects Challenge," *Boston Herald-Traveler*, October 8, 1968, p. 1; other units which had members who joined the suit were the 1002d Sup and Svc Co. (Cleveland, Oh), 448th Army Postal Unit (New York, NY), 1018th Sup and Svc Co. (Schenectady, NY), 74th Field Hospital (New York, NY), and the 173d Petr Co (Greenwood, Miss.). These cases were styled *Morse et al.* v. *Boswell et al.; Berke et al.* v. *MacLaughlin; Felberbaum et al.* v. *MacLaughlin;* and *Looney et al.* v. *MacLaughlin* (393 U.S. 802) (1968).

47. Letter, Lewis C. Brodsky, Chief, Public Affairs Office, to thirty-five addressees, December 10, 1982, Subject: "Request for Historical Information," copies in OCAR Historical Files.

of the role and performance of the Army Reserve in Vietnam.

The stories of the Army Reserve units in Vietnam are varied, but they offer a number of common elements. First, the units themselves were not nearly ready for active participation in the Vietnam War when they were mobilized in May 1968. It required months—sometimes up to six or seven months—of intensive training before the thirty-five units were ready to go to Vietnam. Many of the Army Reserve units that were chosen for the 1968 mobilization had only recently undergone TOE changes, and some of them had changed from one branch of the Army to another.

The maturity of the individuals in the USAR units and the esprit of the unit personnel were major factors in making up for the lack of long-term technical expertise. Most of the men and women in the Army Reserve were older than the typical draftee, and the Army Reservist, if the fragmentary statistics on discipline, AWOL, and courts martial are representative, was less likely to become involved in criminal activities than was the draftee. The personnel of the Army Reserve units were likewise determined to prove to the active Army—and perhaps to themselves as well—that they were as good as anyone in uniform. And they did just that in Vietnam, for Army Reserve units were constantly being lauded and decorated by the men under whom they served.

Members of the thirty-five USAR units in Vietnam received 277 Certificates of Achievement and the following other awards:

Silver Star 1
Legion of Merit 5
Bronze Star 384
Air Medal 7
Army Commendation Medal 779
Purple Heart 20

Additionally, the 231st Transportation Company, Fltg Cft, from St. Petersburg, Florida, was selected as the Army's outstanding transportation unit in Vietnam and received the National Defense Transportation Award. Two Army Reserve units were recommended for the Presidential Unit Citation, thirteen for the Meritorious Unit Citation, and one for the Unit Cross of Gallantry (Vietnam).[48]

---

48. "Awards for Vietnam Service," *The Army Reserve Magazine,* January 1970, p. 7.

208   TWICE THE CITIZEN: A HISTORY OF THE USAR, 1908–1983

There were some problems with Army Reserve units in Vietnam, but they were not problems caused by the units themselves. The biggest gripe from unit personnel was the Army's policy of "infusion," i.e., of taking members out of USAR units and replacing them with non-unit personnel.

As the French military thinker Ardant Du Picq stated:

Four brave men who do not know each other will not dare to attack a lion. Four less brave, but knowing each other well, sure of their reliability and consequently of mutual aid will attack resolutely. There is the science of the organization of armies in a nutshell.[49]

One of the primary strengths of the Army Reserve units in Vietnam was that the men and women in the units knew each other well. Indeed, through years of training together they had developed the highest possible level of esprit, and they were not afraid to "attack a lion" once they got to Vietnam. "Fusion," however, whatever its merits as a means of distributing the individuals with particular Special Skill Identifiers among units or of preventing home-town tragedies, was a destroyer of the esprit built up among the Army Reservists.

The US Army could well have learned a lesson from the British in this regard, for the British Army has long recognized the value of unit integrity and unit identification as a motivator, and even as a means of enhancing combat effectiveness. The US Army now seems with its active Army unit identification system to have taken a step in this direction. The Army Reserve's experiences in Vietnam should serve to confirm and strengthen this trend.

CONCLUSION

The final question that can be asked about the Army Reserve's role in Vietnam is whether it made any difference or not. The individuals and the units mobilized did an "outstanding" job, to use that over-worn Army phrase. The Army Reservists in Vietnam, however, were only a small fraction—less than 5 percent—of the total Army force involved there. They did their jobs, and they did them well.

49. Col. Ardant Du Picq, *Battle Studies: Ancient and Modern Battle.* Translated by Col. John N. Greely and Maj. Robert C. Cotton (New York: Macmillan Company, 1921), p. 110.

But whether they made any *real* difference in the war is debatable.

As this chapter is being written (1983), the United States has just passed through a major transition period on the subject of Vietnam. The Vietnam Memorial has become one of the must-see places on the Mall in Washington, and Vietnam veterans are getting some belated recognition and attention and help. Although the individual members of the Army Reserve who went to Vietnam may have done their duty in anonymity, the men and women of the units mobilized in 1968 and returned from Vietnam in 1969 generally experienced a reception much more akin to that following World War II, when Johnny and Jane came marching home to a hero's or heroine's reception.

If some Army Reservists were subjected to scorn and hostility, most received welcomes like those in Yakima, Washington, or Provo, Utah. Their communities greeted their return as American towns and cities have long greeted returning veterans: with bands and flags and parades. If the public had turned against the war in Vietnam by 1969, the communities where there were Army Reserve units had not turned against their men and women in uniform, just because the War was an unpopular one. It had been a long time in happening, but the Army Reserve unit had become an integral part of the community in much of small-town America, and these true citizen-soldiers were very much in the mainstream of community life and consciousness.

Indeed, the growing involvement of the Army Reserve could well have been the key to what might have been a different course for the Vietnam War. Hindsight is always speculative, of course, but if in 1965 President Johnson had decided to fight the Vietnam War with Reserve Component forces, rather than draftees, he would have been forced to ask for explicit Congressional authorization. The Gulf of Tonkin Resolution, which provided the legal basis for Johnson's actions on Vietnam, would not have given him sufficient authority to call up the Reserve Components without declaring a national emergency. The whole question of our involvement in Vietnam might have been subjected to the sort of public and Congressional debate that never really occurred. Such a debate might well have revealed the painfully learned truth that there was not a deep and enduring national resolve on the question of Vietnam, and it might have foreshortened the US involvement in the war. It would not have been as easy to call up the Reserves as it was to increase the draft calls, and in the history of the Vietnam War, the decision not to mobilize the Army's Reserve Components in 1965 may have been Lyndon Johnson's key decision. Indeed, the Army Reserve ought not to be too easy to mobilize, lest it be used before the crisis has been properly considered. Once a national consensus is reached, however, and the Congress and the President agree on US objectives, the Army Reserve should be ready and able to do its part. Vietnam proves both the truth and the tragedy of this thesis.

10

Toward Greater Partnership

The Army's ability to fight a war without the Reserves is zero. This sums up Lt. Gen. William R. Richardson's remarks to the Association of the United States Army in October 1982 and illustrates the vital role of the Army Reserve in the early 1980's.[1] Only a few years earlier, in spite of the fine performance of duty in Vietnam by the 35 Army Reserve units that were sent to Southeast Asia in 1968, it would have been more accurate to say that the Army Reserve's ability to go to war was near zero.

The Army Reserve ended the 1960's in disrepair and disarray. The Reserve leadership, with the substantial aid of the Reserve Officers Association (ROA), had just fought off Secretary of Defense Robert S. McNamara's attempt to merge the Army Reserve with the National Guard. The Reserve had been stripped of essential materiel for the Vietnam War, and Reservists were characterized as summer soldiers— draft-dodgers in the eyes of some Regulars—who had avoided Vietnam combat through Reserve membership. This innuendo was directed at the Army Reserve even though more than 130,000 Army Reservists were serving on active duty in 1969 at the peak of America's involvement in Vietnam.[2]

---

1. Faith Faircloth, "AUSA Panelists Focus on Reserve Readiness," *ARNEWS*, Release No. 407, Department of the Army, Washington, DC, 1982.

2. *Department of Defense Selected Manpower Statistics, Fiscal Year 1982,* (Washington, DC: Department of Defense, 1983), pp. 199–200.

In addition, more than 70 percent of the Army's Reserve Centers were inadequate,[3] and proper facilities for field training were few and far between. The Army Reserve's share of the Army's budget had fallen to 1.6 percent in 1967 and 1968, the lowest share since the Korean War.[4]

In little more than a decade, from 1969 until today, the Army Reserve underwent a major transformation and emerged as an essential partner in the Total Army. The precipitating event for this transformation was the decision to end the draft in favor of an all-volunteer force, while the event leading up to the formation of the Rapid Deployment Joint Task Force (RDJTF) hammered home the need for a strong Army Reserve.[5]

The policy responsible for the recent enhancement of the Army Reserve—the Total Force Policy—was publicly announced on September 8, 1970, but the genesis of the Total Force Policy came earlier from the decision to achieve an all-volunteer military force. According to a comprehensive study of this subject, "The failure of Congress and the Johnson Administration to reform the draft in 1967 was important to the evolution of the All Volunteer Force. That failure, continued high draft calls, and increased opposition to the war and draft assured that the draft would be a major issue during the 1968 presidential campaign."[6]

Sensing a winning issue, Richard M. Nixon campaigned on the theme of ending the draft, and Nixon's election brought to the White House a man who favored draft reform and a volunteer military.[7] On March 27, 1969, two months after assuming office, President Nixon appointed an Advisory Commission on an All-Volunteer Armed Force under the chairmanship of Thomas S. Gates, Jr., a former Secretary of Defense.

Nixon directed the commission to develop a comprehensive plan to eliminate conscription and move toward an

3. *Annual Report of the Secretary of Defense on Reserve Forces, Fiscal Year 1970,* (Washington, DC: Department of Defense), p. 20.

4. *Annual Historical Supplements,* Chief Office of Reserve Components (CORC) for 1967 and 1968. Also, *OSD Project 80 Report,* Chart 10.

5. For an expansion upon this point, see "RDJTF: Can It Get There Without the USAR?", *Army Reserve Magazine,* (Spring 1982), pp. 8–10.

6. Gus C. Lee and Geoffrey Y. Parker, *Ending the Draft: The Story of the All Volunteer Force,* (Alexandria, Va.: Human Resources Research Organization), p. 29.

7. *Ibid.,* p. 31.

all-volunteer force. The commission was asked to study a broad range of incentives to make military careers more attractive, and the entire issue of a voluntary military was given a high priority within the Nixon administration.[8]

One important point to remember is that Nixon directed the commission to study *how* the All-Volunteer Force was to be achieved, and not *whether* it should be achieved. On February 20, 1970, Gates reported to the President that the commission unanimously believed that the nation's interests would be better served by an All-Volunteer Force than by a mixed force of conscripts and volunteers. The commission was satisfied that such a volunteer force would not jeopardize national security.[9]

In making detailed recommendations to the President, the commission made little mention of the Reserve Components. The emphasis was upon the active forces, where substantially increased pay for junior members was supposed to make the military competitive with civilian industry. The commission recommended that the draft authority be terminated by July 1, 1971, and that $3.3 billion in military pay increases be placed in the 1971 Defense budget.[10]

In its February 1970 report, the commission recognized that the Reserve Components would need special attention in an all-volunteer era but that a lack of data made it difficult to assess the impact of the volunteer army upon the Reserves. The general problem of future Reserve Component strength was dismissed by the committee when it concluded that pre-Vietnam strength levels would not have to be required in the future.[11] The committee thought that the Reserves would be substantially enhanced by the large flow of active duty servicemen being separated between 1970 and 1973.[12] While the move toward an All-Volunteer Force was a political decision stimulated by the civil unrest of the late 1960's, the Total Force policy developed more in response to fiscal realities.

---

8. Statement by the President, March 27, 1969, included on page vii in *Report, The President's Commission on an All-Volunteer Armed Force*, (Washington, DC, 1970).

9. Letter, Gates to Nixon, Feb. 20, 1970, in *Report, President's Commission*.

10. Recommendations summarized by Lee and Parker, *Ending the Draft*, p. 59.

11. *Report, President's Commission*, p. 99.

12. *Ibid.*, p. 117.

DOLLARS DICTATE TOTAL FORCE POLICY

By mid-1969, with the Nixon emphasis upon Vietnamiza-
tion, it was obvious to the military leadership that the post-
Vietnam Army would be reduced in size. Because the Vietnam build-up had been accomplished by adding to the active forces instead of mobilizing the Reserves, there was a
redundancy between the active force and Reserve force in
certain types of units. As the Army scaled down upon with-
drawal from Vietnam, the attractive solution to the force
structure duplication was to remove units from the active
force. By placing support capabilities in the Reserve Components, money could be saved for the modernization of the
active force—a modernization that had been postponed
when Vietnam placed a heavy strain upon the Defense budget.

With the visibility of the Reserve Components expected
to increase in the near future, the Army's Chief of the Office
of Reserve Components initiated a ten point improvement
program for the Army National Guard and Army Reserve in
August 1969, and in November 1969 he directed a special
study of resource allocations to the Reserve Components.[13]

On December 22, 1969, the Chief of Staff of the Army
presaged Secretary of Defense Melvin Laird's Total Force Policy by issuing a memorandum establishing that the Reserve
Components must be considered the initial and primary
source of additional units and individuals in any future rapid
mobilization. He directed that Army planning be predicated
on this concept.[14]

Laird's Total Force Policy simply formalized what Army
leaders had already anticipated. The economic link between
the need to hold down Defense costs and the cost effectiveness of the Reserve Components was very clearly made by
Laird. This policy was enunciated in an August 21, 1970,
memorandum to the service Secretaries in which Laird wrote
that the Selected Reserves of the Guard and Reserve, rather
than draftees, would in the future be the initial and primary
source of augmentation in any emergency requiring rapid

---

13. Army Chief of Staff General William C. Westmoreland claims
that he foresaw Laird's shift in emphasis to the Reserve Component problems in 1969. Westmoreland states that despite the reduction in active
forces, the Army's basic responsibilities did not change. This required
increased emphasis upon Reserve Components. See Westmoreland's *Report
of the Chief of Staff of the United States Army, July 1, 1968, to June 30,
1972.* (Washington, DC: Department of the Army), pp. 35–39.

14. *Annual Report of the Secretary of Defense on Reserve Forces, Fiscal
Year* 1970, p. 6.

and substantial expansion of the active forces. The military departments were directed to consider the Reserve Components as part of the Total Force available to meet security needs.[15] This was a return to traditional reliance on the Reserve Components and a forceful renunciation of the Johnson Administration's failure to mobilize the Reserves in 1965.

SUPPORT WAS NOT UNANIMOUS

The memorandum was made public on September 8 and generated front page stories in major newspapers.[16] The *Washington Post* quoted Laird as saying that "in many instances the lower peacetime sustaining costs of reserve units, compared to similar active units, can result in a larger total force for a given budget, or the same size force for a lesser budget."[17] The *New York Times* pointed out that continued reduction in defense budgets would mean fewer troops on active duty and that an Army Reserve unit could be maintained for one-sixth to one-half of the cost of an active duty unit.[18] The Associated Press said that Laird was reversing President Lyndon B. Johnson's policy on the use of Reserve forces, and that the Total Force Policy was directly linked to Nixon's goal to reduce the budget.[19]

Laird said as much himself on March 9, 1971, while testifying on the 1972 Defense Budget before the House Armed Services Committee:

Lower sustaining costs of non-active duty forces, as compared to the cost of maintaining larger active duty forces, make possible a greater flexibility in planning the Total Force structure. This lower cost of non-active forces allows more force units to be provided for the same cost as an all-active force structure, or the same number of force units to be maintained for lesser cost.

Despite the economic advantages associated with the Total Force Policy, support for the Policy was not unan-

15. *Annual Report of the Secretary of Defense on Reserve Forces, Fiscal Year 1971,* p. 1.

16. Ironically, the *Army Times* did not address the Total Force issue in the weeks immediately following Laird's announcement, and internal Army publications such as *Soldiers* were likewise mute on the subject.

17. "Reserves, Guard Get Buildup Role," *Washington Post,* September 9, 1970, p. 1.

18. "Pentagon to Cut Use of Draftees in Fast Build-ups," *New York Times,* September 9, 1970, p. 1.

19. The Associated Press Story, "Laird Reverses Johnson Policy on Reserve Use," was carried in the September 9, 1970, issue of the *European Stars and Stripes.*

imous. On June 30, 1972, in his final report to the President on the status of the US Army, Gen. William C. Westmoreland wrote that "only Regular Army forces in being can achieve the levels of readiness required." Westmoreland recommended that the Regular Army be considered a cadre that could be expanded rapidly in an emergency. This expansible army would "serve as a hedge against the high risk associated with the heavy reliance on the Reserve Components."[20] The expansible army of John C. Calhoun had been rejected in 1916 and 1920 when the Army took firm steps toward establishing a federal reserve force as a means of expanding the active establishment, but the cadre concept still seemed to enjoy some popularity.

Writing in the August 1972 issue of *Army*, Gen. Hamilton H. Howze proposed that the U.S. Army follow the Israeli Army and establish a 25 percent cadre of Regular Army troops to hold key positions in Reserve Component units.[21] On September 4, 1972, David R. Boldt disputed the value of the Total Force in a *Washington Post* article entitled "Reserve: Force or Farce?" Boldt questioned the value of spending so much on Army Reservists when their training was disorganized, their equipment inadequate, and their cooperation with the active component only minimal.[22]

On February 27, 1973, Col. David R. Hampton concluded that "today's Army Reserve cannot fulfill the requirements imposed by the total force concept." Hampton believed that using Regular Army officers and noncommissioned officers as a cadre for Reserve units was the first change to be made in a system desperately in need of change.[23]

---

20. Letter, Westmoreland to President Nixon, dated June 30, 1972, and included as Appendix D to *Report of the Chief of Staff of the United States Army, July 1, 1968, to June 30, 1972*. It should be noted that Gen. Westmoreland's knowledge of the Reserve Components may be somewhat confused. In his 1976 book, *A Soldier Reports*, he consistently refers to being able to mobilize Reservists for only one year during the Vietnam era, when the operative act of the time, Public Law 69–305 carried no such restriction. Westmoreland also refers to the Army Reserve as US Army Organized Reserves—a term that went out of official use in 1952.

21. Hamilton H. Howze, "Toward Real Reserve Readiness: The Case for the Cadre System," *Army* (August 1972), pp. 12–16.

22. David R. Boldt, "Reserve: Force or Farce," *Washington Post*, September 4, 1972, p. 1.

23. David R. Hampton, *Society and the Army Reserve*, (Army War College, Carlisle Barracks, Pa., 1973), pp. ii and 39.

The cadre concept proposed by Hampton, Howze and Westmoreland is inherently attractive to some individuals because a cadre provides the essential nucleus of an organization without the costs of maintaining the full combat strength of a unit in peacetime. The cadre concept was successful for Prussia in the 19th century, and to a large degree the American divisions of World War I and World War II were built upon cadres of Regulars and previously-trained Organized Reservists and Guardsmen. Following World War II, many US divisions were in effect cadre units, a fact that became evident when they were suddenly thrust into combat at the start of the Korean War. The same situation applied to Vietnam when new units were built around a cadre of veterans and fleshed out with new recruits recently graduated from Advanced Individual Training.

TECHNICIANS FORM A CADRE

As attractive and logical as they are to some, the cadre proposals for the Reserve Components overlooked the fact that a cadre system was already in effect for the part-time forces. This cadre system consisted of technicians and advisors to Reserve units. The role of these technicians and active component advisors, their numbers, and how they were to be organized were greatly debated in the 1970's and early 1980's. The expansion of the full-time support force behind the Army Reserve has been one of the major changes of the last 15 years.

The technician programs as they exist today had their beginnings in the National Defense Act of 1916, which provided for caretakers to feed the Federally owned horses issued to the National Guard. When the Guard became motor-drawn, maintenance personnel were added to the caretaker force and clerks were added to the force just before World War II. After World War II, Reserve Component units became larger and more complex. There was a great emphasis upon training and property accountability, and as a result, administrative personnel were authorized down to the company level. Staff assistant positions were established at battalion and higher.

During the 1950's and 1960's the technician program expanded, and the concept of having technicians carry out essential functions between weekly or weekend training assemblies (drills) became firmly established. By 1971, the Army Reserve was authorized more than 6,400 technicians. By the mid-1970's the whole concept of a technician workforce was under review as greater reliance was being placed upon the Reserve Components.

The October 1976 "ART Study" by the US Army Forces Command (FORSCOM), for example, concluded that the technician force was necessary and that the force should be expanded.[24] Two years later, however, the civilian technician program was under fire. In a May 24, 1978, memorandum to the Deputy Secretary of Defense, Assistant Secretary for Manpower, Reserve Affairs and Logistics John P. White stated that the Army Reserve had the least effective full-time force of any Reserve Component. White criticized the management of the technician program and the fact that many technicians were not mobilization assets because they could not deploy with their units.[25] White contended that readiness is directly linked to the percentage of full-time personnel in a Reserve Component and noted that the Army Reserve's technician force represented only four percent of USAR strength, while the Air Force Reserve had 22 percent full-time personnel. He recommended that the percentage of full-time personnel in the Army Reserve be increased to improve readiness.[26]

The next month, White's office issued an even more critical report on the full-time training and administration of the Reserve Components. The report concluded that the civilian technician force of the Army Reserve was almost unmanageable, mainly because it was administered under competitive civil service rules. White wanted the technician

---

24. *Army Reserve Technician Study (ART),* (Fort McPherson, Ga.: Headquarters, U.S. Army Forces Command, 1976), p. 2.

25. Since 1960, Army Reserve Technicians (ART) had been required to be members of the unit which they supported. If a technician lost his or her Reserve status he had to be placed in a non-technician civil service position. This requirement to meet both civil service and Army Reserve standards became known as dual-status, and dual-status was deemed essential if a technician were to be able to mobilize with a unit and help ease the unit through its transition to active duty. The flaw in this system was that a technician did not lose his or her job if the Selected Reserve status was lost through no fault of the technician. Examples of no-fault loss of military status include retirement from the Ready Reserve upon 20 years of qualifying service or denial of continued military status because of medical disqualification. By 1978, 20 percent of the Army Reserve's technicians had lost their dual status through no fault of their own. They were no longer mobilization assets and were referred to as "status quo" technicians.

26. Memorandum, Assistant Secretary of Defense to Deputy Secretary of Defense, May 24, 1978, p. 4.

force to be either all military or administered under excepted civil service rules.[27]

Although there was no cost saving in converting the technician force from civilian to military, White recommended that this conversion be considered. His argument was that the civil service status of the technician force did not recognize its essentially military nature.[28] He noted that a full-time military force would be available 24 hours a day and that the military considerations of the job must be paramount. White's report and memorandum seconded the December 1977 "Stroud Study", which had recommended excepted status for civilian technicians.[29] However, White went further in suggesting a conversion of the technician force to military status, thereby raising an issue which is unresolved today.

As early as 1975, the United States Defense Manpower Commission had recommended creating a special category of full-time Guardsmen and Reservists on active duty to replace civilian technicians,[30] but the idea of such an active duty force did not gain support until 1978.

In June 1978, the House Armed Services Committee asked the Army to begin a 15-month "Technician Conversion Test" to see if it was desirable to phase out the Army Reserve's civilian technician program. During the test, which ended in June 1980, the Army Reserve brought 1,276 Army Reservists on active duty in an Active

---

27. Under excepted service rules, a civil service employee serves at the pleasure of his employer and literally accepts the requirements laid down by the employer as a condition of continued employment. This is the status of Army National Guard technicians. A civil servant hired under competitive rules has formal, relatively immutable requirements for hire and promotion and a relatively fixed job description. It is also impossible under competitive service to make a military rank and occupation specialty a prerequisite for promotion or selection.

28. *Report on the Study of the Full-Time Training and Administration of the Selected Reserve*, (Washington, D.C.: Department of Defense, 1978), p. 11.

29. Ansel M. Stroud, *Study on the Full Time Personnel Requirements of the Reserve Components*, (Washington, D.C.: Department of the Army, 1977), p. III–37. Stroud also concluded that the Army Reserve had insufficient full-time personnel to meet the workload at the company level and that assigning active duty personnel to augment the civilian force was the least desirable option open to the Army.

30. United States Defense Manpower Commission, *The Total Force and Its Manpower Requirements, Including Overviews of Each Service*, Volume II, (Washington, DC: Government Printing Office, 1976), p. G–11.

Guard—Reserve (AGR) status to fill vacant civilian technician positions. In December 1980, even though the conversion test caused considerable distress among the civilian
force, the Army concluded that conversions should continue
through attrition and that nearly 3,000 more positions
should be converted to AGR status in the next few years.[31]

As a result of the discontentment, however, the conversion program was slowed considerably. By the end of the
1982 fiscal year, only 1,540 civilian positions had been converted to AGR status,[32] and action on the 1983 Defense
Budget restricted further conversion. Specifically, the House
Appropriations Committee objected to FORSCOM plans to
convert the 43 Senior Staff Administrative Assistant
(SSAA)[33] positions to full-time colonel positions; and that
same committee insured that the continuing resolution
which funded the Defense Department for 1983 contained
language prohibiting the SSAA conversion. It also limited
the total number of converted positions to the number already converted. This put a temporary halt to Army plans to
phase out civilian technicians.

FULL-TIME SUPPORT EXPANDS

The Congressional action did not halt, however, the expansion of full-time support to the Army Reserve provided under the AGR program. This expansion, which began in the
1970's and which is projected to increase in the years ahead,
is one of the most important steps taken by the Army in
the Total Force era to improve Army Reserve readiness.

Historically, there have always been a limited number
of Reservists on active duty in support of Reserve Component programs and interests. Starting with the June 4,
1920, amendments to the National Defense Act of 1916,
Congress has authorized a minimum of five Reserve officers

---

31. Office of the Chief, Army Reserve, Press Release 81–3, "Technician Conversion Report," January 12, 1981.

32. Maj. Gen. William R. Berkman, Chief, Army Reserve, *The Posture of the U.S. Army Reserve*, (Washington, DC: Department of the Army,
1983), p. 25.

33. The Senior Staff Administrative Assistant, GS–13, is the highest Army Reserve technician position. As the senior technician for an
Army Reserve general officer command (GOCOM), the SSAA supervises
the daily operations of a command of up to 12,000 men and women.
The SSAA has ultimate supervision over hundreds of technicians and is
frequently called upon to make important decisions on urgent matters
when the commanding general cannot be reached. It is a position of
considerable responsibility.

to be on duty with the Army's General Staff to insure the proper consideration of Reserve-related matters.

Subsequently, Section 265, Chapter 11, Title 10 US Code, authorized each service to have reserve officers on active duty in a status other than training, for the purpose of preparing and administering policies and regulations affecting the Reserve Components.[34] These positions are primarily in Washington, DC, and at major headquarters having responsibility over Reservists. Until the early 1970's, the number of such officers on active duty was limited.[35]

The first major expansion of the 265 program occurred with the Army's 1973 reorganization, known as the STEADFAST program. Under STEADFAST, 200 Reserve Officers were to be brought on active duty to assist in improving Army Reserve readiness, although the Commander of the Continental Army Command (CONARC) doubted that such a large number of qualified Reserve officers could be found.

On the enlisted side, the first move toward an increase in Reservists on active duty came in January 1972. At that time 27 in-service recruiters were stationed at active Army installations to recruit active duty soldiers for Army Reserve units before they were automatically transferred to the Individual Ready Reserve upon separation from active duty. In 1973, 64 Reserve non-commissioned officers were placed at US Army Recruiting Command main stations as liaison NCOs to help with referral of prospective soldiers between the active component and the Army Reserve. Further expansion of efforts took place in 1976, when 654 Army Reserve non-commissioned officers were called to active duty to expand the Army Reserve's recruiting force that had been composed of civil service, dual-status technicians. In July 1977, the recruiting force was expanded to 1,030; and on January 1, 1978, 97 non-commissioned officers were called to active duty to serve as full-time unit training managers.

With the use of full-time enlisted and commissioned Reservists showing positive results, the Army planned a major increase in Reservists on active duty. Reservists were to be added at the company level in maintenance, supply and training, while at battalion level and above, the emphasis

---

34. 10 U.S.C. 265.

35. According to the *1971 Annual Historical Supplement of Office of the Chief, Army Reserve,* as of June 30, 1971, there were 26 Chapter 265 officers on active duty with the Army. This was an increase from 17 the year before.

was on management and planning. The Department of the Army, FORSCOM, and the Continental US Armies (CON-USAs) were authorized additional mobilization planners and coordinators, and active duty installations and service schools were to be assigned full-time Reservists to coordinate Reserve Component support and to support the Total Force concept.

On February 26, 1980, Maj. Gen. William R. Berkman, the Chief, Army Reserve, testified to the Senate Armed Services Committee that the "assignment of full-time military to positions in Army Reserve units has the greatest potential for improving unit readiness." He pointed out that the Army Reserve had historically the lowest percentage of full-time personnel of all of the Reserve Components, and he requested funds to bring the number of full-time Reservists to 5,400 by September 30, 1981.

What had begun as a very minor program was first expanded to solve urgent recruiting problems and to assist with mobilization planning. The divergent active duty statutes for Reservists were combined in February 1979 into a career program commonly known as the Active Guard-Reserve (AGR) Program. Reservists in the AGR program are competitively selected for active duty after a minimum number of years in Reserve status, selectively retained and promoted, reassigned under centralized personnel management and offered an opportunity for retirement after 20 years active duty. The number of Army Reserve AGR personnel is expected to surpass 7,400 by 1984,[36] and a special Army Deputy Chief of Staff for Personnel (DCSPER) study group is expected to make recommendations for additional AGR and full-time support positions in late 1983. In addition to AGR personnel and civilian technicians, the full-time support to the Army Reserve includes active component soldiers. Traditionally, this has been in the form of advisors, evaluators and trainers.

ADVISOR QUALITY QUESTIONED

Regular Army officers were assigned as a skeleton full-time staff to the Organized Reserve divisions prior to World War II. After World War II, full-time advisors were assigned to Reserve Component units down to the battalion level. Although some of the officers assigned to Reserve Component

---

36. *Ibid.*, pp. 24–27.

duty before and after World War II were outstanding professionals,[37] a general feeling developed in the 1960's that Reserve Component duty was not career-enhancing.

By 1970, the CONARC had become concerned about
the quality of officers assigned as Reserve Component advisors. Although CONARC determined that the advisor
program was sound in concept, it published an advisor
handbook in June that year and instituted a 40-hour course
for advisors to familiarize them with their duties. The command also recommended to DA that all advisors in the
grades of lieutenant colonel and colonel be Command and
General Staff College graduates.[38]

The next year, CONARC continued to complain about
the quality of advisors and the lack of Army guidance in
their use. On July 31,1970, CONARC recommended
changes in the advisor chain of command and higher standards for advisors. In December the Army approved more
stringent criteria for assignment to Reserve advisor positions
and raised the priority of advisor assignments, thus increasing the advisor fill from 74 percent to 92 percent of authorized strength.[39]

A few months later, Lt. Gen. Walter T. Kerwin, Jr.,
the DCSPER, admitted to the Under Secretary of the Army
that the advisor program had problems. Not only were the
Reserve Components lacking in advisors, but it was common
for officers to be assigned to positions requiring an officer
two or more grades higher. It was not unusual for first lieutenants to be advising Reserve Component colonels.

In addition, Kerwin admitted to educational deficiencies in the advisor force. For example, only 29 percent of
the captains assigned to Reserve Component duty were college graduates, while 49 percent of captains on active duty
possessed a college degree. For colonels assigned to the Re-

---

37. Future General-of-the-Army and Chief of Staff George C. Marshall was assigned to Reserve Component duty in the 1930's by Chief of
Staff Douglas MacArthur. The assigning of full-time RA advisors to Reserve units was confirmed in an interview with D. Y. Dunn (Lt. Col.,
USAR-Ret.) on April 22, 1983.

38. *Continental Army Command Annual Historical Summary, Fiscal
Year 1970,* (Fort Monroe, Va.: CONARC, 1971), pp. 226–29. By contrast, in 1983, an Army Reserve officer is required to have completed
Command and General Staff College for promotion to colonel, and half
of the Command and General Staff Officer Course must be completed for
promotion to lieutenant colonel.

39. *Continental Army Command Annual Historical Summary, Fiscal
Year 1971,* (Fort Monroe, Va.: CONARC, 1972), pp. 188–92.

serve Components, less than half had college degrees at a time when 97 percent of all active Army colonels were college graduates. Another indicator was that 37 percent of lieutenant colonels in Reserve assignments were Command and General Staff College graduates. Army-wide, 59 percent of the lieutenant colonels were C&GSC graduates in 1971.[40] For senior officers, Reserve Component assignments were terminal assignments and a transition to the civilian world upon retirement.

In December, under pressure from the Army's civilian leadership, Maj. Gen. George W. Putnam, Jr., the Director of Military Personnel Policies, conceded that the demand for quality officers exceeded the supply. Rather than assign command credit for senior advisor duty as was done for advisors to the Vietnamese, Putnam suggested better housing as a way to induce high quality officers to apply for Reserve Component duty. He suggested that Reserve Component tours be stabilized at 30 months, but he resisted the idea that Reserve Component duty was equal in any way to overseas service.[41] The opportunity to upgrade the advisor program came in the Army reorganization that was pending in 1972.

By January 1972, the Army had concluded that outside pressures, particularly from the Department of Defense and the Congress, made a reorganization of CONARC particularly inevitable. The octopus-like CONARC span of control had to be reduced.

A March 31, 1972, Army staff study concluded that the only reasonable course of action was to divide CONARC into a training and doctrine command and a forces command. A project group was appointed under Maj. Gen. J. G. Kalergis to work out the details of the reorganization, and by July 19, 1972, they had accomplished their task.

The principal impact upon the Army Reserve was a complete revision in the manner by which the active Army advised, evaluated and assisted the Army Reserve. While the Army Reserve Commands (ARCOMs) established in the 1968 reorganization remained unchanged, the relationship between the ARCOMs and Continental U.S. Armies (CONUSAs) was strengthened. The CONUSAs would be relieved

40. Letter, Lt. Gen. Walter T. Kerwin, Jr., Army Deputy Chief of Staff for Personnel, to the Under Secretary of the Army, July 16, 1971.
41. Letter, Maj. Gen. George W. Putnam, Jr., Director of Military Personnel Policies, to the Under Secretary of the Army, December 9, 1971.

of all responsibility for active forces and installations and would concentrate upon command of the Army Reserve and the readiness of both the Army Reserve and the Army National Guard.

A series of seminars between August 8 and August 15, 1972, refined the concept, which called for three CONUSAs assisted by nine Readiness Assistance Regions. The Regions were not in the Army Reserve chain of command, but instead consisted of branch teams to assist Reserve units. The Regions would command the advisors dedicated to Army Reserve general officer commands and the National Guard State Adjutants General, and the dedicated advisors at the battalion level would be eliminated to provide the manpower for the regions and their subordinate Readiness Group (RG). The regions and the Readiness Groups were the doers—hands-on workers who were responsible for improving Reserve Component readiness.[42] On August 21, 1972, the Chief, Army Reserve strongly endorsed the region and Readiness Group concept,[43] and on September 21, Chief of Staff Gen. Creighton W. Abrams approved the Readiness Regions and Groups as part of the CONARC reorganization.[44]

The Readiness Assistance Region concept changed slightly before the Regions were finally formed on July 1, 1973. They were renamed Army Readiness Regions (ARRs), and the advisory/assistance functions of the ARR were organized in three echelons:

1. Dedicated advisors at major levels such as Army Reserve Commands, divisions and brigades;
2. Readiness Groups with mobile teams to assist units within specific geographical areas; and
3. Readiness Coordinators who coordinate ARR-wide assistance efforts and who act as a staff for the ARR Commander.

It became Army policy that the best qualified personnel available were assigned to the ARRs and RGs. Such

42. *Continental Army Command Annual Historical Summary, Fiscal Year 1972.* (Fort Monroe, Va.: CONARC: 1973), pp. 57–87. See also, *U.S. Army Forces Command Annual Report of Major Activities, Fiscal Year 1974.* (Fort McPherson, Ga.: FORSCOM: 1976), pp. 1–75.

43. Letter, Maj. Gen. D. V. Rattan, Deputy Chief, Office of Reserve Components, to Lt. Gen. Harris W. Hollis, Chief, Office of Reserve Components, September 20, 1972.

44. Memorandum for Record, Lt. Gen. Harris W. Hollis, Chief, Office of Reserve Components, September 27, 1972.

assignments were equated with the best branch assignments when comparing personnel of similar grade for personnel actions, and ARR and RG personnel were exempt from such duties as casualty assistance officer and line of duty investigations.[45] The Department of the Army seconded the CONARC and subsequent FORSCOM emphasis by instructing promotion boards that Reserve Component assignments were important assignments for active component officers.[46]

Although some Reserve Component commanders were unhappy about losing their battalion-level advisors, the reorganization completely revamped the advisor program and upgraded the quality of active component assistance rendered the Army Reserve. As a result, the Army Reserve began to receive intensive training management.

The Army Readiness Region approach worked well initially and was a drastic improvement over the past. Reserve commanders were able to obtain help from knowledgeable personnel outside of the chain of command, and the dedication of the assistance teams worked some minor miracles in the mid-1970's.[47]

Even though the ARRs and RGs were effective in improving the readiness of many Army Reserve units, there were negative connotations to the reorganization. The 37 new ARRs and RGs had no post-mobilization mission; and when added to the 19 ARCOMs and two Maneuver Area Commands in the Army Reserve structure, there were a total of 8,170 soldiers who had no post-mobilization assignments.[48]

The assumption was that these soldiers would become available as individual replacements, but this assumption

---

45. *Army Readiness Region Concept of Operations*, (United States Army Continental Army Command, Fort Monroe, Va., 1973), pp. 1–6.

46. *Annual Historical Review, July 1, 1975 to Sept. 30, 1976*, (U.S. Army Forces command, Fort McPherson, Ga., 1976), p. 483.

47. In April 1975, one particular Adjutant General Replacement Regulating Detachment was widely reputed to be one of the worst units in the Army Reserve. The unit had flunked three consecutive Annual General Inspections (AGI), failed three straight periods of Annual Training, had no technician support, and had retained a satisfactory strength level only because of the influence of earlier draft-induced enlistments. Personnel, mess and property records were a shambles; however, with the assistance of teams from Readiness Group Meade and hard work by a majority of the unit's members, the unit passed its 1975 Annual Training evaluation.

48. Comptroller General, Report to the Congress of the United States, LCD–79–404, *Can the Army and Air Force Reserve Support the Active Forces Effectively*, (General Accounting Office, Washington, DC, 1979), pp. 76 & 82.

was somewhat tarnished when critics began to ask if the Army could really use 28 major generals who had no post-mobilization assignments—the 9 ARR commanders and 19 ARCOM commanders. The generals became the personification of criticism that the Army had created duplicate levels of management in establishing the active Army ARRs to oversee the readiness of Army Reserve units commanded by ARCOMs.[49]

As a result of criticism from the Congress, Department of Defense, and the General Accounting Office, the Army in late 1978 established a task force to identify problems in the Army command and control system. The result was the Army Command and Control Study—82 (ACCS–82) that presented several alternatives for maintaining the necessary peacetime management while providing an orderly and rapid transition to wartime.[50]

The alternative favored by the ACCS–82 study group would have eliminated the ARCOMs and ARRs and combined them into 11 Army Readiness and Mobilization Commands (ARMC). These ARMCs would be commanded by an active Army major general and would report directly to the CONUSAs. There would be a Reserve Component deputy commander, and the staff of the ARMCs would be a mix of active Army officers, dual-status technicians and part-time Reservists and Guardsmen.[51]

Before the ARMC concept could be tested, FORSCOM proposed an alternative that modified the ARRs by giving them additional mobilization responsibilities. The Office of the Chief, Army Reserve concurred in the FORSCOM alternative which retained the ARCOMs while enhancing the

---

49. The issue of excess major generals presented the Army with a very delicate problem. Many in the Army's senior leadership were concerned about the proper role of these generals after mobilization. For example, while an Army Reserve major general whose background was Civil Affairs was suitable for an ARCOM command, there was a debate as to what role could be assigned him after mobilization. The same question was also addressed to officers with backgrounds in logistics and other combat service support specialities when mobilization designees of their grade and experience were already assigned to the Army staff.

50. Point Paper, DAAR–OT, *Army Command & Control Study–82,* as presented to the Reserve Component Coordination Council, February 1980.

51. Information is based upon the author's experience as a dual-status technician on the staff of an ARCOM that was selected to be included in a test merger of an ARCOM and an ARR. The staffing mix of the ARMC went through several versions before the ARMC idea was dropped in favor of Army Readiness and Mobilization Regions (ARMRs).

role of the ARRs. The FORSCOM alternative was approved in late 1979, and the transition from ARRs to ARMRs was completed in the summer of 1980.

Meanwhile, the issue of excess levels of management did not go away. On December 11, 1979, the Senate Appropriations Committee and House Appropriations Committee conference report on the 1980 Defense Appropriations Act stated that "the Conferees agree that significant savings should be available beginning in FY 81 from eliminating unproductive management layers in the Army Reserve Component support structure."[52] The conferees requested a realignment to reduce excess levels of management be started by September 30, 1980. The Army did not meet the deadline requested by the Congress, but it did continue to work on the problem.

After the Reagan Administration took office, Kenneth P. Bergquist, the new Deputy Assistant Secretary of the Army for Reserve Affairs and Mobilization, proposed sweeping revisions in the Army Reserve's command and control structure. An Army Reservist with a background as a Senate staffer, Bergquist wanted to organize the Army Reserve in peacetime for the way it would fight in wartime. He also wanted to upgrade the management of the Individual Ready Reserve, which he characterized as inadequate and ineffective. Specifically, Bergquist proposed transferring Reservists in the Training Divisions, Reception Stations and Army Reserve Schools to the US Army Training and Doctrine Command (TRADOC) and transferring non-deploying Army Reserve medical units to the Health Services command— moves that would affect 75,000 drilling Reservists.

Bergquist wanted to place Army Reserve units under the peacetime command of the ARMRs. Some ARCOMs would be merged with ARMRs, while others would be given post-mobilization missions. The Bergquist ideas were opposed by the Senior Army Reserve Commanders Association (SARCA) and were little supported by the Army staff. They did, however, stimulate additional thought on the organization of the Army Reserve.[53]

---

52. Point Paper, DAAR–OT.

53. Interview between the author and Secretary Bergquist at the time of the proposal. See also *Washington Update,* Senior Army Reserve Commanders Association, Riverdale, Md., December 1981 issue. The issue of placing training divisions, reception stations, and Army Reserve schools under TRADOC remained alive and was still being pursued by TRADOC in September 1983.

Meanwhile, the Congress continued to press the Army to eliminate one level of the Army Reserve's management structure. There were also particular concerns over the fact that the Chief, Army Reserve did not command the Army Reserve in the manner that his Air Force counterpart enjoyed authority over the Air Force Reserve. In latter 1981, the Senate Preparedness Subcommittee asked the Army to take action to enhance the authority of the Chief, Army Reserve and indicated that legislation to that end would be proposed if the Army failed to act.

A year later, the Army announced that the Army Reserve command and control structure was being reorganized. The ARMRs would be eliminated, and the role of the ARCOMs would be enhanced. The FORSCOM span of control would be increased from three armies to five, and the CONUSAs would assume many of the responsibilities of the disbanded ARMRs. Concurrently, the Army promised to enhance the role of the Chief, Army Reserve.[54]

In March 1983, the Army announced that the Chief, Army Reserve would soon establish an Army Reserve Personnel Center as a field operating agency of OCAR. This center would provide career management to AGR, IRR and Individual Mobilization Augmentee (IMA) personnel. On May 2, came a report that the Army had told FORSCOM to increase the responsibility of major Army Reserve Commands over training force modernization and mobilization planning. According to a story in *Army Times*, FORSCOM was told to give the ARCOMs significant, well-defined, meaningful, post-mobilization missions.[55]

The published plans were explained to the Executive Committee of the Senior Army Reserve Commanders Association on May 5 and 6. Following the briefing, Brig. Gen. Raymond M. Jacobson, SARCA's Executive Director, wrote Army Chief of Staff Gen. Edward Meyer, expressing concern that the ARCOMs would not be given sufficient additional assets to carry out additional responsibilities under the planned reorganization.[56] Meyer's June 8, 1983, reply to Jacobson emphasized that "a key objective of this reorganiza-

---

54. "Reorganization Planned," *CARNotes,* Office of the Chief, Army Reserve, Washington, DC (Jan.–Feb. 1983), pp. 1 and 6.

55. Larry Carney, "FORSCOM Told to Increase Reserve Command's Control," *Army Times,* May 2, 1983, p. 3.

56. Letter, Brig. Gen. Raymond M. Jacobson to Gen. Edward C. Meyer, May 25, 1983, as reprinted in the June 1983 issue of *Washington Update,* Senior Army Reserve Commanders Association, Washington, DC.

tion is to invest Major US Army Reserve Commands (MUS-ARCs) with more responsibility and authority for their own management. This is appropriate recognition of both the increasingly critical role of the Army Reserve in the national defense, and its increased capability."

Meyer also wrote, however, that the need to reduce overall Army manpower spaces, and the need to add two new CONUSAs to the command structure meant that no additional resources would be given to the ARCOMs to carry out their added responsibilities. Meyer suggested that ARCOMs should re-evaluate the manner in which they intended to employ the added full-time personnel planned for them in 1984 under the AGR program.[57] The emphasis upon reducing manpower requirements was seconded in July 1983 when *CARNotes* announced that the elimination of the ARMRs would mean a reduction of 125 military and 75 civilian spaces. According to *CARNotes*, the changes were designed to increase the efficiency of the Total Army.[58] The implication is that the reorganization has more to do with saving dollars and manpower spaces that it does with enhancing the authority of the Chief, Army Reserve or the ARCOMs.[59] However, with the final decision not firm by mid-1983, the net effect of the announced reorganization cannot be predicted.

As important as the full-time support structure is to the Army Reserve, the cadre and support forces and their organization was but one of several major issues facing the Army Reserve in the post-1968 timeframe. Immediately after the 1968 reorganization, the principal Reserve Component concern was materiel readiness. Once the Army entered the All-Volunteer Force era, the concern shifted to personnel strength. After the strength picture improved in the 1980's, the principal concern became materiel readiness and the potential block obsolescence of Army Reserve equipment.

---

57. Letter, Gen. Edward C. Meyer to Brig. Gen. Raymond M. Jacobson, June 8, 1983, as reprinted in the June 1983 issue of *Washington Update*, Senior Army Reserve Commanders Association, Washington, DC.

58. "Army Trims Command Structure," *CARNotes*, Office of the Chief, Army Reserve, Washington, DC, (July–August 1983), p. 1.

59. The reorganization is expected to produce annual savings of $5.5 million. See *Army News Service Release No. 103*, "Reserve Component Command and Control," Department of the Army, Washington, DC, May 26, 1983.

THE AVF BRINGS STRENGTH PROBLEMS

One of the first effects of the All-Volunteer Force policy and the ending of the draft was a drastic reduction in Ready Reserve strength. The paid drill strength of the Army Reserve fell from 263,299 on June 30, 1971, to 239,715 on June 30, 1973. The next year Army Reserve units had a net loss of 14,000 members and the paid drill strength dropped to 191,919 on June 30, 1976. By September 30, 1978, the drill strength was down to 185,753 and it stayed around that total until a steady increase began in 1981.

Concurrently with the unit losses, the Individual Ready Reserve dropped from 1,059,064 on June 30, 1972, to 143,882 on January 30, 1978. The combined effect was that the Ready Reserve, which stood at 1,192,453 men and women when the Total Force Policy was announced in 1970, was down to 338,847 seven years later. The Standby Reserve, which consisted mostly of soldiers in the last year of their six-year military obligation, dropped by more than 300,000 between 1970 and 1977.

The precipitous decline in the Army's Ready and Standby Reserves was a cold, hard reality that threatened the success of the Total Force Policy. Improvements in materiel readiness, training, and mobilization planning were hollow accomplishments when the Army Reserve simply lacked the manpower necessary to carry out its responsibilities to the Total Force.

One of the great ironies of the All-Volunteer Force era and the Total Force Policy is that the net effect of ending the draft was increased Reserve Component responsibilities, and hence greater numerical strength requirements, while the capability to fill the Reserve Component ranks was decreased.[60] This inherent conflict between personnel requirements and the ability of the Reserve Components to obtain volunteers gave rise to a decade of handwringing as the Army attempted to make the Volunteer Army concept work for the Army Reserve.[61]

---

60. This paradox is one of the conclusions drawn by a National War College research group in April 1982. See: James W. Browning II, et al., *The U.S. Reserve System: Attitudes, Perceptions, and Realities,* (Washington, DC: The National War College, 1982), p. 40.

61. Much of what is said here about the Army Reserve applies equally to the Army National Guard. However, the history of the Army National Guard is not the main thrust of this book, and specific policies and examples will be addressed to how they affect the Army Reserve.

The Volunteer Army concept was based upon the assumption that if soldiers were paid a competitive wage the military could attract enough manpower to sustain a volunteer active Army in the range of 800,000 to 1,000,000 men and women. The incentive of higher wages worked reasonably well for the active force, especially when coupled with relaxed personnel policies. The wage incentives, however, failed to maintain Reserve Component strength in the 1970's.

The wage incentives failed because the motivation for joining the Reserve Components was not the same as for joining the active forces. The active components offered a complete benefit package that the Reserve could not offer. The benefits ranged from travel and medical care to paid vacations and a change of lifestyle. This was in addition to providing a wage that allowed a young person to quickly satisfy material wants. Although both the active and Reserve forces could offer initial job training and work experience, the Reserve Components could not meet a young person's day-to-day needs. The fact that the Reserve Components were essentially viewed as a part-time job by their junior personnel and potential enlistees was not recognized until the *Reserve Compensation System Study* was complete in June 1978. In addition to the Defense Department's belated recognition that the Reserve Components required unique incentives to maintain strength without the inducement of a draft, the Reserves entered the 1970's with several handicaps.

THE LEGACY OF VIETNAM HURTS THE ARMY RESERVE

The greatest handicap faced by the Army Reserve in 1970 was the failure of the Johnson Administration to mobilize the Reserve Components to an appreciable degree for Vietnam. This allowed the Reserves to become a haven for individuals seeking to avoid combat duty. While this situation may have allowed the Reserves the luxury of waiting lists and the ability to choose whom they wanted, it also created a Reserve peopled with over-educated and affluent junior enlisted men who had absolutely no motivation to reenlist once their initial tour was over. As a result, there was a mass exodus of first-term Reservists in the early and mid-1970's, and waiting lists disappeared as draft calls were reduced in 1970 and 1971.

Second, the Army Reserve was handicapped by a lack of equipment and adequate training facilities. Because of equipment drawdowns, the supply of equipment to Reserve units was so diminished that it became impossible to train. As a result, Reserve commanders were forced to turn to movies and classroom lectures to fill inactive duty training time. It was quite common for NCOs to read lesson plans to masses of sleepy, bored, college-educated first-termers while the officers and full-time technicians wrestled with administration—which incidentally included drafting detailed lesson plans.[62]

Third, the surfeit of potential enlistees and the practical restraints against realistic training made the Reserve leadership lazy. Commanders, who were responsible for their own recruiting, forgot how to recruit; training officers, who were responsible to their commanders for realistic training, forgot how to plan field training; and the active Army leaders responsible for overseeing or advising Reserve training came to accept poor performance as the norm.[63]

These handicaps created in the public's mind an impression that the Army Reserve could offer very little to prospective enlistees and that there was little to be proud of

---

62. The author's own experience followed this pattern.

63. In May 1973, Maj. Gen. Edward Bautz, Jr., described Army Reserve training this way during an Army and Army Readiness Region Commanders conference:

One of my first IDT visits was to a thousand-bed fixed hospital. When I asked where they stood in their training program I was advised, 'the fourth week of BUT'. When I asked what this really meant for a thousand-bed fixed hospital, there was a fair amount of conjecture among the commander and his principal staff officers. Investigation showed that there was no precise ATP for a thousand-bed fixed hospital . . . . I observed a POL company engaged in a week-long exercise hauling empty 5,000-gallon tankers on a 150-mile turn-around. The men obviously were not getting much out of it . . . . On observing an infantry company ATT, I learned that the company had attacked, withdrawn, and attacked over the same 4 to 5 kilometer stretch of ground—and this was soon to be followed by a helicopter extraction. According to the tactical scenario, a helicopter extraction would have been disastrous . . . . (but) the CONARC Infantry Company Test required a helicopter extraction as the last event.. . . In visiting a POL supply point during AT, I found a very well laid out arrangement. In talking to three men—all college graduates—their primary mission for two weeks was to pump gas into a vehicle fuel tanker whenever one rolled up. The skill level required is equal to that needed in a self-service gasoline station. . . . If this gives you the impression that most Reserve Component units do not know how to train properly, I would have to agree—*but I hasten to point out that in almost every instance I was accompanied by a senior Active Army officer who bore some responsibility for this training. In at least half of these examples the Active Army officer was a general officer.* Quoted from a cleared transcript of remarks in possession of the First US Army Historian.

in Army Reserve membership. This created a difficult hurdle to overcome at a time when the Army Reserve had to compete against the active forces and the civilian employment and education market for volunteers. The Army Reserve has had a difficult time overcoming this hurdle.[64]

THE ARMY TACKLES STRENGTH PROBLEMS

In spite of the handicaps and a negative public perception of the Army Reserve, the Army took a four-pronged approach to solving Army Reserve strength problems in the 1970's:

1. Establish and then increase the size of the recruiter force.
2. Add low-cost incentives to the Reserve benefits package.
3. Take administrative actions to include changing Individual Ready Reserve (IRR) regulations while offering a variety of Reserve enlistment options.
4. Institute a Selected Reserve Incentive Program (SRIP). The first three approaches, which were relatively low cost, were started as soon as it became apparent that the Army Reserve's strength problems were not going to be solved by wishful thinking. Bonuses, with their relatively high cost, were tried last, even though the Army has continued with low-cost initiatives such as asking Congress to extend the total military obligation to eight years.

With enlisted strength dropping rapidly and waiting lists all but gone, 1972 marked the start of Army initiatives to maintain Army Reserve strength. A separate recruiting and retention branch was established within the Office of the Chief, Army Reserve to coordinate the recruiting and retention programs. On January 3, 1972, a 42-man, in-service recruiting force was established at 27 active Army installations to encourage soldiers to join Reserve Component units upon release from active duty.

Aided by an early release program for those joining a Reserve Component unit, the in-service recruiters signed up

---

64. After the Iranian Crisis began in the fall of 1979, Reserve recruiters received a large number of calls from parents wanting to know if their sons could join the Army Reserve so that they would not have to serve in the Army. It appears that the Vietnam legacy of the Army Reserve as a refuge from combat service died slowly. A major finding of the November 1974 Gilbert Youth Survey was that only 13 percent of young men were at that time favorably disposed toward Army Reserve service. See *Attitudes of Male Civilian Youth Toward Military Service*, Manpower Research and Data Analysis Center, 1975, p. ii.

25,000 active duty soldiers for the Army Reserve by March 29, 1972.[65] The Army Reserve backed unit recruiters and in-service recruiters with a national print media advertising campaign starting in January; and unit recruiters were given full-time help starting on July 1, 1972, when the Army Reserve started hiring 365 GS–7 Recruiting Specialists.

In 1973, 64 Army Reserve liaison non-commissioned officers were placed in active Army recruiting main stations to coordinate referrals between the components, and in 1976 the dual-status technician recruiting force was augmented by 654 Reserve non-commissioned officers in an active duty status. In July 1977, the number of Army Reserve Recruiters on active duty was expanded to 1,030, marking a 300 percent increase in the full-time recruiting force in a little over four years.[66]

In August 1978, the Vice Chief of Staff decided to make Army Reserve Recruiting a responsibility of the US Army Recruiting Command (USAREC). The transition of the recruiting mission for FORSCOM to USAREC began October 1, 1978, and was completed in May 1979. Meanwhile, the advertising budget in support of recruiting grew from $2 million in 1972 to $11.1 million in 1979.

Today, USAREC remains responsible for the Army Reserve's recruiting mission, although Reserve unit members are still an important source of leads for recruiters. Army Reserve recruiters and active Army recruiters share recruiting station space. They have similar incentive programs for high production and parallel management structures under the District Recruiting Command. Recruiters commonly share referrals, but proposals to give active Army recruiters full credit toward their monthly enlistment quotas for Army Reserve accessions and vice versa have not been accepted.

BENEFITS ARE INCREASED

No-cost and low-cost benefits to improve recruiting and retention were tried as early as 1972. In that year, the active duty retiree's Survivor Benefit Plan was extended to retirees from the Army Reserve, and drilling Reservists were ex-

---

65. *Department of the Army Annual Historical Summary, FY 1972,* (Washington, DC: Department of the Army, 1976), p. 108.

66. Prior to the second expansion of the full-time recruiting force, units were still responsible for recruiting. They were assisted by the full-time recruiters, but units still had to have trained recruiting teams. A considerable share of the Army Reserve's discretionary active duty for training funds were expended for training and subsequent recruiting duties.

tended unlimited post exchange (PX) privileges during their periods' of inactive duty for training (IDT)—the formal name for weekend drills. The first of these incentives would incur no expense until years in the future, and the PX benefit was of value only if the Reservist's unit trained on or near an active installation.

Effective May 24, 1974, members of the Ready Reserve were authorized full time Servicemen's Group Life Insurance (SGLI), with the normal monthly premiums charged active Army soldiers being deducted from the Reservists' drill pay. This benefit did not appreciably add to the cost of the Army Reserve.

Four days later, Public Law 93–292 made Army Reservists eligible for a burial flag, provided they died while in a Ready Reserve status or after achieving the years of service necessary for a Reserve retirement. The extra cost of this benefit cannot be computed, but it is not thought to be substantial. On September 30, 1978, the Survivor Benefit Program was liberalized for Reservists. Under Public Law 95–397, a Reservist who attained 20 years of creditable service could make a survivor annuity option that would pay benefits to a survivor if the Reservist died before age 60. Under earlier law, there was no survivor benefit if the Reservist died before actually beginning to receive retired pay at age 60. This was a substantial and valuable incentive for Reservists to stay in an active status for at least 20 years.

The gradual enhancement of low-cost or no-cost benefits to Reservists continued even as Army Reserve unit strength improved in 1980. In 1981, Reservists were given a Variable Housing Allowance (VHA) based upon their Annual Training site or location of additional active duty for training, if they were eligible for a housing allowance.

In March 1981, it was announced that Reservists could receive cash awards under the Army suggestion program. Previously, awards were permitted only to full-time military and civilian employees of the Army. Also in 1981, Reservists were authorized payment for use of their personal vehicle if they were required to perform inactive duty for training at a duty station other than their unit's normal place of duty. In September 1981, Reservists were authorized to take advantage of the toll-free Army Family Life Communication Lines as a way of obtaining immediate answers to routine questions. This proved very helpful to spouses who were unsure of their benefits when the Reservist was away on Annual Training and there was no one at the Reserve Center to answer questions.

In March 1982, officials clarified the PX privileges of Reservists. Post Exchange officials effectively doubled the PX shopping privilege by ruling that a Reservist receives one day of shopping for each period of drill performed, or four days per weekend drill. Earlier, the rule had been one day's shopping for each day of inactive duty performed. Officials also ruled that Reservists could take guests to post exchange theaters and purchase uniforms at post exchanges at any time, without regard to privileges earned through inactive duty or active duty for training.[67]

As with earlier low-cost incentives, the more recent benefits do not mark a major advance in overall Reserve benefits if taken individually. However, when combined over a period of years, the low-cost incentives have appreciably enhanced the Reserve compensation package.

In addition to low-cost incentives, the Army quickly turned to administrative actions to fill the Reserve ranks. After a 1972 early release program encouraged soldiers to join Army Reserve units, the Army adopted the Civilian Acquired Skills Program (CASP), which permitted a non-prior service enlistee to gain credit for Advanced Individual Training because of civilian skills or education. Started as a test program on July 17, 1973, the CASP program was made permanent on June 30, 1974. It was especially attractive to women, who were required to take only a two-week basic training orientation under CASP enlistees. By 1975, CASP was producing 60 percent of Army Reserve female enlistments.[68]

In 1974, the Army Reserve was authorized to offer 4×2 and 3×3 enlistments to non-prior service men in the top three mental categories. The 4×2 meant that the Reservist served four years in an Army Reserve unit and two years in the IRR. The 3×3 option allowed three years in each part of the Ready Reserve.

On May 24, 1978, the Army Reserve was permitted to start a split-training option, which remains very popular today with high school and college students. Under split-training, a young man or woman takes basic training one summer and returns 12 months later for Advanced Indi-

---

67. A full description of the sweeping changes in Post Exchange privileges can be found in the March 1982 issue of *CARNotes*, Office of the Chief, Army Reserve, Washington, DC.

68. *Annual Historical Summary, Fiscal Year 1975*, Office of the Chief, Army Reserve, Department of the Army, Washington, DC, p. 17.

vidual Training. In between the two training phases, the Reservist earns IDT pay.[69]

When it became obvious that low-cost enhancements were not effective in increasing Army Reserve unit strength, Congress took the initiative and passed Public Law 95–79 on July 30, 1977. This act authorized enlistment bonuses of up to $1,800, or educational assistance of up to $4,000, for soldiers enlisting in selected critical skills or designated units after October 1, 1977. In 1978, Congress dropped the education assistance part of the program, but it included reenlistment bonuses.

The educational assistance provisions were reinstated in 1980, and the present program (1983) pays up to $1,000 per year for books, fees and tuition for postsecondary education. There is, however, a $4,000 maximum payment for a six-year enlistment. The present enlistment bonus ranges from $1,500 to $2,000, and the reenlistment bonus is $900 to $1,800, depending upon the length of the reenlistment.

Between October 1, 1978, and September 30, 1982, the Army Reserve spent $37 million on the bonuses and educational assistance incentives for the 43,000 USAR members who took advantage of the Selected Reserve Incentive Program (SRIP). Congress has extended the program through 1985, and it is estimated that the program will cost over $15 million in 1983.[70] According to Maj. Gen. William R. Berkman, the Chief, Army Reserve, "the incentives have a two-fold effect: an increase in Army Reserve paid drill strength each year since initiation in FY 79; and the channeling of new members into high priority units."[71] Berkman stated that the SRIP has contributed substantially to Army Reserve strength improvement.[72] Berkman's enthusiasm for SRIP is not shared by the GAO, but it is sup-

---

69. When combined with the Simultaneous Membership program, the split-training option provides a way for a young person to receive up to six years of part-time employment and four summers of paid training while in high school and college. In 1983, this package was estimated to be worth $14,000 to an enlistee who goes on later to take ROTC and receive a commission after his or her sophomore year in college.

70. Data is taken from official questions and answers prepared for the press on Dec. 9, 1982, regarding the SRIP. Memoranda supporting these data are on file in the Public Affairs Office, Office of the Chief, Army Reserve.

71. Testimony, Maj. Gen. William R. Berkman, Chief, Army Reserve, before the Subcommittee on Manpower and Personnel, Committee on Armed Services, US Senate, Mar. 11, 1982.

72. Berkman, *Posture of the U.S. Army Reserve,* FY 1984, p. 12.

ported by the 1981 tracking study of Reserve Component attitudes. This study found that bonuses such as SRIP double the propensity of middle class youths to join the Army Reserve and that the educational assistance aspect of the SRIP is a strong incentive for high school graduates to enlist.[73]

Beginning October 1, 1980, the Army added an Affiliation Bonus to the Reserve Component's incentive arsenal. This bonus pays members of the Individual Ready Reserve and soldiers leaving active duty $25 a month to complete the remainder of their military obligation in a Reserve Component Unit. By the end of 1982, more than 3,000 soldiers had taken advantage of the bonus, receiving an average of $325 each. The benefit of this program is that it creates immediately available troop unit mobilization assets rather than more theoretical assets for Ready Reserve.[74]

The Army also took action, however, to strengthen the Individual Ready Reserve (IRR). The IRR is the primary source of pretrained individuals which the Army depends upon to augment the active forces and Reserve Component units in the event of war or national emergency. As such, the IRR figures prominently in mobilization planning. The number and mix of specialities required early in a mobilization has been the subject of considerable debate both inside and outside the Defense Department. Estimates of IRR needs during the first 90 to 180 days of a conflict range from 200,000 to over a half-million. The latest unclassified figures estimate a need for 400,000 IRR soldiers to flesh out units and to replace casualties during the first 90 days

73. In the fall of 1982, the General Accounting Office prepared a draft report on the Selected Reserve Incentive Program (SRIP). The GAO made three basic findings: the Army allowed overstrength Military Occupation Specialities (MOS) to benefit from the program, some low-priority units were allowed to award the bonuses, and the Army failed to manage SRIP. Because the GAO was working with data over a year old, the report was overcome by events prior to its final publication in January 1983. Beginning October 12, 1982, the Army paid SRIP bonuses by MOS instead of the broader career field, which allowed a few individuals in overstrength MOSs to receive bonuses. Also, the unit priority for SRIP payments was tied directly to a unit's resource priority—which in turn is almost directly linked to its mobilization priority. *Reserve Component Attitude Study, 1981 Tracking Study,* (Philadelphia, Penn.: Associates for Research in Behavior, Inc., 1982), pp. vi and vii.

74. Data is taken from official questions and answers prepared for the press on December 9, 1982, regarding the SRIP. Memoranda supporting these data are on file in the Public Affairs Office, Office of the Chief, Army Reserve.

after mobilization.[75] It should be pointed out that this figure is consistent with the manpower needs that were projected in the mid-1970's.

Manpower for the IRR comes from individuals with prior service in the active and Reserve Components who have a remaining service obligation. IRR strength is therefore almost totally dependent upon the number of soldiers leaving active duty or Reserve Component units. As long as a draft was in effect, there was a constant source of manpower for the IRR as draftees left the active force following their two years of active duty. They were then available to the IRR for three years before being transferred to the Standby Reserve for the last year of their six-year military obligation. When the United States scaled down its involvement in Vietnam in the early 1970's and reduced the size of the active Army, the IRR shrank. With fewer men entering the active force, there were fewer men to be transferred to the IRR following their initial period of service.

The IRR, which stood at 1,059,064 on June 30, 1972, had dropped to a low of 143,882 by January 31, 1978. It had fallen below the critical 400,000 figure as early as 1975, and IRR strength suddenly became a matter of serious concern within DoD.[76] The Army did little, however, to enhance the IRR until 1978.

On February 1, 1978, the Army extended the six-year military obligation to women who joined the military. Previously, women could join the active force or a Reserve unit for three years and then be discharged. The new policy required women to remain in the IRR for three years following their active duty or Reserve Component service. A few months later, the Army stopped transferring soldiers to the Standby Reserve during the sixth year of their military obligation. This policy became law on October 20, 1978, with the signing of Public Law 95–485. In May 1979, the Army began to enlist soldiers directly into the IRR, where they would remain mobilization assets for six years following a short period of active duty for training. Since the IRR direct enlistment option carried few benefits with it, very few young men and women chose this option.

---

75. *Fiscal Year 1984 Defense Manpower Requirements Report*, (Washington, DC: Department of Defense, 1983), p. III–31.

76. By 1976, the projected IRR shortfall was 321,000, and this shortage was considered critical. *See Secretary of Defense's Annual Report on Reserve Forces, FY 1976*, (Washington, DC: Department of Defense, 1976), p. 24.

On October 1, 1979, the Army stopped discharging soldiers for hardship, pregnancy or dependency. Instead, individuals qualifying under these categories were released from active duty or Reserve units and placed in the IRR until the end of their six-year obligation. Members of the Trainee Discharge Program and Expeditious Discharge Program were also sent to the IRR if their command thought they might be of value in a full mobilization.[77]

In 1981, the Army tested an IRR reenlistment bonus which paid soldiers in selected skills $600 to reenlist in the IRR for three years following the end of their six-year obligation. This was a modest success, with 3,815 soldiers reenlisting in the IRR in 1981, but the Congress declined to continue the bonus in 1982.[78] The Army is again proposing direct IRR enlistment and has also sought legislation to extend the basic military obligation of all service personnel to eight years instead of six. Another step to increase IRR strength was taken in 1983 when the Army tacked a two-year IRR obligation on the end of all reenlistments, even if the soldier had already served more than six years.

Faced with severe IRR shortages, the Army has turned to its retirees as a source of mobilization manpower. Soldiers who retire from the active Army after 20 years of service become members of the Retired Reserve and remain mobilization assets. Starting in October 1981, the Army began issuing pre-mobilization orders to selected members of the Retired Reserve. These individuals would be ordered to stateside duty in case of mobilization. These older soldiers have typically been given training, planning, and administrative assignments which would free younger servicemen for field duty.

The Army has assumed that 100,000 recent retirees could be recalled promptly. The use of retirees and an assumed increase in IRR strength over the next few years has enabled the Army to reduce its predicted IRR shortfall to 15,000 by the mid-1980's.[79] These assumptions have not been universally accepted.

---

77. The Trainee Discharge Program permitted the discharge, without bias, of enlistees during Basic Training and Advanced Individual Training if it appeared that they would be unable to succeed in the active force. The Expeditious Discharge Program allowed for quick release of individuals who were unable to adapt to military life following the successful completion of their initial training.

78. Berkman, *Posture of the U.S. Army Reserve, FY 1984*, p. 20.

79. A change of planning assumptions has also enabled the Army to reduce its IRR requirements. The peak demand for IRR members is

The General Accounting Office has been critical of the Retiree Recall Program and the overall status of the IRR. On October 15, 1982, the GAO called the Army's plan for recalling retirees unreliable;[80] and on January 31, 1983, a GAO report stated that the Army has less than one-half of the IRR members needed in wartime.[81] Additionally, the 1982 Military Manpower Task Force Report to the President on the Status and Prospects of the All-Volunteer Force also expressed reservations about the Retiree Recall Program and the IRR.[82] It would appear that current incentives may not be adequate to meet the Army's IRR needs.

WOMAN-POWER INCREASE

As effective as incentives and administrative enhancements have been in building Army Reserve unit manpower in the 1970's and early 1980's, a key to Army Reserve strength improvement has been womanpower.

Women won a permanent place in the American military through the Women's Armed Services Integration Act of 1948 and other legislation at about the same time, but the former act restricted the number of women to two percent of the enlisted force and the number of female officers to 10 percent of female enlisted strength. The strength limitations were removed by Congress in 1967, but female strength in the Army Reserve remained low throughout the early 1970's.

On July 1, 1972, there were 483 members of the Women's Army Corps (WAC) in Army Reserve units and 281 in the IRR. There were also a number of women in a Reserve status in the Medical Corps, Army Nurse Corps, Medical Service Corps, and Medical Specialist Service Corps. At the urging of Maj. Gen. William J. Sutton, then Chief, Army Reserve, Reserve recruiters began a drive to substantially increase the number of women in the Army Reserve. In the first year of that drive, nearly a thousand women

now assumed to occur at M + 120 instead of M + 90. See *Fiscal Year 1984 Defense Manpower Requirements Report, p. III–31.*

80. *The Army's Ability to Mobilize and Use Retirees as Planned is Doubtful,* Report FPCD–83–6, (Washington, DC: General Accounting Office, 1982).

81. *Personnel Problems May Hamper Army's Individual Ready Reserve in Wartime,* Report FPCD–83–12, (Washington, DC: General Accounting Office, 1983).

82. Casper W. Weinberger, *Report to the President on the Status and Prospects of the All-Volunteer Force,* (Washington, DC: Military Manpower Task Force, 1982).

were added to the Army Reserve's rolls, and the number of women in Army Reserve units skyrocketed to 6,669 by June 30, 1974.[83]

To a substantial degree, the rapid increase in female numbers was made possible by the previously-mentioned Civilian Acquired Skills Program (CASP), which allowed an individual to enlist for three years in a civilian-related skill at an advanced grade.[84] A liberal policy allowed the appointment to grade E4 or E5 after completion of a two-week familiarization course, which was supposed to be the equivalent of basic training. (Men, as mentioned, had to undergo eight weeks of training.) Reserve units were supposed to augment the two-week training with a series of mandatory classes, but units frequently skipped these classes and put women to work immediately.

Specialities in the administrative and medical fields were the most popular areas for women joining the Army Reserve under the CASP program as well as under other enlistment options. The CASP criteria were gradually made more strict over the years, and the two-week basic training option was eliminated. Nevertheless, CASP gave the USAR a substantial boost and helped it recruit a substantial number of women in rapid fashion. The program remains on the books today.

After 1974, female membership in the USAR grew steadily, reaching 38,961—16.4 percent of unit strength—by June 30, 1982. The opening of the Reserve Officers Training Corps to women in 1972 dramatically increased the number of female Reserve officers, and there are approximately 5,000 female officers—exclusive of the medical specialities—in Army Reserve units in 1983.

Recruiting statistics released on October 8, 1982,[85] show that women accounted for 28 percent of first-time Army Reserve enlistments during the 1982 fiscal year end-

83. These figures and subsequent personnel figures, unless otherwise noted, are from the Office of the Chief, Army Reserve, *Annual Historical Summary* for the year indicated. Prior to 1972, the Office of the Chief, Army Reserve did not record female and minority strength figures.

84. The provisions of the CASP program are outlined in AR 140–111. The criteria for awarding grade changed over the years, but initially a person was given E4 rank for one year's experience and E5 rank for two year's civilian experience. In some specialities, such as Social Worker, post-high school education could be substituted for work experience. Men were also eligible for CASP enlistments, but had to take eight-weeks of training before being granted accelerated rank.

85. *Selected Reserve Manpower Strength Assessment and Recruiting Results,* News Release 443–82, Department of Defense, Oct. 8, 1982.

ing September 30, 1982. The Army Reserve had 64,388
women in the IRR and Army Reserve units on August 31,
1982, and Army Reserve units are expected to add another
1,000–12,000 women in the next few years.[86]

THE ARMY RESERVE SEEKS MINORITIES

In addition to recruiting more women in the 1970's, the
Army Reserve turned to another almost untouched source of
manpower—minority group members. Although minorities
had been part of the Army Reserve since the first World
War, the percentage of black and Hispanic soldiers in the
Army Reserve was small. In the mainland United States, the
overwhelming majority of Army Reserve units were over-
whelmingly white. This practice of de facto segregation
abruptly changed in 1973.

In 1973 the Army Reserve's official policy became one
of recruiting minority groups so that units would reflect the
ethnic characteristics of the community. As a result, the
number of blacks in Army Reserve units doubled from
6,869 to 13,099 during fiscal year 1973, and the number
of black unit members reached 24,998 two years later. The
number of blacks in the Selected Reserve of the Army Reserve (unit strength plus Individual Mobilization Augmen-
tees) was 59,216—23 percent of the force on June 1, 1983.
Other minorities accounted for 5.8 percent of the force at
that time. Blacks accounted for 26 percent of 1982 enlistments but remain underrepresented in the Army Reserve
commissioned ranks, for only 6.2 percent of Selected Reserve officers are black.[87]

In a final effort to improve unit strength, the Army
Reserve relocated units. Between July 1, 1975, and September 30, 1976, the Army Reserve relocated 88 units to
improve their recruiting base. Every major metropolitan area
was carefully examined, and there was a deliberate effort to
match unit types to the interests and skills of potential enlistees in the area.[88] Today, the ability of an area to sustain a
Reserve unit is one of the principal criteria considered when
the Army looks at potential unit locations.

---

86. Source: Maj. Margaret Novak, Human Resources Action Officer, Office of the Chief, Army Reserve. Women equalled 16.7 percent
of the Selected Reserve on June 1, 1983, and are expected to increase to
18.1 percent by 1988.

87. *Ibid.*

88. *USAR Paid Drill Strength Capped at 237,000,* Press Release
82–88, Office of the Chief, Army Reserve, July 12, 1982.

Army Reserve unit strength problems are minimal in 1983. Although there are some units which are understrength enough to affect their readiness, seriously understrength units are few.

The principal constraint on Army Reserve unit strength is money. On July 12, 1982, the Army Reserve announced that it was holding unit strength at 237,000 for the rest of fiscal year 1982 because there was not enough money to pay for any more members.[89]

On April 6, 1983, Maj. Gen. William R. Berkman testified to the Subcommittee on Preparedness of the Senate Armed Services Committee that the 1984 Army Reserve budget request reflects the Army's decision to hold down personnel costs. According to Berkman, the 1984 paid drill strength of the Army Reserve is being held to the 1983 level and the fiscal year 1983 end strength of 251,500 represents an increase of only four percent over the previous year's authorization. Berkman also testified that Army Reserve unit strength was approximately 50,000 short of wartime requirements.

EQUIPMENT SHORTAGES CONTINUE

Fiscal constraints are also evident in the Army Reserve's equipment posture. As satisfying as recent strength improvements have been, personnel cannot fight effectively if they lack weapons and support equipment. The Army Reserve has traditionally had equipment problems. This was clearly recognized under Secretary of Defense Robert S. McNamara when he decided to abolish the ten Army Reserve divisions which he could not equip. The issue of insufficient equipment for low-priority divisions could be dismissed as *de minimis* in 1964, but a lack of Reserve Component equipment is serious in the Total Force era.

The equipment status of the Army's Reserve Components had been allowed to deteriorate under McNamara, as first priority went to Vietnam and second priority went to NATO. The Reserves were not permitted to requisition major items of equipment in the late 1960's because these requisitions were not going to be filled and the paperwork would only clog the requisition system.[90]

---

89. *Ibid.*
90. Study: *Resource Allocations to Reserve Components,* Chief, Office of Reserve Components (CORC), Washington, DC, 1969, p. 54.

Major items remained unavailable to the Army Reserve through 1970, but an unprecedented issue of equipment was begun in 1971. Issuing $134 million worth of equipment to the Army Reserve that year was made possible when the active Army withdrew from Vietnam. It was made necessary by the Total Force policy.[91]

Considering the technology available and the state of the art of military equipment in 1971, the 1971 equipment issue only serves to underscore the woeful neglect of the Army Reserve under McNamara. Reservists, for example, were still training with M–1 rifles and older weapons that were two or three generations behind the active force. These venerable weapons, veterans of World War II and Korea, were replaced with M14s and M16s. The slush box M211 2½ ton trucks were replaced with M35s, and the Army Reserve started receiving the M151 quarter-ton truck to replace the Korean War-era M38 jeeps. The Army Reserve was issued M60 machine guns to replace the Browning 1919A1 .30 calibre machine guns, and M48A3 tanks began to replace the M48A1 tanks in Army Reserve armor battalions. The Army also started to replace the vacuum tube radios in Army Reserve units.[92]

In 1972, the equipment issue was also $134 million, and in 1973, $105 million was given to the USAR. As a result, the Chief, Army Reserve reported that USAR units had on hand 56 percent of the equipment they needed in wartime.[93] Issues of $71 million, $79 million, and $64 million in the three following years brought the Army Reserve to 71.1 percent of its wartime equipment requirements by 1976.[94]

However, starting in 1978, equipment intended for the Army Reserve was diverted to Europe to build up NATO stocks. As a result, the Army Reserve equipment availability fell to 61 percent of peacetime authorization and only 50 percent of wartime requirements by September 30, 1979. The lack of sufficient modern equipment prevented a substantial number of Army Reserve units from meeting their

---

91. Melvin R. Laird, *Annual Report of the Secretary of Defense on Reserve Forces, Fiscal Year 1971,* (Washington, DC: Department of Defense, 1972), p. 40.

92. *Ibid.*

93. *Annual Historical Summary, 1973, Office of the Chief, Army Reserve,* (Washington, DC, 1974), p. 6.

94. *Annual Historical Summary, 1976, Office of the Chief, Army Reserve,* (Washington, DC, 1977), p. 18.

readiness objectives. These problems were particularly acute for Army Security Agency, Data Processing, and Engineer units. Equipment shortages delayed force structure actions at a time when the Army was trying to align more closely its mix of Reserve units and its war plans.[95] On February 1, 1980, the Chief, Army Reserve reported to the Reserve Components Coordinating Council that 48 percent of Army Reserve units could not meet their mobilization objectives because of a lack of mission-essential equipment. More than 60 percent of Army Reserve units were rated as not combat ready (C4) as of October 15, 1979.[96]

Admittedly, personnel shortages were also a major readiness problem at this time. The Army Reserve was turning the corner on meeting its strength requirements, however, much faster than it was in the equipment area. A 1980 issue of $44 million in equipment improved the situation slightly to 52 percent of wartime requirements,[97] but the over-riding problem was a lack of money for Army Reserve equipment. Army Chief of Staff Gen. Edward C. Meyer spoke of this on February 3, 1981, when he told the Senate Armed Services Committee that the lack of equipment in the Reserve Components was not being addressed as rapidly as necessary because of a lack of money.[98]

The equipment issue cannot be ignored if Army Reserve units are to meet their mobilization objectives as a vital part of the Total Force. The Association of the United States Army expressed the urgent equipment needs of the Reserve Components this way in 1980:

There must be a major increase in early acquisition of current generation equipment right off of the production lines for the Guard and Reserve if our early deploying units are to be compati-

---

95. *Annual Historical Summary, 1979, Office of the Chief, Army Reserve,* (Washington, DC, 1980), pp. 14 and 46.

96. Information Paper, *Overview of USAR Readiness Ratings and Trends,* (Office of the Chief, Army Reserve, DAAR–OT, Washington, DC, February 1, 1980).

97. Information Paper, *USAR Equipment Status,* (Office of the Chief, Army Reserve, DAAR–LO, Washington, DC, December 18, 1980). The information paper stated that "lack of sufficient quantities of modern, first-line equipment continues to prevent the Army Reserve units from attaining their prescribed readiness objectives. Acute major item shortages continue to exist in data processing, heavy engineer, cryptologic and communications and electronic equipment."

98. Transcript of Authorization Hearings on Army Programs, reprinted as Speech File Service, No. 5, Office of the Chief Public Affairs, Department of the Army, 1981. p. 23.

ble with the Active force already deployed or currently deployable.[99]

Citing the House Armed Services Committee report on
the Fiscal Year 1981 Defense Authorization Act, the Association explained the cause of the Reserve Component equipment shortages as follows:

Over the years, the political requirements of budget-making have
overruled the real needs of the military. We now find ourselves
with a backlog of requirements that are essential to national defense and security. Each requirement is urgent in a world becoming more dangerous each day. This backlog of requirements is,
itself, a product of the claim of "unaffordability" in past years.[100]

In 1981, the US Army Forces Command reported favorable increases in Army Reserve deployability because of
an increase in personnel and improved training. Equipment
improvements did not keep pace, however, and FORSCOM
reported that "it was obvious that if DA could match growing personnel strengths with increased issues of now short
items of equipment, there could be a major improvement
recorded over the next several years."[101]

On December 1, 1981, Deputy Assistant Secretary of
Defense (Reserve Affairs) Edward J. Philbin testified before
the Senate Armed Services Committee that the shortages of
Reserve Component equipment were a reflection of overall
shortages of equipment in the Total Force. He admitted that
Reserve forces had obsolete equipment and that much of it
was not deployable, but Philbin stressed that Reserve units
could still effectively perform a variety of missions.[102]

On February 8, 1982, Secretary of the Army John O.
Marsh, Jr., told the House Armed Services Committee that
he intended to place special emphasis upon the Army National Guard and the Army Reserve and that the committee
would see the results of this emphasis in the current and

99. *A Status Report on the Army National Guard and the United States
Army Reserve,* Association of the United States Army, Arlington, VA,
1980, p. 19.

100. *Ibid.,* pp. 18–19.

101. *Annual Historical Review, Oct. 1, 1980–Sept. 30, 1981,* U.S.
Army Forces Command, Fort McPherson, GA, 1982, pp. 305–330.

102. Testimony, Hon. Edward J. Philbin, Deputy Assistant Secretary of Defense (Reserve Affairs), Preparedness Subcommittee, Senate
Armed Services Committee, December 1, 1981, pp. 10 and 18.

coming years.[103] The Army Secretary's 1982 emphasis may produce some materiel gains in future years. On February 25, 1983, Chief of Staff Meyer testified that $750 million worth of equipment would be delivered to Guard and Army Reserve units in 1984, and he projected that $1 billion of the active Army's 1984 procurement would be distributed to the Reserve Components in the years ahead.[104] Shortly thereafter, Lt. Gen. Richard H. Thompson, Army Deputy Chief of Staff for Logistics, gave the following data for the Army's Reserve Component share of future procurement dollars:

FY 1984	$ 906,900,000
FY 1985	885,000,000
FY 1986	769,400,000
FY 1987	1,885,200,000
FY 1988	2,461,700,000[105]

This is a total of $6.9 billion over the next five years. When it is considered that estimates of the Army Reserve's equipment shortages ranged from $3.9 to $5.6 billion[106] early in 1983, it would appear that even $6.9 billion will not cure all Army National Guard and Army Reserve equipment problems. Such a sum, however, would be a major step toward achieving materiel readiness.

There are, however, two problems in anticipating major real gains in Army Reserve equipment status by 1990. First, two-thirds of the billions shown above are planned for the "Out" years of the budget cycle. Procurements planned that far ahead are often revised downward when budget priorities are developed.

Second, the 1983 Army Reserve shortage figures do not consider potential force structure changes. As the Total Force structure is refined each year to meet evolving contingencies, it is quite likely that new units will be added to the Army Reserve and lower priority Reserve units dropped

103. Testimony on the Posture of the Army, reprinted as Speech File Service, No. 3, Office of the Chief Public Affairs, Department of the Army, Washington, DC, 1982, p. 1.

104. Statement, Gen. Edward C. Meyer, before the Committee on Armed Services, United States Senate, February 25, 1983, p. 7.

105. Memorandum for the Secretary of the Army, *Project ALARM,* DALO-PLM, Department of the Army, Washington, DC, 1983, p. 2.

106. Berkman, *Posture of the U.S. Army Reserve,* p. 20. The difference of $1.7 billion between the two figures depends on whether Army Reserve armored battalions are issued the M–1 Abrams tank. If Army Reserve units are equipped with the M60 tank, the value of 1983's equipment shortage is $3.9 billion.

from the force structure. The new units will require equipment that is not on hand today and which cannot be anticipated today. This will add to overall Army Reserve equipment needs as we approach 1990.

As severe as some equipment shortages may be, the clear facts remain that the Army leadership is well aware of the Army Reserve's equipment deficiencies and is attempting to solve the most serious deficiencies within the limits imposed by the Army budget. Equally important is the very substantial progress made in the quality and quantity of equipment on hand between the beginning of the Total Force policy in 1970 and today—1983.

MAINTENANCE IMPROVES

Two subjects closely related to equipment on hand and strongly influenced by the quantity of Army Reserve equipment are maintenance facilities and programs in general and the overall adequacy of Army Reserve facilities. The increased issue of equipment to the Army Reserve in the early 1970's presented problems of maintenance, storage, and training. At the beginning of the decade, units were responsible for their own maintenance, and upper echelon maintenance for Army Reserve equipment was performed by active Army facilities on a space-available and time-available basis. This system worked when Reserve units possessed only a few of their major pieces of equipment, but it broke down under increased equipment issue.

The solution was to increase the number of maintenance facilities operated directly by the Army Reserve. By June 30, 1972, the Army Reserve was reaching maintenance self-sufficiency with 203 maintenance shops and 2,175 maintenance technicians. These shops were known as Area Maintenance Support Activities (AMSAs), and their work was supplemented by assigning Army Reserve direct support units the mission of supporting other Army Reserve units.

In 1977, the Chief, Army Reserve reported that the 212 AMSAs were keeping Army Reserve materiel readiness up to active component standards. In general, the Army Reserve's maintenance capability has not been a negative factor on unit training or readiness. There is still, however, a maintenance backlog for Army Reserve units estimated at $61.2 million in 1981.[107]

---

107. *Annual Historical Review, Oct. 1, 1980–Sept. 30, 1981*, U.S. Army Forces Command, p. 451.

INADEQUATE FACILITIES

The chronic nature of inadequate facilities was evident in 1969 when a resource allocation study determined that at the current rate of construction—$25 million a year—the construction requirements could be met by the year 2016.[108] In 1971, only 287 of 1019 centers were considered adequate, generating total construction requirements of $338,400,000. The unfinanced construction requirement had expanded to $399 million by 1974, at which time the Army declared a 10-year Army Reserve Construction Program to eliminate most of the major problems by 1980.

This plan called for spending $54 million a year on Military Construction Army Reserve (the MCAR appropriation). This figure was approached only once in the next decade—$53.8 million in 1977—and fell to $30 million in 1980. By the time $65 million was available in 1982 and $53 million was requested for 1984, inflation had halved the value of such a sum. As a result, the Army Reserve's construction backlog stood at $848 million in 1982.[109] Even though the Army Reserve possesses many fine, modern Reserve Centers well-equipped with maintenance facilities and training areas, the majority of Army Reserve centers are inadequate. Some centers are inadequate because they are old or too small, while others are inadequate because they are rented facilities that were not designed to house Army Reserve units. There has not been enough money appropriated to replace or upgrade all of the inadequate facilities, and there are Army Reserve units in 1983 training in former automobile showrooms and unused portions of bowling alleys.

The USAR must also build and maintain maintenance facilities and certain training areas. The Army Reserve is responsible in part for the training areas of a number of installations such as Fort Indiantown Gap, Pa. and Fort Pickett, Va., where MCAR monies have been spent on training ranges and other facilities used by Reserve units.[110]

---

108. *Resource Allocation to Reserve Components,* p. 68.

109. The $848 million dollar backlog figure comes from *The Posture of the Army and Department of the Army Budget Estimates for Fiscal Year 1983,* p. 55; other construction figures are found in the Annual Historical Summaries of the Office of the Chief, Army Reserve and *The Posture of the U.S. Army Reserve,* previously cited.

110. Sometimes the planned use of facilities by Reservists can lead to some decisions of dubious long-term value. For example, when the Army Reserve funded the construction of an encampment area on Fort

The adequacy of training areas has a direct impact upon the ability of a unit to train for its mobilization mission, and when a unit must travel several hours to reach a suitable facility for field training, the amount of time remaining for training is seriously reduced. Although there has been an upgrading of training areas in recent years, many units cannot meet their full potential because of a lack of ranges or maneuver areas.

Despite budget constraints which have placed limits on training facilities, equipment issues and personnel strength, the Army Reserve has made considerable progress since 1970 in the critical area of training. In the past 10–12 years, training has become more imaginative, training has become better managed, training–support personnel have been increased, training flexibility has been achieved, and training standards have been upgraded. In addition, the Army has instituted affiliation programs between the active and Reserve Components, and the long-standing Mutual Support Program has enhanced training and readiness.

In 1970, the Army Reserve had two major training problems. The first was an extensive backlog of new Reserve enlistees who had been unable to obtain their initial active duty training. Since the establishment of the REP–63 enlistment program on September 3, 1963, Army Reserve enlistees were guaranteed as much initial active duty as was necessary to complete basic training and become qualified in their military occupation specialty. When the Army was expanded in the mid-1960's, priority for training went to active Army draftees, and Army Reservists were unable to obtain basic training and technical schooling.

Basic training delays of up to two years were not uncommon in the 1960's. By July 1, 1969, 21,652 Reservists—approximately 10 percent of the USAR enlisted force—were awaiting training. The inability to obtain initial training was particularly acute in medical specialities,[111] and this problem was not alleviated until 1971. As the number of new soldiers entering the active Army decreased,

---

Pickett in 1982, the Army denied funds to install heating in the barracks and administrative areas. The rationale was that these facilities would only be used by Reservists on weekends and in the summer during Annual Training. The Fort Pickett commander's entreaties that there just might be a winter mobilization someday were rejected so that a relatively few dollars could be saved.

111. *Annual Historical Summary, July 1, 1970 to June 30, 1971,* Office of the Chief, Army Reserve, Washington, D.C., pp. 7–8.

Reservists were able to obtain training. The REP–63 backlog was down to 1,904 by June 30, 1972, and it ceased to be a problem the next year.

The second major problem in 1970 was that the entire Army Reserve training philosophy and approach seemed to be inadequate. Ever since the Korean War, Reserve units had concentrated on basic unit training (BUT), with the attainment of company-level proficiency as the objective. Once the unit had achieved company-level proficiency, it would take the standard Army Training Test (ATT). Once all of the companies of a battalion passed their ATT, the battalion would start on battalion-level training. This latter, however, rarely occurred.[112]

In theory, units were supposed to be able to progress three weeks along the training cycle toward battalion and higher level proficiency each year. Such progress was in reality almost impossible, because units would have a 20 percent turn-over among their junior enlisted personnel each year. After two or three years, it became necessary to stop company-level training and start over on squad and platoon-level training.

This endless cycle of training was exacerbated in the 1960's by inadequate training facilities, curtailment of Reserve operations and maintenance funds, reduction in advisor support, and the REP–63 backlog. Something had to be done.

In January 1970, following the Chief of Staff's December 22, 1969, memo reaffirming the Reserve Components as the principal source of mobilization expansion, the Department of the Army directed the Continental Army Command (CONARC) to improve Reserve Component training and readiness.[113] After studying the problem, CONARC determined that improvements in the advisor system, an affiliation between active and Reserve units and more mutual support between the components would lead to major improvements in training and readiness.

---

112. In 1970, 31 percent of Army Reserve companies had achieved company-level training. There was little progress though. That year, 11 percent of Army Reserve battalions reported that they had moved from squad-level to platoon-level training and seven percent reported progress from platoon-level to company-level training. See *Annual Historical Summary, Fiscal Year 1971*, Continental U.S. Army Command, Fort Monroe, Va, 1972, p. 187.

113. *Annual Historical Summary, Fiscal Year 1970*, Continental U.S. Army Command, Fort Monroe, Va, 1971, pp. 226–29.

MUTUAL SUPPORT, AFFILIATION, AND CAPSTONE

Mutual support between the components had been in effect in an informal manner for several years. Specialized Reserve units such as Medical, Judge Advocate General or Civil Affairs would provide services to an active Army installation or command in return for physical support during Annual Training or weekend field training.

This beneficial relationship had come to the attention of the Army's Vice Chief of Staff, Gen. Bruce Palmer, who encouraged Gen. James L. Woolnough, the CONARC Commander, to formalize the program. Woolnough agreed, and CONARC forwarded a draft program to Palmer in December 1970.[114] This program gave 23 examples of how active units could support Reserve units and 18 examples of Reserve support to the active force.

The CONARC draft was accepted, and the Mutual Support Program was made official in July 1971 with the publication of Army Regulation 11–22. Although a lack of funds restricted mutual support to units located near each other, the Mutual Support Program (MSP) was well received. Within a year, more than 40 percent of Army Reserve units had formal MSP agreements, and virtually every Reserve unit was involved in MSP by the 1980's.

Affiliation and Roundout programs were also started in 1970. The two differ in that a Roundout Reserve unit replaces an active component unit in an active Army brigade or division, while an Affiliation is a working relationship where the Reserve unit augments rather than replaces an active component unit.[115]

The Army Reserve's Roundout relationship began in 1970 when the 8th Battalion, 40th Armor was assigned as a Roundout battalion of the 1st Armored Division. This was expanded in February 1973 with the 100th Battalion,

---

114. For correspondence, between Palmer and Woolnough, see *Annual Historical Summary, Fiscal Year 1971*, pp. 184–86. Palmer initiated the correspondence, but when Woolnough agreed and asked for a formal program, Palmer replied that the current fiscal situation did not allow expenditures for mutual support programs.

115. Roundout is not without risk. The FORSCOM *Annual Report of Major Activities, Fiscal Year 1975*, summarizes Roundout risks and benefits this way: "On paper, the Roundout concept seemed to offer a method of increasing Active Army mobilization deployment combat strength at an attractively low cost. The only problem was whether or not these Reserve units could ever be brought to a combat readiness condition which would allow them to function . . . effectively and responsively in a sudden mobilization." See page 396 of that report.

442nd Infantry in Hawaii being named to roundout the 25th Infantry Division. By September 30, 1978, every stateside active Army division had Army Reserve or National Guard Roundout units assigned, although by and large this is a National Guard role as opposed to one for the Army Reserve.[116]

Affiliation as a formal program developed in the mid-1970's. Affiliation as a concept had been approved in 1973 and studied in detail in 1974. As with Roundout, Affiliation was very attractive because of its cost effectiveness. The Army concluded that Affiliation was preferrable to keeping additional units on active duty.[117] This led to an adjustment of the Department of the Army Master Priority List (DAMPL) and a major restructuring of the Army Reserve's forces in 1976, 1977 and 1978.

During those three years, 782 Army Reserve units underwent a realignment of some nature—activation, deactivation or reorganization. Seventeen Army Reserve units were brought into Affiliation in 1978, and 50 more were added in 1979.[118]

In 1980, the Affiliation concept was expanded to include every unit in the Army Reserve, and a new program was coined. This was the CAPSTONE program which aligned Reserve units with the active and Reserve Component units with which they are likely to be deployed. CAPSTONE relationships were formalized into discrete mobilization packages based upon NATO requirements in the D to D + 90 timeframe and the Total Force.

---

116. *Ibid.*

117. See Robert A. Gessert, *Problems of Implementing Reserve Component—Active Army Augmentation/Affiliation,* (McLean, Va.: General Research Corp., 1974). This study asserts that formal Affiliation became necessary because the Army had a 40 percent manpower shortfall in the active Army and was unable to meet JSOP planning objectives without extensive use of Reserve Components in the D to D + 90 time-frame of a NATO contingency. In supporting Affiliation as a solution, according to Gessert, the Army made several assumptions. These include assumptions of company-level proficiency for Reserve units, four weeks lead time for mobilization, equipment compatibility between active and Reserve Components, and strength figures that would allow a deployment strength of 86 percent TOE. Affiliation as a formal program was authorized by Chief of Staff Memorandum 73–135—132, dated November 21, 1973.

118. Realignment and Affiliation data is from the OCAR *Annual Historical Summaries* for 1976 through 1979.

CAPSTONE created a training and planning relationship that focused upon wartime missions and left no doubt as to the wartime organization of every unit in the total peacetime force. CAPSTONE thereby became the basis for much mobilization planning. This planning is an extraordinarily complex task involving manning, equipping, training and deploying more than 4,000 separate military units to more than 50 different installations.[119]

Mutual Support Programs have proven beneficial, and Roundout and Affiliation solved an Army force structure problem. Roundout and Affiliation led to CAPSTONE, but Roundout and Affiliation did not alter the fact that Army Reserve unit training did not seem to progress very quickly.

Unit commanders were given more flexibility in training in 1972 when the number of mandatory and general subjects was reduced to allow more emphasis upon mission-related training. In 1974, the Army started to move away from the Army Training Test and began to develop the Army Training and Evaluation Programs—ARTEPs. The ARTEPs defined unit training status by the ability of a unit to perform a number of mission-related tasks. The ARTEP was different for each type of unit and gave the commander a guide by which to tailor his training program. More importantly, the ARTEP concept made it easier to define training readiness. The ARTEP concept abolished the practice of estimating how many weeks a unit had progressed during the year. Instead, a unit's training readiness was measured by the proportion of major and minor training tasks the unit could or did accomplish. Thus, the training portion of the overall readiness equation became more objective and less subjective.

FORSCOM EMPHASIZES REALISTIC TRAINING

At the same time the Army was developing the ARTEPs, the Steadfast reorganization was having an effect upon Army Reserve training and readiness. The new FORSCOM emphasized field exercises, the use of aggressor forces for realistic training, field skills such as camouflage, cover and conceal-

---

119. Testimony, Maj. Gen. William R. Berkman, Chief, Army Reserve, before the Committee on Armed Services, U.S. Senate, Feb. 26, 1980. See also, *Department of the Army Historical Summary, FY 1980,* (Draft), Department of the Army, Washington, DC, pp. II–6 and VIII–28.

ment, adventure training, and the realistic use of training aids. In 1974, FORSCOM's second year, the new command emphasized mission-related training for Army Reserve units during weekend IDT. Reserve combat support and combat service support units were urged to perform actual support missions on weekends. The next year, FORSCOM required Army Reserve units to conduct at least two weekend field training exercises, and units were told to minimize parades, details and fatigue work during IDT. Looking carefully at typical Reserve unit training, FORSCOM personnel concluded that half of IDT was not directed toward mission training. Two weekends each year were devoted to preparation for the Annual General Inspection (AGI); two went into recruiting; one was lost to ceremonies and parades; and one was spent in MOS testing. Annual Training (AT) time was also lost to administration, weekend passes, parties, PX visits, issue and turn-in of equipment and travel. It was estimated that only 8 to 9 days of useful training were being accomplished during the 14-day AT period.[120]

The problem was that many of the diversions from mission-related training were either justifiable or desirable. In the mid-1970's, the Army Reserve was having tremendous recruiting and retention problems. Reserve commanders recognized that benefits such as making use of the PX and active Army recreation facilities during AT were inducements for Reservists to remain in the Army Reserve. Commanders realized that having the middle weekend off reduced family objections to Annual Training, and a final night party was good for morale.

The administrative problems were a fact of life. This was before the Army Reserve started to receive additional help under the full-time manning program. Paperwork requirements—generated by the active Army—had exploded, and the increased administrative workload was a direct result of the Total Force policy. With the increased reliance upon the Reserve Components, Reserve units were subjected to the full weight of active Army requirements with little or no change in the full-time manpower to support this workload.[121]

---

120. *Annual Report of Major Activities, Fiscal Year 1975*, U.S. Army Forces Command, Fort McPherson, GA, 1976, pp. 423 and 424.

121. C. F. Briggs, *1980 Reduction of Administrative Workload at the Reserve Component Unit Level*, final report, RCCC Task Force, Department of the Army, Washington, DC, 1980, p. 4–2.

There simply was not time enough in 280 training hours a year to achieve all desirable training objectives while accomplishing all *required* administrative tasks. When faced with a choice between looking good on an AGI, which concentrated on administration, or improving training readiness, which was still very subjective, unit commanders chose to pass their AGIs.[122]

Although recognizing the dilemma that strict training policies created, FORSCOM continued to demand more realistic training. In 1978, Reserve commanders were required to conduct 88 hours of mission-related training during AT. This mission-related time could not include travel, equipment issue and turn-in, pay call, physical training testing, marksmanship, or even clearing of post at the end of AT. As a result, unit commanders began to schedule evening and overnight training to achieve the mandatory 88 hours. The increased night-time training was what the Reserve units needed, and the end result was an improvement in field training.

In 1979, Reserve units were told to emphasize night training and to concentrate upon mission essential training—those tasks which had to be done to perform the wartime mission. Since then, mission-essential training has been the watchword, and units have concentrated on likely wartime missions, in contrast to achieving every capability identified for their type of unit. Army Reserve training readiness thus made major improvements between 1970 and 1983 because of stricter standards, increased active Army assistance, the adoption of the ARTEP system, and a clearer identification of wartime responsibilities as defined by CAPSTONE relationships. An increase in the number of full-time personnel has helped reduce the administrative problems faced by commanders, and advances in mobilization planning have more clearly identified the tasks that units need to accomplish in peacetime.

---

122. The Briggs report urged the army to reduce the administrative workload at the unit level. A watchdog organization was set up within The Adjutant General's (TAG) Office, but by 1983 its accomplishments have been more form than substance. Probably the two biggest changes which have slightly reduced unit administrative requirements are the lengthening of the minimum Officer Evaluation Report (OER) time to 120 days and dropping the monthly serial number check of weapons. Weapons are now counted monthly, and the serial number check is done quarterly.

MOBILIZATION

Estimates of readiness aside, the key to Army Reserve unit usefulness is the ability to mobilize. At least one-half of the Army's war-making capability is in the Ready Reserve, and the entire Total Force policy is predicated upon the ability of the Reserve Components to mobilize quickly. Mobilization is a complex process requiring that people and equipment be brought together in the right proportions at the right time. Mobilizing a Reserve unit means assembling all of its members, separating them from their families and civilian jobs, gathering all of their personal gear and unit equipment, moving this assemblage in a few days to a mobilization station, performing last minute training, perhaps going overseas, and, finally, arriving at the wartime destination able to perform the unit mission. Obviously, much can go wrong with this process.[123] It is an undertaking fraught with opportunities for failure and confusion. Experience with Reserve Component mobilization for World War II, Korea,

---

123. The stark necessity for mobilization exercises is vividly illustrated by the experience of the 3397th US Army Garrison during MOBEX 78. This Chattanooga, Tenn., Army Reserve unit was assigned to operate Camp Shelby, Miss. At the time, the press described Camp Shelby as a swampy, mosquito-ridden camp, some 45 miles north of Biloxi, Miss., which had not been used by active units since the end of World War II. It was one of some 15 semi-active or state-operated installations which would have to be used for mobilization purposes in cases of full mobilization.

The garrison's mission in MOBEX 78 was to prepare Camp Shelby to receive five Reserve Component combat brigades that were coming to Shelby for final training before overseas deployment. The garrison's first problem was that Camp Shelby had only enough barracks for one brigade, and even these were wooden, temporary World War II buildings. The garrison attempted to requisition tents, but the requisition was cancelled by an improperly-programmed computer. The computer problems proved meaningless anyway, because the Army did not have enough tents for four mechanized brigades. Actually, however, the garrison didn't need tentage for four brigades, because the units coming to Shelby were 4,000 men understrength.

The garrison tried to requisition trained men to flesh out the brigades. However, at the time, the Army had three different personnel requisitioning systems in effect—one each for active Army, National Guard and Army Reserve. These systems could not be made compatible. In the end, there was a 40 percent error rate on the personnel assigned as fillers.

According to outside observers at the time, it was difficult to see how the troops could have been given final training at Camp Shelby. There was no ammunition available for firing, and Shelby had no place to store the diesel fuel needed for maneuvers. There was no way to get the M60 tanks and armored personnel carriers to Camp Shelby because of

Berlin, and Vietnam has shown that it is very easy for the process to break down.

Though each mobilization has gone more smoothly than the previous one, even the small Vietnam mobilization was far from perfect. This tendency was recognized in the early 1970's, so the Army decided to practice mobilization. The result has been a series of mobilization exercises (MOBEXs) in 1976, 1978, 1980 and 1982 which have led to changes in Army Reserve administration and training while fine-tuning mobilization planning.

The first exercise, MOBEX 76, was the first large-scale test of mobilization plans since the Berlin mobilization provided a real world practical exercise in 1961. The 1976 exercise was a free-play command post exercise representing a deliberate full mobilization for general war in Europe. Nearly 300 Army Reserve units participated in the exercise, which simulated alert, mobilization at home station, and movement to the mobilization stations. Even though MOBEX 76 was only a paper exercise, the Army learned from it. As a result, mobilization and deployment plans were revised, and the Army took steps to correct the deficiencies it revealed.

MOBEX 78 was code-named "Nifty Nugget". The crisis situation portrayed in Nifty Nugget involved a short warning, fast breaking attack on NATO forces in Europe. In such a crisis, the United States would have to use the forces in being, and there would be little time to improve the readiness of the Reserve Components. This exercise was DoD wide and involved several other departments of the federal government. As in 1976, Reserve personnel and equipment did not actually move, but took part through representative player cells who provided real-world data for the exercise. As in 1976, Nifty Nugget showed that the United States had severe mobilization problems. First, existing mobilization plans were a hodgepodge of old and unconnected Presidential emergency orders, policies, regulations and procedures. Second, although contingency plans as-

---

a shortage of flatcars. Further, even if the necessary 300 heavy-duty flat cars could be found, the one decrepit rail line leading to Shelby was incapable of handling them. In addition, the telephone system at Camp Shelby did not work. The entire mobilization at Shelby would have been a disaster.

In the end, FORSCOM concluded that there was nothing grievously wrong at Camp Shelby that couldn't have been cured by the efficient application of sufficient resources. (Adapted from pp. 402–404 of FORSCOM's *Annual Historical Review, Oct. 1, 1980 to September 30, 1981*).

sumed that units would be at their desired levels of personnel and equipment, Reserve Component units were seriously short of personnel and equipment in 1978. On the civil side, the federal government was in disarray. Civil emergency planning had concentrated only upon natural disasters and nuclear attack. There was no coordination on the industrial base, and the public health sector was unprepared for mobilization.[124] Following Nifty Nugget, the Federal Emergency Management Agency was formed to coordinate government-wide emergency planning.

The next MOBEX, in 1980, was known as "Proud Spirit". Like its predecessors, Proud Spirit revealed that the mobilization preparation of the United States was woefully inadequate.[125] From the Army Reserve's point of view, Proud Spirit confirmed the inability of active Army installations to support a rapid influx of Reserve units. The exercise did identify problems to be attacked by the Army Readiness and Mobilization Regions (ARMRs). The exercise was carried out during the Iranian Crisis and after the decision to form the Rapid Deployment Joint Task Force (RDJTF). As a result, the exercise gave valuable clues as to the steps required to make the RDJTF a true rapidly-deployable force.[126]

The most recent such exercise, MOBEX 83, took place in the fall of 1982, and was actually three exercises in one. Three different warplans were played in successive weeks, and officials reported very extensive improvements in mobilization capabilities. The exercise focused on the Army's Reserve and National Guard and found them able to deploy despite continued equipment shortages.[127]

MOBEX–83, moreover, confirmed the results of an earlier exercise that dealt with accessions. This exercise, Grand Payload, indicated that TRADOC would have difficulties in

---

124. July 23, 1980, the Department of Defense released an unclassified 24-page report on Nifty Nugget. The findings of this report are summarized in "Exercise Reveals Defense Problems," *Pentagram News,* Washington, DC, July 31, 1980, pp. 1–4.

125. See John J. Fialka, "The Pentagon's Exercise Proud Spirit: Little Cause for Pride," *Parameters, Journal of the U.S. Army War College,* Vol. XI, No. 1, pp. 38–41. See also, Maj. Richard B. Crossland, "Suppose the Balloon Goes Up: Then What," *Army Reserve Magazine* (Winter 1981), pp. 24–27.

126. See John J. Fialka, "U.S. Again Fails Test of Ability to Mobilize," *Washington Star,* Dec. 21, 1980, pp. A–1 and A–6.

127. "U.S. Crisis Exercise Reports Major Gains in Ability to Mobilize," *New York Times,* Dec. 12, 1982. Also, Capt. Robert Pratt, "Mobilization: No Straight A Report Card," *Army Reserve Magazine* (Summer, 1983), pp. 22–23.

expanding the training base upon mobilization. For example, Army Reserve reception stations did not possess the automatic data processing equipment required to rapidly process new soldiers into the Army. The Army Reserve training divisions were not fully prepared to expand the training base because of a lack of equipment, and the Army's training requirements and resourcing systems were unable to cope with a partial mobilization.[128]

By taking part in these exercises, Reservists gained valuable experience in the mobilization process. On a larger scale, the federal Government gained an appreciation of the need for better mobilization planning. Although changes have come slowly, the federal Government in general and the military departments in particular have placed greater emphasis upon mobilization planning in recent years. For the Army Reserve, the increased emphasis upon mobilization has made mobilization capabilities a top consideration in day-to-day decisions. Training activities and administration are now being conducted in light of how these actions will enhance mobilization.

On the practical level, mobilization planning was clearly defined for Army Reservists with the August 1982 publication of the *Reserve Component Commanders Handbook for Mobilization*. For the first time, every peacetime action that a unit commander must take to prepare for mobilization is indicated.

The Mobilization Personnel Processing System (MOB-PERS) has been compiled out of the experiences of the MOBEXs. These exercises have finally helped the Army achieve the ability to swiftly and smoothly mobilize the Reserve Component, including the Retired Reserve. The Army has also established the Army Mobilization and Operations Planning System (AMOPS) as the single, integrated mobilization and deployment planning system for the Army.

The new systems and procedures they represent have been a quantum leap ahead for Army Reserve readiness. Because a sturdy framework of mobilization concepts has been established and because additional personnel assets have been devoted to mobilization planning in recent years, the Army Reserve is better able to mobilize in 1983 than at any other time in its history.

---

128. For the results of Grand Payload, see *Evaluation Report, Exercise Grand Payload* (Arlington, Va.: Systems Research and Applications, Corp., 1982). Proud Saber Reports are outlined in After Action Reports, HQ, TRADOC, MOBEX—83.

THE IMPACT OF THE IRANIAN CRISIS

Finally, any history of the Army Reserve in the 1970's and
early 1980's would be incomplete without an overview of the
impact caused by the Iranian Crisis and the Soviet invasion
of Afghanistan. The November 4, 1979, seizure of the
American embassy in Tehran underscored this country's inability to project conventional forces into the Middle East,
while the December 27, 1979, Soviet invasion of
Afghanistan raised the issue of American capability to counter Russian threats in the Persian Gulf region. President
Jimmy Carter committed the United States to the defense of
the Persian Gulf in his January 23, 1980, State of the
Union Address. The RDJTF was officially established on
March 1, 1980, with the mission of executing that commitment.

As soon as planners began to draw up contingency
plans, it became obvious that Reserve units were going to
be key elements of the Rapid Deployment Force—Army
(RFD–A) troop list. A decision to employ the task force
would require a call-up of Reserve units in excess of the
50,000-man authority that had been in the law since May,
1976.[129] Defense officials immediately sought an increase in
the 90-day call-up authority. Congress responded quickly,
and in December 1980, Carter signed Public Law 96–584
giving him authority to mobilize up to 100,000 members
of the Selected Reserve without a declaration of war or national emergency. Concurrently, the Army revised its former
Mobilization Designee (MOBDES) program and instituted
the Individual Mobilization Augmentee (IMA) program.
These individuals were included in the Selected Reserve,
thus making them eligible for the 100,000 call-up.

The 100,000 figure had a direct relationship to the
number of Reservists of all services that would be needed to
sustain the RDJTF. In answering questions from the floor
during the convention of the Association of the US Army in
October 1981, Lt. Gen. Robert C. Kingston, the RDJTF
commander, said that he would need almost the entire call-
up authority to move and sustain a corps-sized RDJTF in
the Middle East.

---

129. On May 14, 1976, the Reserve Forces Call-Up Authority, became Public Law 94–286. It permitted the President to mobilize a maximum of 50,000 Selected Reservists for a period of up to 90 days without declaring a national emergency. This authority was necessary to add
teeth to the Total Force policy of heavy reliance upon the Reserve Components.

A few months later, Kingston told the midwinter conference of the Reserve Officers Association that "the Rapid Deployment Joint Task Force is one of the foremost 'customers' of the Reserve Components. If this force is ever deployed in anger, a sizable portion of my forces—particularly combat support and combat service support forces—will come from the Reserve and the National Guard."

Kingston stated that the Army Reserve was absolutely critical to the success of the RDJTF, pointing out that 80 percent of his psychological operations capability came from the Army Reserve. He told the ROA that Army Reserve units would be among the first of those deployed with the RDJTF and that Reserve commanders had to do everything within their capability to get their units ready for immediate deployment.[130]

The exact number of Army Reserve units earmarked for the RDJTF—now called the US Central Command—in 1983 is classified. However, in March 1981, Maj. Gen. Berkman testified before Congress that "the importance of the Army Reserve continues to grow. An increasing number of reserve units have been assigned high priority because of the essential combat service and logistical support needed early upon mobilization and deployment, and for support of the Rapid Deployment Force. Recently, 83 Army Reserve units have been identified for inclusion in the Army's portion of the Rapid Deployment Force because of the essential combat support and combat service support they represent."[131]

Following their inclusion in the RDJTF, Army Reserve units came under intensified management. The RDJTF units went to the top of FORSCOM's Intensified Management Force List, which had previously been led by Roundout units. These USAR RDJTF units had their mobilization plans updated and their equipment priority adjusted upward.[132]

130. Prepared remarks, Lt. Gen. Robert C. Kingston, for delivery to the Reserve Officers Association Midwinter Conference, Feb. 15, 1982.

131. Testimony, Maj. Gen. William R. Berkman, Chief, Army Reserve, before Subcommittee on Military Personnel and Compensation, House Armed Services Committee, March 11, 1981.

132. For details on the increased priority of USAR units and cross-leveling of assets, see Maj. Richard B. Crossland, "RDJTF: Can It Get There Without the USAR?," *Army Reserve Magazine*, (Spring 1982), pp. 8–10.

Despite the fact that Army Reserve units moved higher on the Army's resource list, it would be naive to assume that all of the Army Reserve's RDJTF–identified units are at full readiness. Many of these units are in doubtful condition for immediate deployment because of severe equipment shortages.

There is a hard core of shortage items for these priority units, and many of these pieces of equipment will not be available until at least 1985. There are unique units with unique equipment needs for which equipment has not even been type-standardized, let alone procured. In other cases, funds are not available to buy needed items such as landing craft and lighterage.[133]

Defense guidance and projections reveal that equipment problems will continue in future years. Unclassified portions of the 1983–87 Program Objective Memorandum (POM) state that a significant portion of the RDJTF combat support package will remain in the Reserve Components, even while those components remain underequipped. The Army leadership has consistently testified that the Reserve Components will remain a vital part of the Army for the foreseeable future, and there has been no mention of a diminished RDJTF role for the Army Reserve. It would appear that the Army Reserve will have high-priority contingency missions for a long time to come.

In summary, the Army Reserve's integration into immediate deployment plans is an indication of how far the Total Force policy progressed between 1970 and 1983. In this short span of time, the Army's Reserve Components have changed from being back-up forces to be deployed 90–150 days into a crisis, to being a part of the first units to deploy in case of an emergency. Since 1970, the training and equipping of the Army Reserve have improved more than in any similar period of American history. The citizen-soldier concept has matured in late 20th century America, and the blending of the traditional American reliance upon Reserve Components with the practical military needs of today's risky world represents an evolution of the citizen-soldier concept and a triumph for American democracy.

133. The problem of lighterage and watercraft is discussed in the November–December issue of *Army Logistician* and is included in Secretary of the Army John O. Marsh, Jr.'s 1983 Army posture statement.

Epilogue

The days when this country could be defended by men who put down their plows, picked up their rifles, and went off to meet the enemy are gone forever. Warfare today is simply too complicated, and weapons systems are too sophisticated for the United States to depend upon an *ad hoc* system like the one that served so well in the colonial period. Today, few people lay down their plows and march off to war, but the Army Reservist may well shut down an eighteen-wheeler, turn off a computer console, or leave an assembly line to answer the call of duty. The tools of war have changed, and the jobs we hold are different, but the selflessness that characterized the Minutemen is still a vital part of the forces that defend our country today.

As we researched this book and talked with scores of individuals whose entry into the Army Reserve in 1917 or 1918 coincided with the "War to end all wars," we became convinced that the Reservist is indeed "twice the citizen." The dual responsibility is shown clearly in the history of the Army Reserve, as, indeed, it is in that of the other Reserve Components of this nation. Especially among the earliest Reservists, men who received little pay and often less encouragement, one is struck by the patriotism they display. This was not, we found, a blind chauvinism or mindless xenophobia, but rather a well-reasoned belief that the United States—whatever its flaws—was worth fighting for.

We have been impressed by the Reservists who served in the early years of this century, men like D. Y. Dunn of

Murray, Kentucky, who at the age of ninety-two was selected to represent these early Reservists. Lt. Col. Dunn has been an educator all his life, and in an interview with the staff of the US Department of Education's *American Education* magazine, he expressed the idea that he served in the Army Reserve to help preserve his right to educate. As Dunn put it, "If we cannot defend America, we will lose our way of life. Someone else will be coming over here and telling us what to teach, say, and think." Men like Dunn were the heart of the Army Reserve between World Wars I and II, and after WWII they were joined by women who did their part as Reservists defending this country. They all sacrificed mightily, perhaps more than do those who serve in 1983.

Being an Army Reservist today, however, while maintaining a civilian career is not easy. Reservists are expected to retain the skills gained through their active duty training while learning additional skills as they advance in the Army Reserve. For officers, many years of night classes and summer training are required to complete military education courses ranging from officer basic branch courses to Command and General Staff College to Army War College. For enlisted personnel, the Army Reserve is a constant series of courses designed to improve technical knowledge and leadership skills.

Though the Army Reserve receives additional full-time support every year, career (non-active duty) Reservists must devote extra evenings and days to the Army Reserve beyond the weekend drills and Annual Training time. This extra time is demanded because Army Reserve units and members must meet the same standards as the active Army, and there simply is not enough training time to perform all of the work necessary to meet these high standards.

As we have shown in this volume, support for the Army Reserve has not always been strong where it was needed. There are those today who doubt the wisdom of the Total Force policy. Gen. William C. Westmoreland's fears of over-reliance on Reserve Components in 1973 have been seconded even by Reserve Component officers who fear that America may be expecting more of part-time soldiers than they can reasonably achieve. In addition, there are critics of the Total Force policy who contend that budgetary considerations more than anything else are behind the reliance upon the Reserve Components. At the same time, however, the Reserve Components are unable to meet their defense obligations because of insufficient funding.

There is some truth to this argument. Looking at Defense trends since the time of Secretary of Defense McNamara, funding increases concomitant with increased Army Reserve responsibility have not been forthcoming. Despite increased Reserve Component emphasis during the 1970's, the Army Reserve's share of the Army budget has not changed appreciably in 15 years, though the Army Reserve today is described as "vital" to the national defense. A look at the Army's future plans for the Army Reserve, too, shows its increased responsibility as a part of the Total Force. Increased budgetary support and desperately needed equipment replacement are indicated.

Looking toward Defense plans for the 21st century, nothing indicates a diminishing dependence upon the Army Reserve for a substantial portion of the Army's combat support and combat service support. If anything, this dependence may increase. It is likely that the Army Reserve will play an even greater role in day-to-day Army plans. A few months ago, for example, it was revealed that the number of Army Reserve units on the Rapid Deployment Force—Army (RDF–A) list had doubled to 189 in less than two years, and for the first time, Army Reserve Military Police, Military History, Public Affairs and Signal Corps units are included on this list. Army Reserve units are also being prepared for a wider range of contingencies. Recent exercises have for the first time indicated major Army Reserve responsibilities outside of NATO, Korea and the Rapid Deployment Joint Task Force (US Central Command).

Reservists will continue to be a bridge between the government, the Army and the people, that Trinity of War that Clausewitz described as so essential for military strength. A reasonable guess for the future is that the Army is going to have to reconcile its Total Force policy with its fiscal priorities. As Chief of Staff Gen. Edward C. Meyer said, "Army leaders need to sit down and decide what great leap they can take over a period of time to improve the readiness of the Army Guard and Army Reserve." It is evident that the issue of Reserve Component readiness is growing more acute. The irony of the present situation, however, is that as the capabilities of the Reserve Components have increased, the perceived need for improvement has accelerated at a far greater pace.

Regardless of how the Army addresses Army Reserve needs in the future, we believe that the citizen-soldier tradition will endure. The heavy dependence upon Reserve Components is basic to American military policy and is a part of this country's grand heritage. Reservists will continue to serve and will gladly bear an added burden to preserve America's freedoms. The only question is whether the American people will provide the resources necessary for the Army Reserve to fulfill its responsibilities to today's citizens and to generations of Americans yet to come.

Appendix A

Chiefs of the Army Reserve[1]

* MAJ. C. F. THOMPSON, Chief of Reserve Section, G–2, June 12–July 1, 1923.

* MAJ. WALTER O. BOSWELL, Chief of Reserve Section, G–2, July 2, 1923–July 31, 1924.

* COL. DOUGLAS POTTS, Chief of Reserve Branch, G–2, August 1, 1924–December 30, 1925.

* LT. COL. J. C. PEGRAM, Chief of Reserve Branch, G–2, December 31, 1925–August 14, 1926.

* LT. COL. FRED B. RYONS, Chief of Reserve Branch, G–2, August 15, 1926–September 30, 1926.

* COL. STANLEY H. FORD, Chief of Reserve Branch, G–2, October 1, 1926–February 10, 1927.

COL. DAVID L. STONE, Executive for Reserve Affairs, March 5, 1927–June 30, 1930.

BRIG. GEN. CHARLES D. HERRON, Executive for Reserve Affairs, July 1, 1930–June 30, 1935.

---

1. Memo, War Department General Staff, G–2 to Col. Hartshorn, June 27, 1935, RG 319, Entry 343, Box 97; War Department Order, AG 008 O.R.C. (6–11–41), dated June 16, 1941, RG 319, Entry 343, Box 104; Memorandum, (with additions in pen) The Adjutant General to Executive for Reserve Affairs, May 1, 1941, Subject: Data re Tenure of Office of Executives for Reserve Affairs, RG 319, Entry 343, Box 104; James E. Hewes, Jr., *From Root to McNamara: Army Organization and Administration, 1900–1963* (Washington: Center of Military History, United States Army, 1975), p. 400; Files of the Chief, Army Reserve, the Pentagon.

* Performed function in addition to other duties.

BRIG. GEN. EDWIN S. HARTSHORN, Executive for Reserve Affairs, July 1, 1935–September 15, 1938.

BRIG. GEN. CHARLES F. THOMPSON, Executive for Reserve Affairs, September 16, 1938–June 9, 1940.

BRIG. GEN. JOHN H. HESTER, Executive for Reserve Affairs, June 21, 1940–March 23, 1941.

BRIG. GEN. FRANK E. LOWE, Executive for Reserve and R.O.T.C. Affairs, June 5, 1941–August 10, 1942.

BRIG. GEN. EDWARD W. SMITH, Executive for Reserve and R.O.T.C. Affairs, September 16, 1942–October 14, 1945.

BRIG. GEN. EDWARD S. BRES, Executive for Reserve and R.O.T.C. Affairs, October 15, 1945–November 30, 1947.

BRIG. GEN. WENDELL WESTOVER, Executive for Reserve and R.O.T.C. Affairs, December 1, 1947–November 14, 1949.

MAJ. GEN. JAMES B. CRESS, Executive for Reserve and R.O.T.C. Affairs, January 1, 1950–January 31, 1951.

BRIG. GEN. HUGH M. MILTON, Executive for Reserve and R.O.T.C. Affairs, February 24, 1951–November 18, 1953.

BRIG. GEN. PHILIP F. LINDEMAN, Executive for Reserve and R.O.T.C. Affairs, November 19, 1953–December 6, 1954, and Chief, Army Reserve and R.O.T.C. Affairs, December 7, 1954–July 31, 1957.

MAJ. GEN. RALPH A. PALLADINO, Chief, Army Reserve and R.O.T.C. Affairs, August 1, 1957–May 31, 1959.

MAJ. GEN. FREDERICK M. WARREN, Chief, Army Reserve and R.O.T.C. Affairs, September 1, 1959–February 12, 1963, and Chief, Army Reserve, February 13, 1963–August 31, 1963.

MAJ. GEN. W. J. SUTTON, Chief, Army Reserve, September 1, 1963–May 31, 1971.

MAJ. GEN. J. MILNOR ROBERTS, Chief, Army Reserve, June 1, 1971–May 31, 1975.

MAJ. GEN. HENRY MOHR, Chief, Army Reserve, June 1, 1975–May 31, 1979.

MAJ. GEN. WILLIAM R. BERKMAN, Chief, Army Reserve, June 1, 1979–present.

NOTE: BRIG. GEN. JOHN MCAULEY PALMER is sometimes regarded as the "Father of the Army Reserve." Though his influence on the evolution of the Army Reserve cannot be over-emphasized, Palmer was never in an official position within the Army Reserve structure.

Appendix B

Army Reserve (Organized Reserve Corps) Appropriations

Army Reserve Appropriations (in millions of dollars)

Fiscal Year	Army Reserve Appropriation	Total Army (War Dept.) Appropriation	% Army Reserve
1917	$ 11.5	$ 2,864.4	0.4
1918	10.3	5,730.9	0.2
1919	7.0	1,406.3	0.5
1920	4.2	1,622.0	0.3
1921	3.4	1,118.1	0.3
1922	3.9	457.8	0.9
1923	4.9	397.1	1.2
1924	7.3	357.0	2.0
1925	9.4	371.0	2.5
1926	10.3	364.1	2.8
1927	10.4	369.1	2.8
1928	9.6	401.0	2.4
1929	11.1	425.9	2.6
1930	11.5	464.9	2.5
1931	13.4	486.1	2.8
1932	13.3	476.3	2.8
1933	13.0	434.6	3.0
1934	12.3	408.6	3.0
1935	8.4	488.0	1.7
1936	12.8	618.6	2.1
1937	15.4	628.1	2.5
1938	16.2	644.3	2.5
1939	18.3	695.3	2.6
1940	20.5	907.2	2.3
1941	136.5	3,939.0	4.1
1942	7.6	14,325.6	0.01
1943	5.5	42,525.6	0.01
1944	2.1	49,438.3	<0.01
1945	(*)	50,490.1	<0.01
1946	(*)	27,986.8	<0.01

Fiscal Year	Army Reserve Appropriation	Total Army (War Dept.) Appropriation	% Army Reserve
1947	$ 72.8	$ 9,172.1	0.8
1948	92.9	7,698.6	1.2
1949	146.2	7,862.4	1.9
1950	140.0	5,789.5	2.4
1951	154.9	8,635.9	1.8
1952	132.8	17,452.8	0.6
1953	123.1	17,054.3	0.9
1954	121.5	13,515.4	0.9
1955	133.9	9,450.4	1.8
1956	211.3	9,274.3	2.3
1957	344.0	9,704.8	3.5
1958	339.6	9,775.9	3.5
1959	314.8	10,284.1	3.1
1960	349.8	10,294.0	3.4
1961	321.5	11,102.6	2.9
1962	309.9	12,425.9	2.5
1963	313.7	11,499.0	2.7
1964	305.3	12,050.0	2.5
1965	346.6	13,999.3	2.5
1966	344.6	20,919.1	1.6
1967	415.1	24,810	1.7
1968	397.4	25,290	1.6
1969	400.4	26,684	1.5

	RPA	OMAR	MCAR	USAR Tot.	Army Tot.	% Army Reserve
1970	$ 338.7	$ 129.3	$ 10.0	$ 478.0	$ 23,580	2.0
1971	374.5	140.7	10.0	525.2	20,300	2.6
1972	431.5	171.3	33.5	636.3	22,480	2.8
1973	461.6	203.0	38.2	702.8	21,820	3.2
1974	465.5	253.9	40.7	760.1	21,650	3.5
1975	489.9	284.0	43.7	817.6	21,580	3.8
1976	478.8	323.5	50.3	852.6	24,040	3.5
1977	479.8	364.7	53.8	898.3	26,810	3.4
1978	532.6	391.5	50.5	974.6	28,770	3.3
1979	566.8	420.3	37.1	1,024.2	31,570	3.2
1980	659.3	440.4	30.0	1,102.7	34,580	3.2
1981	865.5	520.7	43.2	1,429.4	44,030	3.2
1982	1,071.0	666.0	65.0	1,802.0	53,040	3.4
1983	1,247.0	705.0	42.0	1,994.0	57,220	3.5

* Organized Reserve Corps funding was only $200.00 each for the years 1945 and 1946.

RPA   Reserve Personnel, Army
OMAR   Operations, Maintenance, Army Reserve
MCAR   Military Contruction, Army Reserve

Note: There were apparently no separate appropriations for the Medical Reserve Corps and the Organized Reserve during the years 1908–1916. During the years 1917–1969 the figures given for the Army Reserve appropriation include funds for the Officers' Reserve Corps, the Enlisted Reserve Corps, the Reserve Officers' Training Corps, and the Citizens' Military Training Camps.

Sources: Chart 10, *OSD Project 80 Report, Part VII (Reserve Components),* pp. VII–B–24 and VII–B–25; Russell F. Weigley, *History of the United States Army* (New York and London: Macmillan Publishing Co., Inc. and Collier Macmillan Publishers, 1967), p. 561; *Annual Historical Supplement, Department of the Army* (various years); *Annual Report of the Secretary of the Army* (various years); and from the files of the Comptroller Division, Office of the Chief, Army Reserve.

It should be understood that other figures purporting to represent the same information are available from other sources. Budget figures may vary substantially, depending upon whether one is talking about appropriations, total obligation authority, or actual spending for a given year.

Appendix **C**

Army Reserve Units Mobilized in 1968[1]

Unit	Home Station
277th MI Det	Phoenix, Ariz.
*978th Army Postal Unit (Type U)	Ft. Smith, Ark.
*HHC 336th Ord Bn (Ammo) (DS)	Little Rock, Ark.
*231st Trans Co., Fltg Cft (SRF)	St. Petersburg, Fla.
*319th Trans Co. (Light Truck)	Augusta, Ga.
*413th Fin Sec (Disbursing)	Atlanta, Ga.
100th Bn, 442d Inf	Ft. DeRussy, Hawaii
*482d Med Det (Equip Maint)	Aurora, Ill.
724th Trans Co. (Medium Trk Petr)	Forest Park, Ill.
890th Trans Co. (Medium Trk Cargo)	Ft. Wayne, Ind.
*1011th Sup & Svc Co. (DS) (−)	Independence and Emporia, Kans.
*842d QM Co. (Petr Dep)	Kansas City, Kans.
*950th Army Postal Unit (Type F)	Lexington, Ky.
*472d Med Det (Amb) (SRF)	Rockville, Md.
*HQ & Main Spt. Co., 513th Maint Bn (DS)	Boston, Mass.
241st MI Det	Boston, Mass.
*424th Pers Svc Co. (Type B)	Livonia, Mich.
*452d Gen Spt Co (−)	Worthington & Winthrop, Minn.
*173d Petr Co. (Oper) (Type B)	Greenwood, Miss.
*172d Trans Co. (Med Trk Cargo)	Omaha, Neb.
*295th Ord Co. (DS/GS) (SRF)	Hastings, Grand Island & New York, Neb.
*1018th Sup & Svc Co. (DS)	Schenectady, N.Y.
*448th Army Postal Unit (Type Z)	Garden City, N.Y.

1. "Army Reserve Units Respond to Call-Up," *Army Reserve Magazine,* (May 1968), pp. 6–7; News Release, Office of the Assistant Secretary of Defense (Public Affairs), January 23, 1969, Subject: "Final Army Reserve Component Unit Arrives in Vietnam."

Unit	Home Station
*237th Maint. Co. (DS)	Ft. Hamilton, N.Y.
*316th Med Det (Blood Dist)	New York, N.Y.
*74th Field Hosp	New York, N.Y.
203d Trans Co. (Light Truck)	Garden City, N.Y.
*312th Evac Hosp (Semi-mobile)	Winston-Salem, N.C.
*1002d Sup & Svc Co. (DS)	Cleveland, Ohio
*311th Field Hosp	Sharonville, Ohio
*630th Trans Co. (Med Truck Cargo)	Washington, Penn.
*357th Trans Co. (Aircraft Maint) (DS)	Greencastle, Penn.
*305th Med Det (Ortho)	Philadelphia, Penn.
*378th Med Det (Neurosurgical)	Memphis, Tenn.
*238th Maint Co. (DS)	San Antonio, Tex.
*HHC, 259th QM Bn (Petr)	Pleasant Grove, Utah
304th Med Det (Equip Maint) (SRF)	Richmond, Va.
*313th Med Det (Surg)	Richmond, Va.
*889th Med Det (Surg)	Richmond, Va.
*737th Trans Co. (Med Truck Petr)	Yakima, Wash.
*377th Light Maint Co. (DS)	Manitowoc, Wisc.
*826th Ord Co. (Ammo) (DS/GS) (–)	Madison & Baraboo, Wisc.

Units identified by an asterisk were deployed to Vietnam. The other Army Reserve units were assigned to the Strategic Army Forces (STRAF).

NARRATIVE HISTORIES OF CERTAIN USAR UNITS IN VIETNAM

HHC, 336th Ordnance Battalion (Ammo) (DS)—Little Rock, Arkansas

Following its activation on May 13, 1968, this unit went to Fort Carson, Colorado, where it underwent four months of intensive training. The unit was augmented by an Explosive Ordnance Disposal Unit upon its arrival at Fort Carson. The training ended on September 25, 1968, when HHC, 336th Ord Bn was deployed to Vietnam. The unit was assigned to Da Nang, where the men of the unit constructed their own buildings for billeting and operational functions. The battalion supplied Class V (ammunition) for all Army units in the I Corps area, and it received the Meritorious Unit Commendation for its performance on duty.[2]

---

2. Letter, Cdr, HHC 336th Ordnance Battalion (Ammo) (DS/GS) to Lewis C. Brodsky, Chief of Public Affairs, OCAR, January 15, 1983, Subject: "336th Ordnance Battalion Historical Information," OCAR Historical Files; General Orders No. 783, Headquarters, United States Army Vietnam, March 30, 1970, "Award of the Meritorious Unit Commendation."

319th Transportation Co. (Light Trucks)—Augusta, Georgia

The 319th was mobilized on May 13, 1968, and convoyed to Fort Lee, Virginia. Upon arrival at Fort Lee the unit TOE was reorganized from 55–17F to 55–17G; it was further reorganized on May 25 when it gave up one truck platoon. The "G" series reorganization resulted in an equipment change from 2½ ton "slush box" trucks to 5 ton multifuel trucks, but the unit met the challenge and was fully prepared when it arrived in Vietnam on September 26, 1968.[3]

While in Vietnam the 319th achieved an enviable record while operating from "TC Hill," Long Binh. The unit drove a total of 1,073,641 miles and hauled 92,375 tons of supplies. It supported the 1st Infantry Division, the 1st Air Cavalry, the 9th Infantry Division, the 25th Infantry Division, the 199th Light Infantry Brigade, the 11th Armored Cavalry Regiment, the Royal Thai Volunteer Force, and the 1st Australian Task Force. The 319th had anything but a boring tour in Vietnam, for its convoys were ambushed on seven occasions.[4]

The men of the 319th had gone to Vietnam, they stated proudly in a Public Information Release, without "unfavorable Congressional Inquiries or Court Injunctions . . . initiated . . . prior to or after arrival in Vietnam." Once in Vietnam, however, they were subject to something described by the unit as "one of the most demoralizing [situations] the unit faced." This was the "infusion" policy initiated by the Army for Reserve units in Vietnam. Infusion was accomplished by pulling men out of the Reserve units and sticking them into similar units elsewhere, while simultaneously putting non-unit personnel into the Reserve unit. "The infusion policy," stated the 319th, "severely hampers the unit morale, efficiency, and esprit." The reasons given for the infusion policy were two: (1) to prevent a local tragedy in the event of severe casualties and (2) to reduce the effects of having an entire unit pull-out at once. One of the real strengths of the Army Reserve, however, is the esprit de corps and the sense of unit integrity and teamwork that is

3. Letter, Cdr, 319th Transportation Company (LT) (5T) to Cdr, 544th S&S Bn (GS) (FWD), September 10, 1968, Subject: "Operational Report of the 319th Transportation Company (LT) (5T) for Period Ending 26 August 1968 (RCS CSFOR-65 (R–1)), copy in OCAR Historical Files.

4. Public Information Release, 319th Transportation Company (LT) (5T), July 31, 1969, copy in OCAR Historical Files

built up over the years, and infusion was not conducive to these qualities. The 319th, like many other Reserve Component units, was out "to overcome the stigma of the citizen soldier fighting the professional man's war."[5] It definitely overcame that stigma, but infusion did not help the process.

The 319th received a Meritorious Unit Citation for its work in Vietnam, and individual unit members received 2 Bronze Star Medals with "V", 8 other Bronze Stars, 3 Army Commendation Medals with "V", 62 other ARCOMs, and 3 Purple Heart Medals.[6] The members of the unit received a rousing welcome when they came home from Vietnam, too, for more than 300 wives, children, parents, and friends were on hand when the unit landed in Augusta.[7]

HQ and Main Spt Co, 513th Maintenance Bn (DS)— Boston, Massachusetts

The 513th Maintenance Battalion, as already related, was a hot-bed of opposition to the Vietnam mobilization. Despite the protests that had accompanied the departure of the 513th for Vietnam in October 1968, however, there was no protest from the unit after that time. "We supported 77 tactical units and worked seven days a week. Once we got out of the United States the morale was good. We had a job to do," said the commander of the 513th, Lt. Col. Eugene Martinez.[8]

In Vietnam the 513th was assigned to the 26th General Support Group at Phu Bai and provided maintenance services to non-divisional units in the supported area, which reached north from the Hai Van Pass to LZ Nancy and from Laos to the sea. The battalion participated in four campaigns while in Vietnam and returned to Boston in October 1969, almost a year after it had left the United States.

---

5. Public Information Release, 319th Transportation Company (LT) (5T), July 31, 1969, copy in OCAR Historical Files. Letter, Commander, 81st US Army Reserve Command, to Commanding General, Third US Army, March 4, 1970, Subject: "After Action/Lessons Learned Report—319th Transportation Company (Lt Trk), WSZ0AA, for Period 11 April 1968 through 19 September 1969, RCS CS FOR-65 (RZ)," copy in OCAR Historical Files.

6. "Citations Go To 319th at Ceremony," *The Augusta Chronicle,* August 20, 1969, copies of both in OCAR Historical Files.

7. "Army Reservists Welcomed Home from Vietnam Tour" *The State,* August 15, 1969, Section C, p. 1, copy in OCAR Historical Files.

8. "Boston Unit Returns from Viet," *Sunday Herald-Traveler,* October 5, 1969.

Upon its return the members received a tremendous welcome from some 450 relatives and friends.[9]

452d General Spt Co—Worthington and Winthrop, Minnesota

The 452d spent four months at Fort Riley, Kansas, training and preparing for deployment to Vietnam. In Vietnam the unit was stationed at Da Nang, where it operated Class II (Individual equipment, general supplies) and Class IV (construction materials) supply sites. After a month in Da Nang the Class I (rations) Platoon moved to Phu Bai and operated the subsistence supply point there. The 452d left Vietnam in August 1969 and returned to Fort Riley.[10]

172d Transportation Co (Medium Truck Cargo)—Omaha, Nebraska

After four months of training at Fort Lewis, Washington, the 172d left for Vietnam and arrived at Cam Ranh Bay on October 10, 1968, with its trucks and other equipment. The unit became fully operational within seven days and began running convoys to the Central Highlands. Convoy destinations were Ban Me Thuot (154 miles one-way; two day round-trip), Bao Loc (169 miles one-way; four day round-trip), and Dalat (119 miles one-way; two day round trip). During the period from October 10, 1968, to August 18, 1969, the 172d participated in thirty-six convoy operations, hauling 79,977 tons a total of 659,051 miles. There were no incidences of AWOL during the time the 172d was in Vietnam, a total of only twenty-four punishments under Article 15 of the Uniform Code of Military Justice, and only two court martial convictions. Both of the latter were men who had been assigned to the 172d as a result of the Army's infusion program. No original member of the unit was ever court martialed.[11]

9. Unsigned memorandum, HQ, 513th Maintenance Battalion (DS), December 9, 1968, Subject: "Summary of Unit History 5 Jan 66 to 31 Nov 68," copy in OCAR Historical Files; Department of the Army Lineage and Honors, Headquarters and Headquarters Detachment, 513th Maintenance Battalion, copy in OCAR Historical Files; "Boston Unit Returns from Viet," *Sunday Herald-Traveler,* October 5, 1969.

10. Unit History, 452d General Supply Co. (GS), copy in OCAR Historical Files.

11. Letter, Lt. Col. Edward Honor, Cdr, 36th Transportation Battalion (Truck) to Cdr, US Army Support Command, August 18, 1969, Subject: "Nomination for Meritorious Unit Commendation," copy in OCAR Historical Files.

The 172d was the only unit in the 36th Transportation Battalion to receive a Meritorious Unit Commendation. According to Lt. Col. Edward Honor, the 36th Bn Cdr,

The Unit's enthusiasm was immediately apparent. In many instances, drivers made twice as many runs per shift as compared with regular drivers from other units. The unit was determined to prove itself . . . . The unit passed its Annual General Inspection (AGI) with a rating of excellent. It also passed its CMMI with a rating of satisfactory and the best overall score in the battalion. The Inspector General made a point of praising the unit for its high caliber of administration in the orderly and supply rooms. This can be attributed, in part, to the mature attitude of most of the reservists in the unit as well as in the innate ability of the high caliber individuals called to duty.[12]

The men of the 172d sent word from Vietnam that they did not want any parades when they returned home, and that they wanted to be treated "like guys returning with lunch buckets after a hard day's work." Their families and friends would not accept the idea of an austere homecoming, however, and the 172d was greeted with a full-fledged ceremony, complete with the Strategic Air Command's band.[13]

237th Maintenance Co (DS)—Fort Hamilton, New York

The 237th Maintenance Company (DS) performed its pre-Vietnam training at Fort Meade, Maryland, though individual members of the unit were sent to Army service schools at Forts Dix, Gordon, Monmouth, Belvoir, and Lee. The 237th reached Vietnam on October 21 and 22, 1968, and was assigned to provide maintenance support to the 108th Artillery Group and electronics maintenance support to the Third Marine Division. Company Headquarters with service and evacuation sections soon moved to Quang Tri, and the electronics, maintenance, and armament sections moved to Dong Ha. These locations were within a few miles of the De-Militarized Zone (DMZ), and the unit came under enemy fire on numerous occasions.[14]

---

12. *Ibid.*, letter, SSG Armand K. Gibbons, Unit Historian, 172d Transportation Co. to Office of the Chief, Army Reserve, December 24, 1982, in OCAR Historical Files.

13. "Like It or Not, 172d Greeted as Heroes," *Sunday World-Herald,* October 5, 1969, p. 1.

14. Letter, 1Lt. George H. Wills, Cdr., 237th Maintenance Co and CW4 Louis E. Lorenzo, Unit Historian, 237th Maintenance Co, to

The 237th was responsible for all armament, electronics, and motor maintenance support in the area from Quang Tri north to the DMZ, east to the South China Sea, and west to the Laotian border. Unit personnel constructed their own air conditioned repair shop to assist in their electronics repair work and each day sent repair teams to remote fire bases. Tube changes on 175 mm guns and 8 inch howitzers, repair of hydraulic leaks, welding of cracked spades, and similar repair operations were all routinely accomplished with the weapon in firing position. This procedure minimized down-time and resulted in maximum availability of the weapon.[15]

The 237th Maintenance Company distinguished itself as one of the top outfits of its type in Vietnam, and it was awarded the Meritorious Unit Commendation for its fine work. Unit personnel received 5 Bronze Star Medals, one Air Medal, and 7 Army Commendation Medals.[16] The 237th was greeted with an elaborate welcoming ceremony upon its return from Vietnam, and John V. Lindsay, Mayor of New York City, sent the unit a letter of congratulations and thanks.[17]

316th Medical Detachment (Blood Distribution)—New York, New York

This unit was organized in January 1968 and mobilized in May of the same year. The 316th moved to Vietnam in October 1968 and was attached to the 9th Medical Laboratory. Personnel from this unit were widely dispersed throughout Vietnam, where they did an outstanding job of blood distribution. This particular Army Reserve unit was unusual in that it had no officers authorized. The 316th, like all of the units in the 77th US Army Reserve Command, received an elaborate welcome home upon its return from Vietnam. The ceremony for the 316th was combined with that of the 74th Field Hospital, also a 77th ARCOM unit.[18]

OCAR Public Affairs Office, January 28, 1983, Subject: "Historical Information," in OCAR Historical Files.

15. *Ibid.*

16. General Orders No. 288, HQ, US Army Vietnam, February 1, 1970; "Awards and Decorations," in "Historical Information," 237th Maintenance Company, copies of both in OCAR Historical Files.

17. *Welcome Home Ceremony, 237th Maintenance Company* and letter, Mayor John V. Lindsay, October 10, 1969, copies of both in OCAR Historical Files.

18. *Welcoming Home Ceremony for 74th Field Hospital and 316th Medical Detachment,* copy in OCAR Historical Files.

74th Field Hospital—New York, New York,

Members of the 74th Field Hospital were among the individuals who participated in court action in an attempt to avoid being sent to Vietnam. Nevertheless, the entire unit was shipped to Southeast Asia, where its primary mission was caring for wounded prisoners of war. The 74th was stationed at Long Binh, where it was the only prisoner of war hospital in the III Corps and IV Corps Tactical Zones.[19]

The 74th met every medical challenge that came its way, from high velocity wounds of the chest to amputations to grafts of the femoral vein. The one problem it never could overcome, however, was the excessive temperature of the wards. There were days when ward temperatures reached 118°F and weeks when they did not go below 90°F at any time of the day or night. Nevertheless, the quality of care given by this Army Reserve unit was impressively high. A Swiss representative of the International Red Cross visited the 74th and remarked that the level of professional medical treatment given the prisoners was "equal to and perhaps even better than" that given civilians in many Western nations.[20]

While in Vietnam the 74th, as Army units have done in every war, "adopted" a local orphanage as its own civic action project. In addition to providing medical support to the Tan Lap Orphanage, the men and women of the 74th Field Hospital contributed money and school supplies to the orphans.[21] The men and women of the 74th were not ignored when they returned from Vietnam, either, for the 77th ARCOM staged an impressive ceremony to welcome them back to New York.[22]

312th Evacuation Hospital (Semi-mobile)—Winston-Salem, North Carolina

In April 1968 Sue Walker was working as Assistant Director of Nurses in a civilian hospital in Winston-Salem, North

---

19. Letter, Maj. Gen. Victor J. Mc Laughlin, Cdr, US Army Quartermaster Center and Fort Lee to Maj. Joseph P. Cillo, Cdr, 74th Field Hospital, October 14, 1968, Subject: "Letter of Commendation," copy in OCAR Historical Files; "Welcoming Home Ceremony for 74th Field Hospital and 316th Medical Detachment."

20. "Welcoming Home Ceremony for 74th Field Hospital and 316th Medical Detachment."

21. *Ibid.*

22. *Ibid.*

Carolina, when a friend called to tell her that her Army Reserve unit was being called up for Vietnam. Lt. Col. Walker checked with her unit commander, but he had not heard the news. The 313-member hospital unit was mobilized in 1968, however, and after three months training at Fort Benning, it was off to Southeast Asia. The 312th was based at Chu Lai, on the South China Sea coast, and it provided medical support to US and allied forces in the Northern I Corps Tactical Zone.[23]

The unit arrived while Chu Lai was under rocket attack, but this did not deter the men and women of the 312th and its attached units (889th Medical Detachment, USAR; 378th Medical Detachment, USAR; and 305th Medical Detachment, USAR) from taking over existing hospital facilities without any disruption in patient care. After only one month the 312th had expanded the hospital's capacity from 120 beds to 400 beds. On several occasions when the hospital came under direct, heavy fire, the hospital's personnel refused to take cover and continued to provide medical services to the massive number of wounded. The men and women of the 312th also participated in numerous civic action programs in which they provided surgical instruction and consultation to local Vietnamese health care centers.[24]

Lt. Col. Walker also spoke of the Army's infusion program, which she said they referred to in Vietnam as the "confusion" program. "They seemed to take our best quality personnel," said Walker, "and send us ones who were not so good." It hurt morale in the 312th, said the Chief Nurse, to have friends and co-workers, with whom a real team spirit had been developed, transferred to some other unit in Vietnam.[25]

The 312th received the Meritorious Unit Commendation for its performance of duty in Vietnam. When the members of the 312th returned to Winston-Salem, however, it was anything but a warm homecoming. There was a brief official ceremony, recalled Lt. Col. Walker, but when the ceremony was over "we were afraid to wear our uniforms. It

23. "At 48 She Answered Call to Vietnam War," *Messenger* (Madison, NC), March 30, 1983; General Orders No. 206, HQ, United States Army, Vietnam, January 24, 1970; copies in OCAR Historical Files.

24. *Ibid.*

25. Interview of Lt. Col. Sue Walker (USAR-Ret.) by Maj. James T. Currie, June 27, 1983, notes in OCAR Historical Files.

hurt a lot at first," she said, "but then you realized they [people who did not approve of her going to Vietnam] just didn't know any better." The hostility soon ended, however, and what has remained with Walker was the knowledge that she and the other members of the 312th had done their job when they were called upon. As an Army Reservist, she said in an interview, "we had something to prove, and we proved it."[26]

357th Transportation Co (Aircraft Maintenance) (DS)— Greencastle, Pennsylvania

The 357th spent five months at Fort Benning after its mobilization in May 1968, after which the 186-member unit went to Vietnam. The 357th was headquartered at Bien Hoa, where it performed direct support aircraft maintenance for such units as the 11th Armored Cavalry. The unit was recognized by award of the Meritorious Unit Commendation and Vietnam Gallantry Cross with Palm. Individual unit members received a Legion of Merit, 2 Bronze Star Medals with "V", 5 other Bronze Star Medals, 19 Army Commendation Medals, and 2 Purple Heart Medals. The unit returned to the United States on September 29, 1969, and on October 9 it was honored with a welcome home ceremony attended by some 400 people.[27]

378th Medical Detachment (Neurosurgical)—Memphis, Tennessee

This small unit of seven members (four officers and three enlisted personnel) spent 4½ months at Fort Carson, Colorado, before going to Vietnam in October 1968. The 378th was immediately attached to the 312th Evacuation Hospital, and the personnel of the 378th became regular members of the operating room team. The 378th received the Meritorious Unit Commendation for its performance of duty in Vietnam, and upon its return to Memphis in August 1969, the returnees were met by Mayor Henry Loeb, Brig. Gen. Leonard S. Woody (Cdr, 121st ARCOM) and other dignitaries.[28]

---

26. "At 48 She Answered Call to Vietnam War;" General Orders No. 206; Interview, Lt. Col. Walker and Maj. Currie.

27. "357th Transportation Company (DS) Vietnam," copy in OCAR Historical Files.

28. Movement Orders No. 17, HQ, 5th Infantry Division (Mechanized) and Fort Carson, Colorado, July 24, 1968; General Orders No.

259th Quartermaster Battalion (Petroleum)
HHC, 259th Quartermaster Battalion (Petroleum)—
Pleasant Grove, Utah

The questionable process by which Army Reserve units were chosen for duty in Vietnam is brought into focus when the HHC, 259th is considered. This unit was mobilized in May 1968 after being converted from Infantry to Quartermaster on February 12. The unit trained at Fort Leonard Wood for four months, then it departed for Vietnam. HHC, 259th QM Bn was first located at Quang Tri, then moved to Phu Bai in November 1968.[29]

The 259th was assigned to the 26th General Support Group, Da Nang Support Command, 1st Logistical Command. The battalion was formed from four Army Reserve units that were mobilized in 1968: HHC, 259th QM Bn; 173d Petr Co (Oper); 737th Trans Co. (Med Trk); and 842d QM Co (Petr Dep). The battalion operated 73 miles of 6-inch pipelines: Quang Tri–Dong Ha; Colco Island–Phu Bai; and Colco Island–Quang Tri. It also operated two bolted steel tank farms with a combined capacity of 390,000 gallons and two packaged product yards. Line haul by 5000 gallon tank trucks delivered fuel from the bulk storage areas to the using units in the field.[30]

HHC, 259th went to Vietnam with a total strength of 91 personnel. Shortly after January 1, 1969, the unit was alerted for personnel infusion, and the first members left the 259th in April. Additional unit personnel were transferred out in May and June, but the infusion process stopped in July. The unit was thereafter stabilized, with some members getting an early release from Vietnam to return to school or accept seasonal employment. Unit personnel received one Legion of Merit, 16 Bronze Star Medals, 19 Army Commendation Medals, and 43 Good Conduct Medals. Upon their return from Vietnam, the members of HHC, 259th QM Co were met at Salt Lake City Airport on September 16 by a welcoming party that included Utah Governor Calvin L. Rampton. This was followed on September 18 by a motor parade through Pleasant Grove, Orem, and Provo, Utah. At a ceremony in Provo awards were presented to in-

206, Headquarters, United States Army Vietnam, January 24, 1970; Press Release, HQ, 121st United States Army Reserve Command, August 2, 1969; copies in OCAR Historical Files.

29. "Historical Supplement, HHC, 259th Quartermaster Battalion (Petroleum)," copy in OCAR Historical Files.

30. *Ibid.*

dividual members of the unit. The quality of personnel in the 259th was exemplified by the fact that members of the battalion won the 1st Logistical Command's Soldier of the Month competition three times in a row. The 259th received a Meritorious Unit Commendation for its service in Vietnam.[31]

173d Petroleum Company (Oper)—Greenwood, Mississippi

Personnel from this unit were among the Army Reservists who filed suit to prevent their being sent to Vietnam. The suit, as previously discussed, was unsuccessful, and the unit went to Southeast Asia on schedule. The company was headquartered at Phu Bai and operated pipelines between Phu Bai and Camp Evans and the Phu Bai Tank Farm. The company operated a pump station in Hue and one at Camp Evans.[32]

842d QM Co (Petr Dep)—Kansas City, Kansas

This unit operated the pipeline from Camp Evans to Quang Tri and one from Quang Tri to Dong Ha. It also operated a 59,000 barrel tank farm at Quang Tri and line-hauled bulk fuel to combat bases as far south as Camp Evans and northwest to Camp Vandergrift near Khe Sanh.[33]

737th Transportation Co (Med Truck Petr)—Yakima, Washington

The 737th was mentioned in Chapter Nine in connection with the fine send-off it received from citizens in the Yakima area. After several months of training at Fort Lewis, Washington, the unit left for Vietnam in September. The unit with its equipment landed at Da Nang and transferred to Quang Tri, where it immediately began convoy operations. The 737th supported the 1st Air Cavalry Division (Airmobile) with POL (petroleum, oil, and lubricants) for two months, after which the 101st Airborne Division moved

31. *Ibid.;* General Orders No. 205, Headquarters, United States Army Vietnam, January 24, 1970; *The Northern Log,* March 15, 1969, p. 5; copies in OCAR Historical Files.
32. "Historical Supplement, HHC, 259th Quartermaster Battalion (Petroleum)," p. 5, copy in OCAR Historical Files.
33. *Ibid.*

in. On January 6, 1969, the Company, minus the 3d Platoon, was moved to Chu Lai and assigned to the 57th Transportation Battalion. The 3d Platoon remained in Phu Bai until the unit returned to the US in August 1969.[34]

The 737th received the Meritorious Unit Commendation, and individual unit members won one Bronze Star Medal with "V", 6 other Bronze Star Medals, and 2 Purple Hearts. Upon returning to Yakima, the men of the 737th were given a "welcome home" ceremony by a crowd of 1000 people. Yakima Mayor Jack Larson proclaimed a day of honor for the returnees, and everyone dined on roast beef dinners.[35]

377th Light Maintenance Co (DS)—Manitowoc, Wisconsin

The 377th began calendar year 1968 as the 377th Ordnance Company (DAS). It was redesignated the 377th Light Maintenance Co (DS) on January 31, 1968, and in April it was notified that it was going to be mobilized. The post-mobilization training period at Fort Riley was not without problems. The 377th was first placed under a supply and service battalion, but it did not receive adequate training in this arrangement. On July 15, therefore, the unit was put under a maintenance battalion, and the quality and type of its training immediately improved. The change and confusion at Fort Riley resulted, however, in the 377th having the longest time between mobilization and arrival in Vietnam— seven months—of any Army Reserve unit.[36]

In Vietnam the 377th was assigned to the 69th Maintenance Battalion (GS), US Army Support Command, Cam Ranh Bay. The unit provided direct support maintenance to sixty-seven units of the 1st Logistical Command in the II Corps area. The unit's primary repair responsibilities were in the area of wheeled and tracked vehicles, towed and self-propelled artillery, small arms, refrigeration equipment, office machines, and chemical equipment. The 377th was awarded the Meritorious Unit Commendation for its service

34. "Unit History of Mobilization," 737th Transportation Company (MDM TRK) (PTRL), copy in OCAR Historical Files.

35. General Orders No. 408, HQ, U.S. Army Vietnam, February 4, 1971; "Unit History of Mobilization;" "Long, long trail ends—737th home," *Yakima Herald-Republic,* August 14, 1969, p. 1; copies in OCAR Historical Files.

36. 377th Light Maintenance Company (DS), "Unit History— 1968," copy in OCAR Historical Files.

in Vietnam, and individuals in the unit were awarded 7 Bronze Star Medals and 34 Army Commendation Medals.[37]

826th Ord Co (Ammo) (DS/GS) (–)—Madison and Baraboo, Wisconsin

The 826th performed five months of post-mobilization training at Fort Knox, Kentucky, from May 16, 1968, to October 13, 1968. Upon arriving in Vietnam the company was assigned to the 3d Ordnance Battalion (Ammo), Long Binh Ammunition Supply Depot. After a short period of orientation, the 826th took over Sub-Depots I and III at Long Binh and worked a two-shift, twenty-four hour day. The unit established a ten-month record of 450,000 short tons of ammunition lifted, as well as a twelve-hour lift record of 2250 short tons. The United States Army Support Command, Saigon, awarded the 826th its Certificate of Achievement. Personnel of the 826th received 14 Bronze Star Medals with "V", 12 other Bronze Star Medals, 2 Army Commendation Medals with "V", 58 other ARCOMs, and one Purple Heart. The unit left Vietnam for Fort Riley, Kansas, on October 2, 1969.[38]

37. "Unit History (Annual Supplement) 377th Light Maintenance Company (DS), 1969;" General Orders No. 752, Headquarters, United States Army Vietnam, March 25, 1970; copies in OCAR Historical Files.

38. "826th Ordnance Company (Ammo) (DS/GS) Annual Historical Supplement (1968)," "Annual Historical Supplement, 1969" and copy of Certificate of Achievement, all in OCAR Historical Files.

Appendix D

Post-Vietnam Emergency Use of the Army Reserve

In the fourteen years since the last Army Reserve unit returned from Vietnam, units of the USAR have been used during at least four emergencies, none of which were directly related to national defense. These four occasions were the following: (1) the Postal Strike of March 1970, (2) Tropical Storm Agnes, June 1973, (3) the Vietnamese refugee influx of 1975, and (4) the Cuban refugee operations in 1980. Each of these episodes was unique, and each one of them provided mobilization, training, and perhaps command experience for individuals involved.

1. *Postal Strike*—Operation Graphic Hand

On March 17, 1970, postal employees in New York City began a wildcat strike that soon spread to cities in nine other states. A Federal judge's injunction was ignored in New York City, as was President Richard M. Nixon's March 21 plea to the strikers. On March 23, Nixon declared that a "national emergency" existed as a result of the strike and thereafter some 28,100 Army personnel were ordered to duty in New York City. Army Reservists comprised almost exactly half (14,000) of the force, while the National Guard (11,600), the active Army, and other reserve components supplied the remainder.

The 77th Army Reserve Command, a major USAR headquarters, was mobilized on March 24 to provide com-

---

1. *History, First United States Army, Annual Supplement, Calendar Year 1970,* p. 66; see also *Ibid.*, pp. 43–66.

mand and control of particular USAR units, as well as certain Marine Corps Reserve and Navy Reserve units. Other USAR commands involved in the operation were the 11th Special Forces Group, 301st Support Brigade, 411th Engineer Brigade, 353d Civil Affairs Area (A) and 818th Hospital Center.

Military personnel served in the New York City Post Office until June 30, providing what were described as "essential postal services," including certain mail collection and processing activities, limited deliveries, and limited window service. Postmaster General Winston M. Blount was lavish in his praise for the job done by the Reservists and others during Operation Graphic Hand. The Reservists themselves seemed to have few complaints about being called to duty, the biggest gripe centering about the cold "C" rations they were served at noon. The exercise was generally considered a successful use of Reserve Component forces in an unusual situation, and according to the official First United States Army History, it "appeared to justify the conclusion that the military forces, both active and reserve, are prepared on very short notice to perform any conceivable assigned mission."

2. *Tropical Storm Agnes*—Operation Noah II

Tropical Storm Agnes, which originated off the Yucatan Peninsula in the Gulf of Mexico in mid-June 1972, reached the Virginia coast on the afternoon of June 21. The storm took the scenic route up the Virginia and Maryland coasts, causing rainfalls of one inch per hour. It passed Delaware and New Jersey, swept through New York City, and then looped back down through Pennsylvania on what might be called a "Honeymooners Tour" of the Poconos and Williamsport. Agnes then visited Niagara Falls and followed the St. Lawrence River to the ocean.

The greatest damage was in central Pennsylvania, where residential property losses were estimated at $570 million, and industrial, commercial, and public property damage was placed at $2 billion. From June 22 to September 15, 1972, a total of 28 Army Reserve units with 1466 men took part in disaster relief efforts in Pennsylvania and adjoining states.

2. Col. John F. McElhenny, *After Action Report: Tropical Storm Agnes–Operation Noah II*; Col George H. Russell, DCSOT to various addressees, Subject: "After-Action Report—Tropical Storm Agnes."

Joining the unit members were some 3000 individual Army Reservists.

Seventeen USAR units served in Pennsylvania, performing such tasks as cleaning debris from streams and rivers, building bridges, transporting food and water, and providing medical and law enforcement support. Most of the work of disaster assistance fell naturally to the National Guards of the states concerned, but the Army Reserve also played a vital and well-appreciated role.

3. *Vietnamese Refugees*—Project New Arrivals

With the collapse of the South Vietnamese government in the spring of 1975, the United States was soon on the receiving end of what appeared to be a nearly-inexhaustible stream of refugees. The United States Army Forces Command (FORSCOM) was soon given responsibility for the refugee operations at Fort Chaffee, Arkansas, and Fort Indiantown Gap, Pennsylvania. Active Army personnel did most of the work with the refugees, but in the civil affairs area the Army Reserve had to become involved. The 96th Civil Affairs Battalion was the only such unit in the active Army, so FORSCOM sought volunteers from USAR personnel who were qualified civil affairs specialists.

Thirty volunteer Army Reservists at Fort Chaffee were organized into the Directorate of Civil Military Affairs, while the twenty-five USAR members at Fort Indiantown Gap comprised the Civil Affairs Support Battalion (Composite/Provisional). According to a story that appeared in *Army Reserve Magazine,* USAR personnel "set up English, American customs, and history classes. Several WACs are giving classes on the women's liberation movement and how it differs from the traditional role of the Vietnamese woman."

Finally, it should be pointed out that the operations at Fort Chaffee and Indiantown Gap were funded under Army Reserve Operation and Maintenance (OMAR) appropriations. This was apparently the only source of flexible funding available to the Army at the time, though one would be hard-pressed to show how the refugee operations were of di-

---

3. Frank W. Pew, *The Role of the U.S. Army Forces Command in Project New Arrivals: Reception and Care of Refugees from Vietnam* (Fort McPherson, Georgia: Historical office, Office of the Chief of Staff, U.S. Army Forces Command, 1981), pp. 20–21, 173-75, 212; "The New Arrivals," *Army Reserve Magazine* (November-December 1975), pp. 16–18

rect benefit to more than the few Army Reservists who volunteered for duty.

4. *Cuban Refugees*

Barely four years after the Vietnamese refugee camps at Forts Chaffee and Indiantown Gap were emptied and closed, the Army had to reopen them, plus Fort McCoy, Wisconsin, to take care of thousands of refugees from Fidel Castro's Cuba.

Army Reserve units, which operated under FORSCOM, were involved in refugee operations from the beginning. At Fort Chaffee, Arkansas, the 369th Station Hospital, a USAR unit from Puerto Rico, was particularly effective because its members were Spanish-speaking. Three Army Reserve Military Police units from Indiana—the 222d MP Co, 396th MP Co, and 496th MP Co—were also used at Chaffee.

At Fort McCoy, Army Reservists from the 432d Civil Affairs Group worked with the refugees, as did members of the 432d PSYOP Battalion, USAR.

More Army Reservists served at Fort Indiantown Gap than anywhere else. Army Reserve Civil Affairs units in the First Army area were especially active at the "Gap," spending their two weeks of annual training, plus many weekend drills, working with the refugees there.

According to the after action report on activities at the Gap, "The performance of individual Reservists ranged from outstanding to unsatisfactory. For the first months of the operation, Reserve Civil Affairs personnel augmented by Reservists from other branches ran the seven alien compounds. . . . Generally speaking, their performance was more than satisfactory . . . . The most serious drawback to the use of Reservists was the necessity for changing Area Commanders every two weeks . . . ."

---

4. Jean R. Moenk, Frank W. Pew, and Maj. Charles Bishop, *Annual Historical Review, United States Army Forces Command, United States Army Forces, Readiness Command, 1 October 1980–30 September 1981 (RCS CSHIS–6 (R–3)) (U)* (Fort McPherson, Georgia: Historical Office, Office of the Chief of Staff, U.S. Army Forces Command, 1981), pp. 342–54; "First Army Reservists Find Themselves 'Doing Real Thing' at Fort Indiantown Gap," *The Officer*, August 1980, p. 12; *Task Force, Fort Indiantown Gap After Action Report*, Vol II, p. 3.

Appendix **E**

Strength of the Army Reserve (Medical Reserve Corps, Organized Reserve) Prior to World War II

End of Fiscal Year	Med. Res. Corps	Army Reserve[1]		
1909	364			
1910	420			
1911	922			
1912	1105			
1913	1205	8		
1314	1254	16		
1915	1426	17		
1916	1903	27	4621[2]	
		ORC	ERC	Total
1917	4855	21,543	35,000	61,398
1918	20,855	86,262	80,000	187,117
1919		45,573	none	45,573
1920		68,232	none	68,232
1921		66,905	1	66,906
1922		67,390	480	67,870
1923		76,923	1557	78,480
1924		81,706	3400	85,106
1925		95,154	5115	100,269
1926		103,829	5775	109,604
1927		110,014	5735	115,749
1928		114,824	5464	120,288
1929		112,757	5192	117,949
1930		113,523	4721	118,244

	Active ORC	Inactive ORC	ERC	Total
1931	80,399	27.811	4837	113,047
1932	83,808	31,028	4872	119,709
1933	86,338	33,147	5028	124,513
1934	88,107	26,250	4646	119,003
1935	91,955	20,635	4323	116,913
1936	95,619	19,550	3897	119,066
1937	96,545	14,624	3189	114,358
1938	100,116	18,796	2998	121,910
1939	104,575	12,144	3054	119,773
1940	104,228	12,408	3233	119,869
1941	110,931	22,028	2149	135,108[3]

[1] Created by the Army Appropriation Act of August 24, 1912.

[2] Consists of individuals furloughed to the reserve from the Regular Army under the provisions of the Army Appropriation Act of August 24, 1912.

[3] Includes 57,309 Officers' Reserve Corps members on extended active duty.

ORC   Officers' Reserve Corps of the Organized Reserve
ERC   Enlisted Reserve Corps of the Organized Reserve

All figures are taken from the reports of the Secretary of War, The Adjutant General, and The Surgeon General for the appropriate years.

Appendix F

Strength of the Army Reserve (Organized Reserve Corps) after World War II

End of Fiscal Year	Paid Drill	IRR	Total Ready Reserve	Standby Reserve	Retired Reserve	Total Army Reserve
1946	none					none
1947 (Dec. 31)	none					729,289
1948	none					752,271
1949	196,427					588,972
1949 (Dec. 31)	245,585					580,459
1950	186,541					613,526
1951	154,816					278,327
1952	135,003					340,580
1953	117,323					798,026
1953 (Dec. 31)	127,613		883,820	23,463	38,320	945,603
1954	136,918					1,108,967
1954 (Dec. 31)	153,932		1,290,833	9,828	43,584	1,344,245
1955	163,137		1,593,419			1,648,626
1955 (Dec. 31)	173,196			8,209		
1956	197,340		1,917,250			1,975,559
1956 (Dec. 31)	225,345					1,814,333
1957	260,377		1,008,438			1,839,474
1958	272,683		955,462			2,034,598
1959	314,173		1,008,837			2,282,550
1960	301,081		1,024,549			2,217,472
1961	301,796		1,028,168	772,543	93,036	1,893,747
1962	261,456	580,034	841,490	496,762	107,649	1,445,901
1963	284,182	382,899	667,081	293,283	132,470	1,092,834
1964	268,524	453,485	722,089	255,592	154,180	1,131,782
1965	261,680	456,758	718,438	233,916	176,212	1,128,566
1966	250,794	546,845	797,819	233,683	190,663	1,222,165
1967	261,957	444,204	706,161	312,503	199,320	1,217,984
1968	244,239	629,237	873,476	230,875	230,879	1,335,230

End of Fiscal Year	Paid Drill	IRR	Total Ready Reserve	Standby Reserve	Retired Reserve	Total Army Reserve
1969	261,322	818,471	1,079,793	262,000		1,304,000
1970	257,490	931,715	1,192,453	344,00		1,386,000
1971	262,299	991,039	1,254,338	335,000		1,605,000
1972	235,192	1,059,064	1,294,256	382,215	327,189	2,003,660
1973	235,499	757,675	993,174	415,268	344,457	1,752,989
1974	239,715	532,575	772,290	340,481	357,591	1,470,362
1975	225,057	355,099	580,156	282,696	365,489	1,228,341
1976	191,919	217,621	409,540	184,478	376,037	970,055
1977	189,420	149,427	338,847	152,784	386,368	877,999
1978	185,753	168,607	354,360	82,677	391,304	828,341
1979	189,990	201,783	391,773	30,544	400,825	823,142
1980	195,146	215,810	410,946	19,047	413,431	843,784
1981	225,003	212,925	437,928	5,014	449,406	892,348
1982	256,659	218,991	475,650	357	464,634	940,641
1983 (Jan. 31)	256,379	223,904	480,283	614	466,936	947,833

Strength figures in this appendix are based upon the reports of the Secretary of Defense. Because the reports varied in format from year to year, there are some unavoidable gaps in the chart. There was no paid drill in the Organized Reserve Corps prior to FY 1949. The ORC did not exist at all in 1946, and figures for 1947 reflect only the most tenuous of military connection for the members of the Corps.

Appendix **G**

Army Reservists on Active Duty— 1948–1982 (excluding active duty for training)

End of Fiscal Year	Number	End of Fiscal Year	Number
1948	39,090	1966	74,373
1949	54,149	1967	100,115
1950	44,107	1968	127,513
1951	205,338	1969	134,025
1952	118,444	1970	121,575
1953	115,119	1971	102,592
1954	107,791	1972	71,905
1955	102,688	1973	66,507
1956	106,016	1974	55,798
1957	124,779	1975	53,373
1958	104,773	1976	51,432
1959	74,976	1977	51,636
1960	63,018	1978	52,307
1961	58,762	1979	52,924
1962	128,884	1980	53,078
1963	64,897	1981	53,252
1964	67,976	1982	49,071
1965	68,808		

Source: *Department of Defense Selected Manpower Statistics, Fiscal Year 1982,* pages 199 and 200.

Appendix H

Examples of US Army Reserve Units as a Percentage of the Total Army Unit Structure

Type of Unit	The Army Reserve's Percentage of All Army Units
Training Divisions	100
Training Brigades	100
Strategic Military Intelligence Detachments	100
Civil Preparedness Support Detachments	100
Army Reserve Schools	100
Maneuver Area Commands	100
Maneuver Training Commands	100
Railway Units	100
Judge Advocate General Detachments	98
Civil Affairs Units	97
Psychological Operations Units	89
Smoke Generator Companies	86
Petroleum Supply Companies	72
Petroleum Operating Companies	63
Hospitals	61
Terminal Transfer and Service Companies	58
Conventional Ammunition Companies	51
Chemical Decontamination Units	47
Watercraft Units	45
Pathfinder Units	43
Medical Units other than Hospitals	40

Source: Berkman, William R., *The Posture of the U.S. Army Reserve,* Office of the Chief, Army Reserve, Washington, D.C., 1983, p. 3.

Select Bibliography

MANUSCRIPT SOURCES

National Archives of the United States, Washington, DC
  Record Group 319—Records of the Army Staff (Records of the Executive for Reserve and ROTC Affairs; Records of the Chief, Army Reserve [1922-1954])
  Record Group 407—Records of the Adjutant General, United States Army
Washington National Records Center, Suitland, Md.
  Record Group 319—Records of the Army Staff (Records of the Chief, Army Reserve)
National Archives and Records Center, National Personnel Records Center, St. Louis, Mo. (Personnel Records of Individual Reservists)

INTERVIEWS

Colonel Milton Barall (USAR-Ret.) by Major James T. Currie, February 4, 1983.
Colonel A.S. Behrman (USAR-Ret.) by Major James T. Currie, April 11, 1983.
Captain Kenneth Carson (USAR-Ret.) by Major James T. Currie, April 1, 1983.
Lieutenant Colonel D.Y. Dunn (USAR-Ret.) by Lieutenant Colonel Richard B. Crossland, April 23, 1983.
Colonel Frank B. Gregory (AUS-Ret.) by Major James T. Currie, July 27, 1983.
Lieutenant Colonel Sue Walker (USAR-Ret.) by Major James T. Currie, June 27, 1983.

COMPTROLLER GENERAL REPORTS

The Army's Ability to Mobilize and Use Retirees as Planned Is Doubtful (Report No. FPCD–83–6, 1982).

Can the Army and Air Force Reserve Support the Active Forces Effectively? Report No. LCD–79–404, 1979).

Critical Manpower Problems Restrict the Use of National Guard and Reserve Forces (Report No. FPCD–79–71, dated 20 August 1979).

Personnel Problems May Hamper Army's Individual Ready Reserve in Wartime. (Report No. FPCD–83–12).

CONGRESSIONAL HEARINGS AND PRINTS

Hearings before the Committee on Armed Services, House of Representatives, Eighty-third Congress, First Session, Pursuant to H.R. 122, Reserve Officers Personnel Act.

Merger of the Army Reserve Components. Subcommittee No. 2, Committee on Armed Services, United States House of Representatives. Washington: GPO, 1965.

Report of Subcommittee No. 3 on Military Posture. Committee on Armed Services, United States House of Representatives, 87th Congress. Washington: GPO, 1962.

United States-Vietnam Relations, 1945–1967. Twelve Volumes. Printed for the use of the House Committee on Armed Services. Washington: GPO, 1971. "The Pentagon Papers."

BOOKS AND MONOGRAPHS

A Chronological History of Our Reserve Components. Compiled by an *ad hoc* group from OCMH, NGB, CORC, and OCAR, 19 Nov 1965, at the request of Lt. Col. John P. Parker, Projects Division, DC & A, Office of the Chief of Staff, Army. (Copy in CMH Files).

Ambrose, Stephen E. *Upton and the Army.* Baton Rouge: Louisiana State University Press, 1964.

Association of the United States Army. *A Status Report on the Army National Guard and the United States Army Reserve.* Arlington: AUSA, 1980.

Baskir, Lawrence M. and Strauss, William A. *Chance and Circumstance: The Draft, the War, and the Vietnam Generation.* New York: Alfred A. Knopf, 1978.

Berger, Carl. *Broadsides and Bayonets.* San Rafael, Calif.: Presidio Press, 1976.

Bradley, Omar N. (Gen. of the Army) and Blair, Clay. *A*

General's Life: An Autobiography. New York: Simon and Schuster, 1983.

Brayton, Abbot A. *Military Mobilization and International Politics.* Unpublished Ph.D. dissertation, University of Arizona, 1971.

Browning, James W., II, *et al, The U.S. Reserve System: Attitudes, Perceptions and Realities.* The National War College, 1982.

Byrnes, James F. *Report on Future of Guard and Reserves.* Washington: Department of the Army, 1949.

Carlton, John T. and Slinkman, John F. *The ROA Story: A Chronicle of the First 60 Years of the Reserve Officers Association of the United States.* Washington: ROA, 1982.

Clausewitz, Carl von. *On War.* Ed. by Michael Howard and Peter Paret. Princeton: Princeton University Press, 1976.

Clifford, John G. *The Citizen Soldiers: The Plattsburg Training Camp Movement, 1913–1920.* Lexington: University Press of Kentucky, 1972.

Coakley, Robert W., *et al. U.S. Army Expansion, 1961–62.* Office of the Chief of Military History, Department of the Army. Originally SECRET, but declassified Dec. 12, 1972.

Coakley, Robert W. *Highlights of Mobilization, Korean War, Prepared in the Office of the Chief of Military History, Department of the Army, 10 March 1959.* Copy in CMH Files.

Cocke, Karl. *The Reserve Components.* Manuscript at CMH, undated.

Coffey, Kenneth J. *Strategic Implications of the All-Volunteer Force.* Chapel Hill: University of North Carolina Press, 1979.

Department of Defense Selected Manpower Statistics, Fiscal Year 1982. Washington, 1983.

Du Picq, Ardant (Col.). *Battle Studies: Ancient and Modern Battle.* Trans. by Col. John N. Greely and Maj. Robert C. Cotton. New York: Macmillan Company, 1921.

Eliot, George F. *Reserve Forces and the Kennedy Strategy.* Harrisburg, Penn.: Stackpole Co., 1962.

Ellis, O.O. (Maj.) and Garey, E.B. (Maj.). *The Plattsburg Manual.* New York: The Century Co., 1918.

Endicott, John E. and Stafford, Roy W. (eds.). *American Defense Policy.* 4th Ed. Baltimore: The Johns Hopkins University Press, 1977.

Galloway, Eilene. *History of the United States Military Policy on Reserve Forces, 1775–1957.* Washington: GPO, 1957. Prepared for use of the Committees on Armed Services.

Gerard, Francis R. (Maj. Gen.). *Vista 1999, A Long-Range Look at the Future of the Army and Air National Guard.* Washington: National Guard Bureau, 1982.

Goodpaster, Andrew J. (Gen.). *Toward a Consensus on Military Service.* New York: Pergamon Press, 1982.

Gray, Gordon (Chairman). *Reserve Forces for National Security.* Washington: Department of Defense, 1948. This is the "Gray Board Report."

Hagood, Johnson (Maj. Gen.). *Can We Defend America?* Garden City, NY: Doubleday, Doran & Co., 1937.

Halberstam, David. *The Best and the Brightest.* New York: Random House, 1969, 1971, 1972.

Harrison, Gordon A. *United States Army in World War II. The European Theatre of Operations. Cross-Channel Attack.* Washington: Office of the Chief of Military History, Department of the Army, 1951.

Heinl, Robert D., Jr. *Dictionary of Military and Naval Quotations.* Annapolis: Naval Institute, 1966.

Hewes, James E., Jr. *From Root to McNamara: Army Organization and Administration, 1900–1963.* Special Studies Series. Washington: Center of Military History, United States Army, 1975.

Higham, Robin (ed.). *A Guide to the Sources of United States Military History.* Hamden, Conn.: Archon Books, 1975.

Holley, I.B., Jr. *General John M. Palmer, Citizen Soldiers, and the Army of a Democracy.* Westport, Conn. and London: Greenwood Press, 1982.

Johnson, Lyndon Baines. *The Vantage Point: Perspectives of the Presidency, 1963–1969.* New York, Chicago, and San Francisco: Holt, Rinehart, and Winston, 1971.

Joint Chiefs of Staff. *The History of the Joint Chiefs of Staff. The Joint Chiefs of Staff and the War in Vietnam, 1960–1968, Part II.* Historical Division, Joint Secretariat, Joint Chiefs of Staff. This is an unpublished study that is currently classified TOP SECRET.

Kaufmann, William W. *The McNamara Strategy.* New York: Harper and Row, 1964.

Kriedberg, Marvin A. (Lt. Col.) and Henry, Merton G. (1st. Lt.). *History of Military Mobilization in the United States Army, 1775–1945.* Washington: Department of the Army, 1955. (DA Pam 20–212).

Lee, Gus C. and Parker, Geoffrey Y. *Ending the Draft: The Story of the All Volunteer Force.* Alexandria, Va: Human Resources Research Organization, 1977.

Levantrosser, William F. (Col., USAR). *Congress and the Citizen Soldier: Legislative Policy-making for the Federal Armed*

Forces Reserve. Columbus, Ohio: Ohio State University Press, 1967.

Lynch, Charles M., *et al. The Medical Department of the United States Army in the World War.* Washington: GPO, 1923.

Marshall, George C. (Gen. of the Army). *The Winning of the War in Europe and the Pacific.* Washington: War Department, 1945.

Matloff, Maurice (Gen. ed.). *American Military History.* Washington: Office of the Chief of Military History, United States Army, 1969.

O'Connor, Raymond G. (ed.). *American Defense Policy in Perspective: From Colonial Times to the Present.* New York: John Wiley & Sons, Inc., 1965.

Office of the Chief of Military History, Department of the Army. *Historical Resume, Division Force Structure, Active and Reserve, 1935–1963.* Copy in CMH Files.

Office of the Chief of Military History, Department of the Army. *Problems Encountered in Bringing units up to Strength and Condition of Readiness for Korea.* Copy on microfilm, CMH.

Order of Battle, United States Army, World War II, European Theater of Operations, Divisions. Paris: United States Army, 1945. Copy in Army Library, The Pentagon.

Palmer, John McAuley (Brig. Gen.). *America in Arms.* New Haven: Yale University Press, 1941.

Palmer, Robert R., Wiley, Bell I., and Keast, William R. *United States Army in World War II. The Army Ground Forces. The Procurement and Training of Ground Combat Troops.* Washington: Historical Division, Department of the Army, 1948.

Pate, Robert I. *U.S. Army Reserve Components—Peacetime Assessment and Management to Meet Mobilization Requirements.* Unpublished Paper, U.S. Army War College. Copy in Army Library, The Pentagon.

Perry, Ralph Barton. *The Plattsburg Movement.* New York: Dutton, 1921.

Pew, Frank W. *The Role of the U.S. Army Forces Command in Project New Arrivals: Reception and Care of Refugees from Vietnam.* Fort McPherson, Ga: U.S. Army Forces Command, 1981.

Powicke, Michael. *Military Obligation in Medieval England: A Study in Liberty & Duty.* Oxford: Clarendon Press, 1962.

Public Papers of the Presidents of the United States. Lyndon B. Johnson. Containing the Public Messages, Speeches, and

Statements of the President. 1965. II. Washington: GPO, 1966.

Public Papers of the Presidents of the United States. Lyndon B. Johnson. Containing the Public Messages, Speeches, and Statements of the President, 1968–69. I. Washington: GPO, 1970.

Riker, William H. *Soldiers of the States: The Role of the National Guard in American Democracy.* Washington: Public Affairs Press, 1957.

Risch, Erna. *Special Studies. Supplying Washington's Army.* Washington: Center of Military History, United States Army, 1981.

Salmond, John A. *The Civilian Conservation Corps, 1933–1945: A New Deal Case Study.* Durham: Duke University Press, 1967.

Sarnoff, David (Brig. Gen.). *Final Report to the Congress, National Security Training Commission.* Washington: GPO, 1957.

Schnabel, James F. *United States Army in the Korean War. Policy and Direction: The First Year.* Washington: Office of the Chief of Military History, United States Army, 1972.

Schnabel, James F. and Watson, Robert J. *The History of the Joint Chiefs of Staff. The Joint Chiefs of Staff and National Policy. Volume III — The Korean War, Part I.* Unpublished.

77th ARCOM. *Welcoming Home Ceremony for 74th Field Hospital and 316th Medical Detachment.* Copy in OCAR Historical Files.

77th ARCOM. *Welcome Home Ceremony, 237th Maintenance Company.* Copy in OCAR Historical File.

Sharpe, A.C. (Lt. Col.). *Making a Soldier.* Cleveland: The Acme Publishing Co., 1908.

Sherry, Michael S. *Preparing for the Next War: American Plans for Postwar Defense, 1941–45.* New Haven and London: Yale University Press. 1977.

Sparrow, John C. (Maj.). *History of Personnel Demobilization in the United States Army.* Office of the Chief of Military History, United States Army. 1951.

Stebbins, Richard P. *The United States in World Affairs, 1961.* New York: Harper & Brothers, 1962.

Stillwaugh, Elva (Maj.). *Personnel Policies in the Korean Conflict.* Unpublished manuscript, microfilm, CMH.

Taylor, Maxwell D. (Gen.). *The Uncertain Trumpet.* New York: Harper & Brothers, 1960.

Taylor, William J. *et al. Defense Manpower Planning: Issues for the 1980s.* New York: Pergamon Press, 1981.

Treadwell, Mattie E. *United States Army in World War II. Special Studies. The Women's Army Corps.* Washington: Office of the Chief of Military History, Department of the Army, 1954.

Trewhitt, Henry L. *McNamara.* New York: Harper & Row, 1971.

Upton, Emory (Maj. Gen.). *The Military Policy of the United States.* Washington: GPO, 1916.

Watson, Mark Skinner. *United States Army in World War II. The War Department. Chief of Staff: Prewar Plans and Preparations.* Washington: Historical Division, United States Army, 1950.

Weigley, Russell F. *History of the United States Army.* New York and London: Macmillan Publishing Co., Inc. and Collier Macmillan Publishers, 1967.

————. *Towards an American Army: Military Thought from Washington to Marshall.* Westport, Conn.: Greenwood Press, 1962.

Weinberger, Caspar W. (Chairman). *A Report to the President on the Status and Prospectus of the All-Volunteer Force.* Washington, 1982. Military Manpower Task Force.

Westmoreland, William C. (Gen.). *A Soldier Reports.* Garden City, NY: Doubleday and Company, Inc., 1976.

Whisker, James B. *The Citizen Soldier and U.S. Military Policy.* North River Press, 1979.

Wood, Leonard (Maj. Gen.). *Our Military History, Its Facts and Fallacies.* Chicago: Reilly and Britton, 1916.

Wright, Robert K., Jr. *Army Lineage Series. The Continental Army.* Washington: Center of Military History, 1983.

————. (ed.). *The American Military: Readings in the History of the Military in American Society.* Reading, Mass.: Addison-Wesley Publishing Co., 1969.

Zurcher, Louis A. and Harris-Jenkins, Gwyn (Eds.). *Supplementary Militias, Auxiliaries.* Beverly Hills, Calif.: Sage Publications, 1978.

ARTICLES

"Address by Senator Margaret Chase Smith to the 29th National Convention, Reserve Officers Association." *The Reserve Officer,* August 1955, pp. 12–13, 19.

"AGF Initiates Reserve Training Mobilization in Six Army Areas." *The Reserve Officer,* August 1946, pp. 7–9, 30–31.

"Army Reservists Welcomed Home from Vietnam Tour." *The State* (Columbia, SC). August 15, 1969.

"Army Trims Command Structure." *CARNotes*, July–August 1983, p. 1.

"Army's Revision of Reserve Units and Guard Begins." *New York Times*, December 5, 1962, pp. 1, 25.

"At 48 She Answered Call to Vietnam War." *Messenger* (Madison, NC). March 30, 1983.

"Awards for Vietnam Service." *The Army Reserve Magazine*, January 1970, p. 7.

Beecher, William. "Pentagon to Cut Use of Draftees in Fast Build-Ups." *New York Times*, September 9, 1970, p. 1.

"The Big Slice." *The National Guardsman*. May 1962, pp. 6–7.

Boldt, David R. "Reserve: Force or Farce?" *The Washington Post*, September 4, 1972, p. 1.

"Boston Reservists Fight Viet Duty." *Boston Herald-Traveler*. October 4, 1968. p. 1.

"Boston Unit Returns from Viet." *Sunday Herald-Traveler* (Boston). October 5, 1969, p. 1.

"Building the Strength of the Army Reserve." *Army Reservist*, November, 1963, pp. 3–4.

Carney, Larry. "FORSCOM Told to Increase Command's Control." *Army Times*, May 2, 1983, p. 3.

"Choices Available to Fulfill Enlisted Service Obligation." *Army Information Digest*, February 1956, pp. 36–37.

"Citations Go to 319th at Ceremony." *The Augusta* [Georgia] *Chronicle*. August 20, 1969.

Colby, Elbridge. "Elihu Root and the National Guard." *Military Affairs*, Spring 1959, pp. 28–34, 20.

Crossland, Richard B. (Maj.). "RDJTF: Can It Get There Without the USAR." *Army Reserve Magazine*, Spring 1982, pp. 8–10.

————. "Suppose the Balloon Goes Up: Then What?" *Army Reserve Magazine*. Winter 1981, pp. 24–27.

"Dissidents in Uniform: Supreme Court Rejects Challenge." *Boston Herald-Traveler*. October 8, 1968, p. 1.

"Eisenhower, Dwight D. (Gen.). "The Reserve Component and Our Future Security." *The Reserve Officer*, July 1946, pp. 9–10.

"Exercise Reveals Defense Problems." *Pentagram News*, July 31, 1980, pp. 1–4.

Fialka, John J. "The Pentagon's Exercise Proud Spirit: Little Cause for Pride." *Parameters: Journal of the US Army War College*, Vol. XI, No. 1, pp. 38–41.

————. "U.S. Again Fails Test of Ability to Mobilize." *Washington Star*, December 21, 1980, pp. A–1 and 6.

"Fight Is Brewing on Reserve Role." *New York Times*. December 17, 1961, p. 17.

"First Army Reservists Find Themselves 'Doing Real Thing' at Fort Indiantown Gap." *The Officer,* August 1980, p. 12.

"General Officer Appointments in the Organized Reserve." *The Officer.* June 1947, pp. 16–17, 22.

Havell, George F. "A Fighting 98th Division Will Be Built." *The Reserve Officer,* November 1948, pp. 14–15, 22.

Heymont, Irving (Col.). "Today's Citizen Soldier: Ready for Tomorrow's War?" *Army,* January 1974, pp. 16–22.

Hill, R.A. (Lt. Col.). "Reserve Policies and National Defense." *Infantry Journal,* January–February 1935, pp. 57–62.

House, Art (Capt.), "Defense Honors Four-Decade Backer of Reserve and Guard," *Army Reserve Magazine,* Spring 1983, pp. 33–34.

House, Jonathan M. "John McAuley Palmer and the Reserve Components." *Parameters: Journal of the US Army War College,* September, 1982, pp. 11–18.

Howze, Hamilton H. (Gen.). "Toward Real Reserve Readiness: The Case for the Cadre System." *Army,* August 1972, pp. 12–16.

"Laird Reverses Johnson on Reserve Use." *European Stars and Stripes,* September 9, 1970.

Levantrosser, William F. (Col.). "Army Reserve Merger Proposal." *Military Affairs,* Fall 1966, pp. 137–39.

"Like It or Not, 172nd Greeted as Heroes." *Sunday* [Omaha, Neb.] *World-Herald,* October 5, 1969, p. 1.

"Long, long trail ends- 737th home." *Yakima* [Washington] *Herald-Republic,* August 14, 1969.

Lyons, Gene M. and Masland, John W. "The Origins of ROTC." *Military Affairs,* Spring 1959, pp. 1–12.

"Most in Congress Relieved by the President's Course." *New York Times,* July 29, 1965, p. 1.

"The New Arrivals." *Army Reserve Magazine,* November-December 1975, pp. 16–18.

"Noted Doctors Join Army Medical Corps." *New York Times,* November 30, 1908.

Pace, Frank, Jr. "The Reserve Forces of the Army." *The Reserve Officer,* March 1952, pp. 6–8, 22–23.

Peers, William R. (Lt. Gen.). "New Priorities for Guard, Reserve," *Army.* October 1971, pp. 71–77.

"Pentagon Maps Cut in Army's Reserves." *New York Times,* December 3, 1961, pp. 1, 11.

"Plan to Shift Reservists Faces a Fight at Capitol." *New York Times,* December 11, 1964.

Pratt, Robert (Capt.). "Mobilization: No Straight A Report Card." *Army Reserve Magazine,* Summer 1983, pp. 22–23.

"President Eisenhower's Reserve Statement." *The Reserve Officer,* August 1955, p. 2.

"Reorganization Planned." *CARNotes,* January–February 1983, pp. 1 and 6.

"Reserve and Guard Hassle." *Army-Navy-Air Force Register,* January 13, 1962, p. 14.

"Reserve Drop Fight on Revision." *New York Times,* December 6, 1962, p. 25.

"Reserve Officers Accuse Pentagon of Call-Up Libel." *New York Times,* December 22, 1961, pp. 1, 11.

"Reserves Facing Ten-Division Cut." *New York Times,* December 14, 1961, p. 1.

"Reserves, Guard Get Buildup Role." *The Washington Post,* September 9, 1970, p. 1.

Reston, James, Jr. "A Bigger Role for the Reserves and Guard." *New York Times,* September 13, 1970, Sec. 4, p. 16.

"Senate Preparedness Committee Blasts Merger." *The Officer,* June 1966, pp. 5–6.

"737th earns proud sendoff from Yakima." *Yakima* [Washington] *Herald-Republic,* May 15, 1968.

"737th Mobilizes at Center." *Yakima* [Washington] *Herald-Republic,* May 14, 1968.

Smith, Terence J. (Col.). "The Army's Role in the Success of the CCC." *The Retired Officer,* July 1983, pp. 30–34.

"Ted Pleads for Boston Reservists." *Boston Herald-Traveler,* October 8, 1968, p. 1.

"U.S. Crisis Reports Major Gains in Ability to Mobilize." *New York Times,* December 12, 1982.

Vaughan, Harry H. (Maj. Gen.). "National Guard and Reserve Must Be Unified." *The Reserve Officer,* October 1947, pp. 4–5.

Walsh, Ellard A. "One Federal Force? No." *The Reserve Officer,* June 1949, pp. 6–7, 23.

"Where Are They Now? Activated Reservists Just Waiting Around." *Wall Street Journal,* March 15, 1968, p. 1.

Whichard, W. K. "Administering the Reserves." *The Reserve Officer,* December 1946, pp. 13, 30.

Williams, John D. (Maj.). "Public Affairs Aspects of the 1968 Reserve Mobilization." *Air University Review Air Force Review,* November-December 1971, pp. 59–67.

"Your Association Wins Promotions for Officers Reverting to Inactive Status." *The Reserve Officer,* November 1945, pp. 4–5.

DEPARTMENT OF DEFENSE AND DEPARTMENT OF THE ARMY REPORTS AND STUDIES

Altmann, R.G., Director. *Reserve Compensation System Study, Reserve Compensation Study Group.* Washington: Department of Defense. 1978.

Army Reserve Technician Study. Fort McPherson, Ga: U.S. Army Forces Command, 1976.

The Army Study of the Guard and Reserve Forces, Final Report. Washington: Department of the Army, 1972.

Briggs, C.F. (Brig. Gen.). *Final Report, 1980 Reduction of Administrative Workload at the Reserve Component Unit Level.* RCCC Task Force. Washington: Department of Defense, 1980.

Conti, Louis J., Chairman. *The Reserve Forces of the 1990s.* Washington: Reserve Forces Policy Board, 1980.

Department of Defense. *Manpower Requirements Report, FY 1984.* Washington, 1983.

Gates, Thomas S., Jr., Chairman. *The Report of the President's Commission on an All-Volunteer Armed Force.* Washington, 1970.

Gessert, Robert A. *et al. Problems of Implementing Reserve Component-Active Component Augmentation/Affiliation* (SECRET). McLean, Va: General Research Corp., 1974.

Hackett, Robert (Lt. Gen.). *Reserve Realignment Staff Simplification.* Washington: Headquarters, Department of the Army, 1965.

Hampton, David R. *Society and the Army Reserve.* Carlisle Barracks, Penn.: Army War College, 1973.

Lee, Gus C. and Parker, Geoffrey Y. *Ending the Draft: The Story of the All Volunteer Force.* Alexandria, Va: Human Resources Research Organization, 1977.

McElhenny, John F. (Col.). *After Action Report: Tropical Storm Agnes-Operation Noah II.* Harrisburg, Penn.: U.S. Army Corps of Engineers, Susquehanna District, North Atlantic Division, 1972.

Odegard, Donald C. (Col.). *Non-Mobilization and Mobilization in the Vietnam War.* Carlisle Barracks, Penn.: Strategic Studies Institute, U.S. Army War College, 1980.

Office of Reserve Components. *Resource Allocations to Reserve Components*. Washington: Headquarters, Department of the Army, 1969.

OSD Project 80: Study of the Functions, Organization, and Procedures for the Department of the Army. Washington: Department of the Army, 1961.

Parker, David S. (Maj. Gen.), Chairman. *Report of the Special Review Panel on Department of the Army Organization*. Washington: Headquarters, Department of the Army, 1971.

Report on the Study of Full-time Training and Administration of the Selected Reserve. Washington: 1978.

Reserve Component Attitude Study, 1981 Tracking Study. Philadelphia: Associates for Research in Behavior, Inc., 1982.

Stroud, Ansel M. (Brig. Gen.), Director. *Study on the Full Time Personnel Requirements of the Reserve Components*. Washington: Department of the Army, 1977.

U.S. Army Audit Agency. *Report of Audit: U.S. Army Reserve Activities* (No. MW 70), 3 April 1970.

United States Defense Manpower Commission. *The Total Force and Its Manpower Requirements, Including Overviews of Each Service*. Washington: GPO, 1976.

White, John P. *Report on Full-time Training and Administration of the Selected Reserve*. Washington: Department of Defense, 1978.

Wilson, Dwight L. (Maj. Gen.), Chairman. *Army Command and Control Study—82 (ACCS–82)*. Washington: Headquarters, Department of the Army, 1979.

The Authors

LT. COL. RICHARD B. CROSSLAND is a professional Reservist with over twenty years of service in the three Army components. After enlisting in the Delaware National Guard, he was commissioned in 1965 and served as a Guard officer until he was called to active duty in late 1966. He served in the active Army in field artillery, air defense artillery, infantry, and intelligence until he became a full-time Reservist in 1975. He served in Vietnam and was wounded twice. He is a graduate of the Army's Command and General Staff College and the Army's Advanced Public Affairs Course at the University of South Carolina. He has a B.A. degree in history from the University of Delaware and has done graduate work in journalism and political science. He is currently assigned to the US Army Training and Doctrine Command. His awards include the Bronze Star Medal, Meritorious Service Medal, Air Medal, Army Commendation Medal, Purple Heart with Oak Leaf Cluster, Combat Infantryman Badge, and the Vietnamese Cross of Gallantry.

MAJ. JAMES T. CURRIE is a military historian and member of the Army Reserve. Currie received his B.A. degree *Summa cum Laude* from the University of Mississippi and his M.A. and Ph.D. degrees from the University of Virginia. He has been a college professor and was the first historian for the United States Department of Education. Currie is a prolific writer, and his articles have been published in *Prologue: The Journal of the National Archives*, *The Journal of Negro History*, *Military Review*, *The Journal of Mississippi History*, *American*

315

Education, and elsewhere. He received the Charles Thomson Prize from the National Archives in 1978, and his first book (*Enclave: Vicksburg and Her Plantations, 1863–1870*) was nominated for the Frederick Jackson Turner Prize. Currie served three years on active duty and four years with a troop unit of the USAR. He is an Individual Mobilization Augmentee at the US Army Center of Military History and is Associate Historian in the Office for the Bicentennial of the US House of Representatives.

Index

MILITARY UNIT INDEX

ALPHABETICAL SUBJECT INDEX